Noah's Art

Zoo, Aquarium, Aviary and Wildlife Park Graphics

Quon Editions

Design & Production
Studio 3 Graphics
Cover Illustration
Grace Fong
Cover Photography
James Sew
Linotronics
Contemporary Type
Printer
Tien Wah Press, Singapore

Contents

To May, Ann, Laura & Katie who have shared their great moments with me at the zoos

Special thanks to:

All the zoos, aquaria, aviaries and wildlife parks who have sent a wealth of material for this book,

Masterfile Corporation *Stock Photo Library*

Paul Bluestone *John G.Shedd Aquarium,*

Larry Matthews *National Zoo,*

Charles Beier *Bronx Zoo,*

William Noonan *San Diego Zoo,*

Mary Yeow,

Sheila Laughton,

Della Shellard

Preface

At one time or another, we have all visited a zoo or an aquarium or an aviary. At these venues, we are usually so preoccupied with the animals on display that some of the important graphic features that make the institutions tick are often gone unnoticed.

From the billboards, advertisements, and brochures that attract the crowds of visitors to the directional signs and interpretive display panels, these graphics are always carefully and deftly created to inform, educate and entertain the visitor.

With budget cuts and increasing pressure from animal activists, zoos are becoming endangered species themselves. *Noah's Art* documents the work of many designers who have contributed considerable time and talent to sustaining these institutions.

Some 56 organizations are represented, including the oldest American zoo in Philadelphia and the newest aquariums in Chicago and Osaka, Japan. Twenty of these are dealt with in detail, each featuring directional signs, wayfinding systems, interpretive displays, interactive displays, vehicles, posters, billboards, print material, logos and symbols, etc.

Noah's Art provides an armchair travelogue to the major zoos, aquariums, aviaries and wildlife parks of the world.

Wei Yew

Telegraph Colour Library/Masterfile

Zoo Atlanta Georgia, USA

Zoo Atlanta was incorporated in 1985 as a non-profit organization. Occupying 37 acres near downtown Atlanta, it is home to 278 species, totalling 951 specimens. Its bio-park atmosphere features winding trails, surprise views, and mixed-species exhibits in naturalistic habitats.

The Zoo's philosophy emphasizes conservation, education, recreation and research. Its commitment to these principles is exemplified by active participation in breeding programs for animals such as western lowland gorillas, black rhinos and Sumatran tigers.

The graphics department has a full-time staff of two, working under the guidance of the Director of Education. Its 1991 budget is in the range of $50,000.

Map & Information station

Designer
Richard Washington

Theatre sign with changeable time/subject velcro strips

Designer
Richard Washington

Schedule/map with changeable magnetic feature

Designer
Richard Washington
Copywriter
Angelle Cooper

Sandblasted petting zoo sign

Designer
Richard Washington

Sandblasted sign with changeable velcro strip features

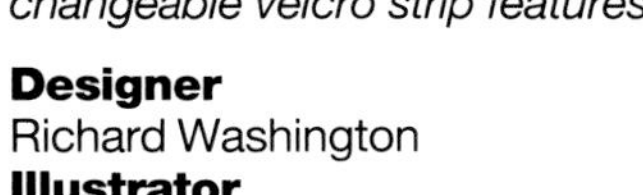

Designer
Richard Washington
Illustrator
Reginald Sanders

Sandblasted interpretive sign

Designer
Richard Washington
Copywriter
Craig Piper

Tiger view building sign

Designer
Richard Washington

Fund raising progress 'thermometer'

Designer
Richard Washington
Illustrator
Mark Sandun

Interpretive signs for monkey exhibit

Designer
Richard Washington
Copywriter
Craig Piper

"Field notes" interpretive signs located throughout the exhibits

Designers
Richard Washington,
Barbara McGrath
Copywriter
Barbara McGrath

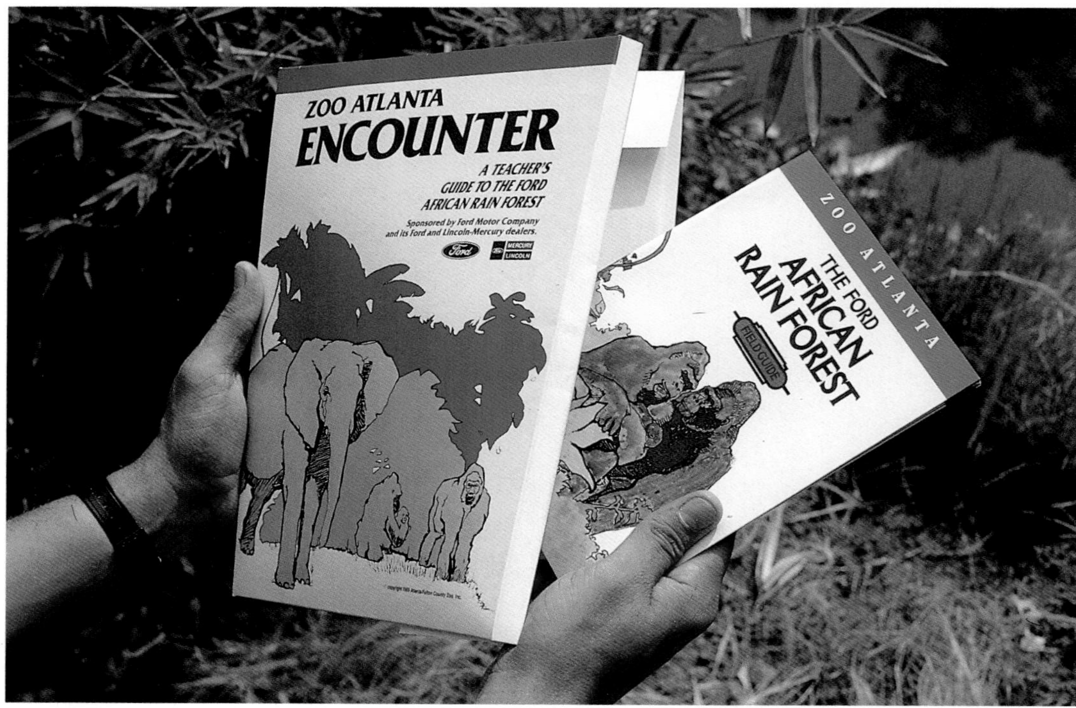

Teacher's packet with field guide

Designer
Richard Washington
Illustrator
Kendall Portis

Visitor information station

Designer
Richard Washington
Illustrator
Reginald Sanders

Cafe & Gift shop sign

Designer
Barbara McGrath
Design Firm
Coe Lee Robinson Roesch, Inc.
Illustrator
Barbara McGrath
Fabricator
John Luttmann

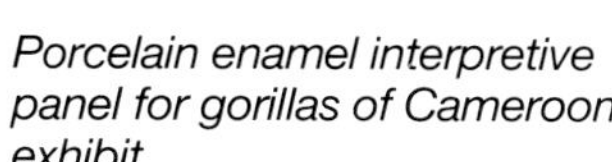

Porcelain enamel interpretive panel for gorillas of Cameroon exhibit

Designer
Barbara McGrath
Design Firm
Coe Lee Robinson Roesch, Inc.
Illustrator
Joe Sebo
Copywriters
Jon Coe, Barbara McGrath

Screen-painted display for new elephant exhibit

Designer
Joe Clark
Design Firm
Coe Lee Robinson Roesch, Inc.
Illustrator
Bob Milnazik
Copywriter
Jon Coe

Jim Haynes/Audubon Zoological Garden

Audubon Zoological Gardens New Orleans, USA

Set in one-hundred-year-old Audubon Park, Audubon Zoological Garden occupies 56 acres of lush, beautifully landscaped, oak-shaded park land. Habitat-style exhibits showcase animals (2000 specimens of 419 species) in naturalistic environments. The zoo is now visited by more than one million guests annually, but this was not always so.

The master plan which drove the renovation in the 1970's is now complete. It included the development of the award-winning Louisiana Swamp Exhibit. Its crowning achievement was the Odenheimer Complex, which broke new ground in zoo planning with its natural history exhibit Pathways to the Past.

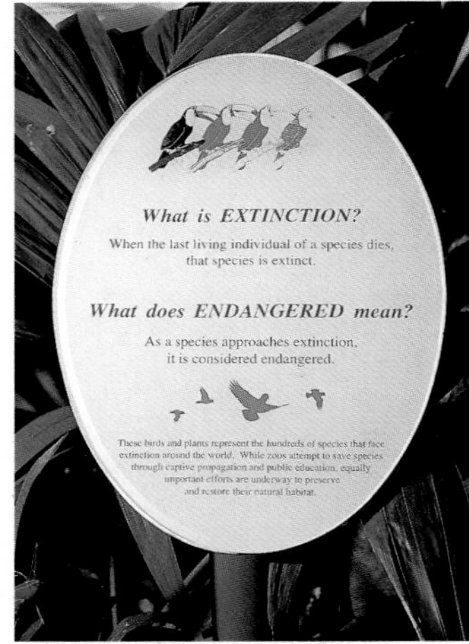

Sun Bear exhibit – interpretive and interactive

Designers
Roger Isles, Steven Dorand
Illustrator/Fabricator
Susan Miceli

Tropical Bird House field guide

Illustrators
Susan Miceli, Terry Kenney
Fabricator
Greve Technical

With the expansion of the Zoo and the Institute, the Design and Exhibitry Department has grown from an initial crew of two, to a staff of 10 full-time designers and craftsmen. Their duties encompass the full range of artistic endeavour for two-dimensional printed pieces to multi-sensory exhibitry. The museum shop now designs, produces, and maintains architectural signage, interpretive graphics, and interactive exhibits for the Zoo and the Aquarium. The operating budget of approximately $200,000 is augmented by capital funding for new exhibits and by allocations from other departments for special projects.

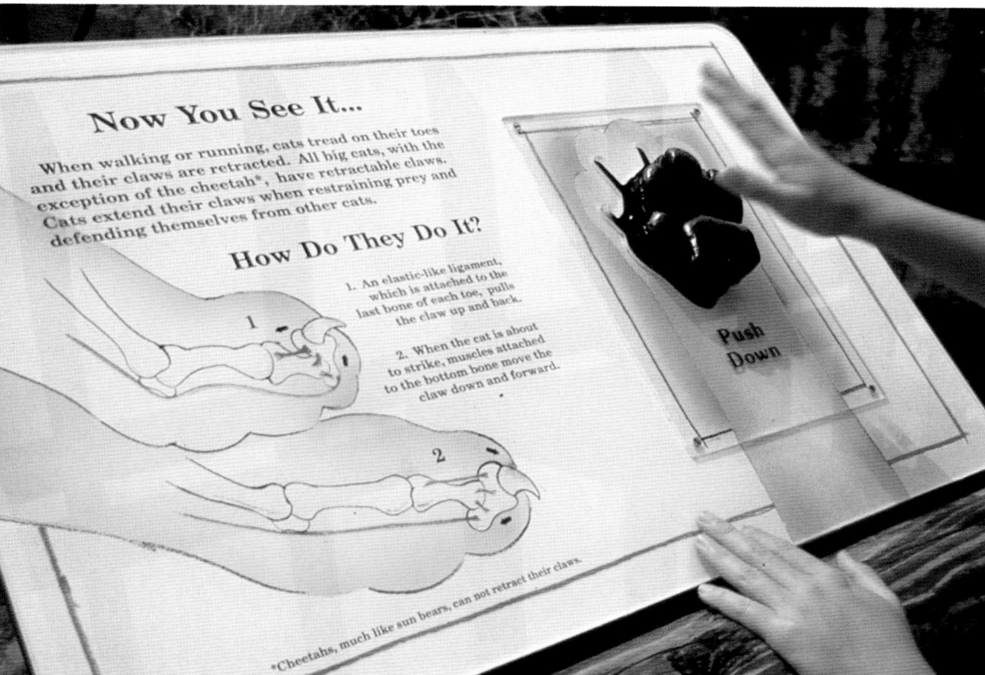

Tiger claw interactive display

Illustrator
Susan Miceli
Fabricator
Greve Technical

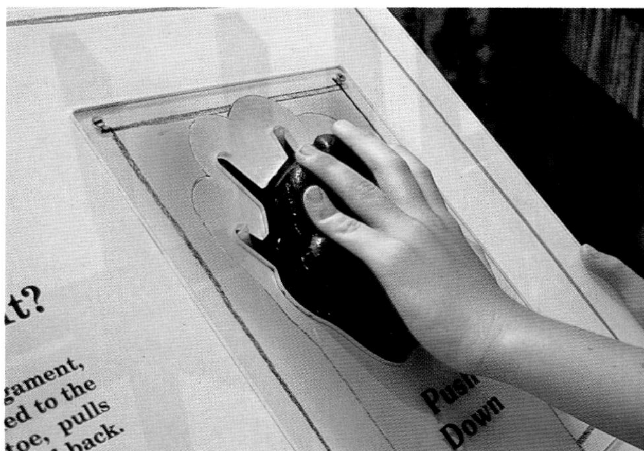

Changeable bird panel

Illustrator
Terry Kenney

Louisiana swamp exhibit – sandblasted panel

Designer
Steven Dorand
Illustrator
Pamela Mathes

Elephant information panel

Illustrator
Susan Miceli

Train stop – Sandblasted post with plexi-sign

Train station banner

Designer/Illustrator
Terry Kenney

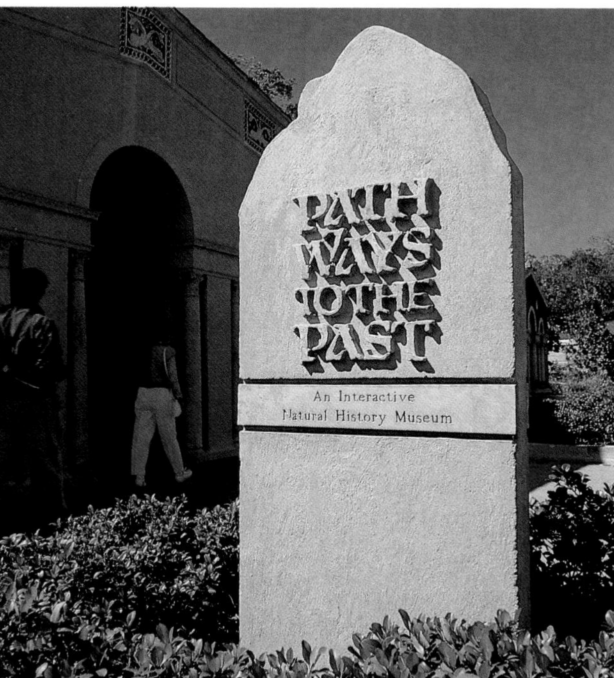

Exhibit sign post

Designer
Steven Dorand
Logotype
Carol Lavallee Rice

Sandblasted flamingo information panel with plexi-sign

Designer
Carol Lavallee Rice
Illustrators
Pamela Mathes

Posters

Designers
Steven Dorand, Alford Agency
Illustrators
Jim Haynes, Karel Havlicek

Richard Laird – FPG/Masterfile

Baltimore Children's Zoo Maryland, USA

The Baltimore Zoo is the third oldest in the United States, established in 1876. The 8-acre Children's Zoo is part of the 160-acre zoo, located in Baltimore's Druid Hill Park. The Maryland Wilderness portion of the Children's Zoo features more than 50 species of animals native to the State of Maryland. Familiar domesticated animals are displayed in the Farmyard.

The Children's Zoo is a microcosm of the State's diverse habitats, from the Western mountains to Eastern Shore marshes. Natural habitat exhibits and interactive devices such as the oriole's nest and the lily pad walk are integrated into this complex project, 3 years in the making.

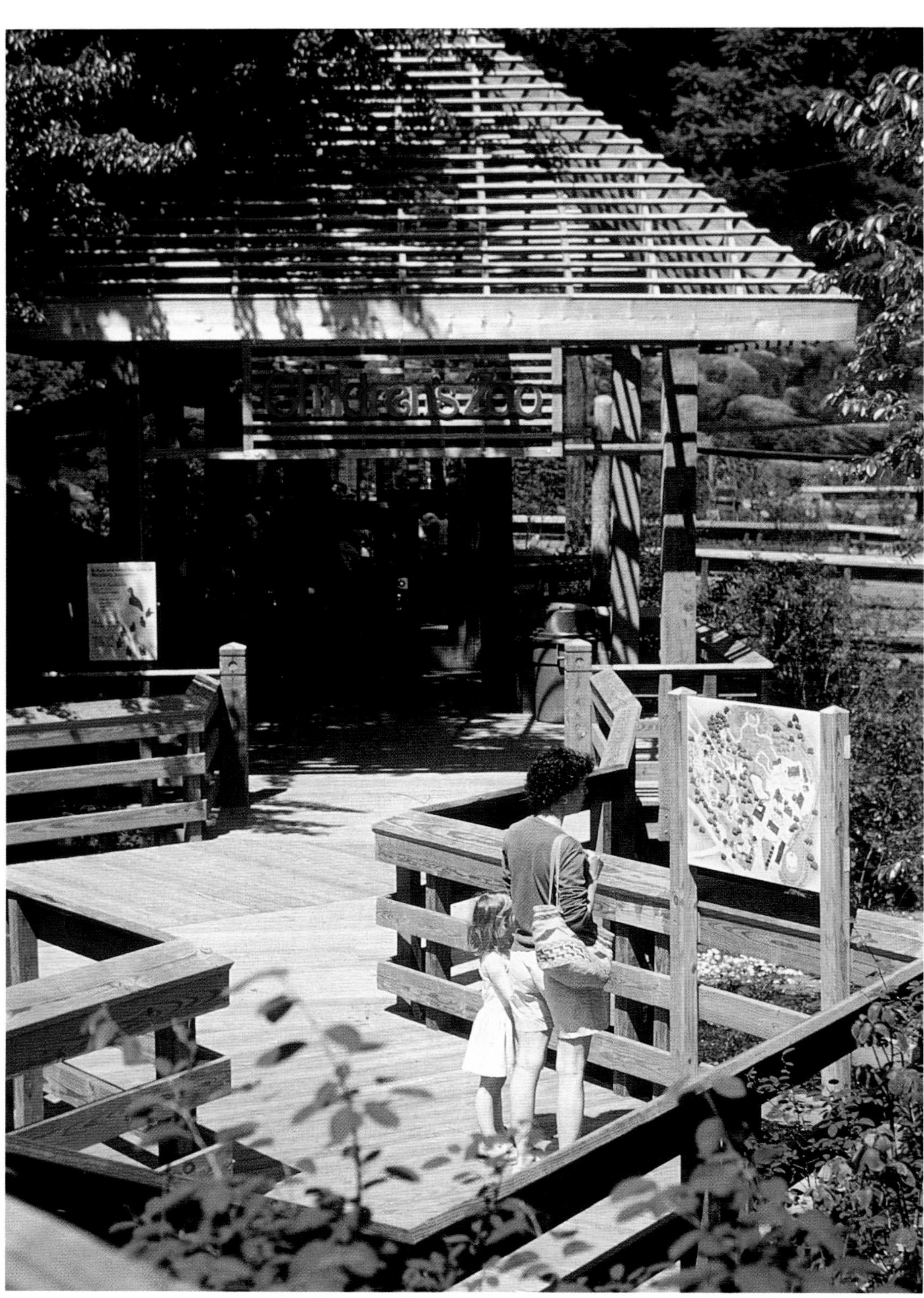

The entrance pavilions and entry signs reflect the Victorian character of the nearby Village Green. Most of the 116 signs and graphics for this eight-acre $6.5 million exhibit are of porcelain enamel on steel.

Art Director
Eileen Tennor
Designers
Eileen Tennor, Brian Rutledge
Design Firm
LDR International, Inc.
Illustrators
Thom Cloffi, Kim Neval,
Anne Greve, Eileen Tennor
Photographers
Patrick Mullaly, Joe McSharry
Copywriters
Brian Rutledge, Sue Stone

The exhibit graphics contribute to the fun of the learning experience. Pictures and simple vocabulary communicate the message of conservation even to the very young. A wide range of materials and techniques was used, from internally illuminated graphics for cave and tree interiors, to slate for a sign in the Farmyard.

Bird's eye perspective illustrations orient visitors and identify the major exhibit areas

Tress native to Maryland can be identified with this rotating wheel in the wooded area of the Children's zoo

At the entrance pond, visitors use this rotating wheel to identify native Maryland birds

In each habitat exhibit – marsh, stream, cave, woods, meadow, and farm – an illustration identifies the animals and plants of that ecosystem

Nest like a heron.

Graphics encourage visitors to participate in the interactive exhibits like the stick nest in the marsh

whitetail deer
black bear
weasel
gray fox
caddis fly nymphs
water line
mayfly
beaver lodge
snail
beaver
mottled sculpin
otter
kingfisher
bobcat
raccoon
ferns
rainbow trout
bullhead catfish
mussels

There are many opportunities to pretend ....and to make new discoveries about animals in these exhibits and graphics

Nest like
an oriole.

Burrow like a woodchuck.

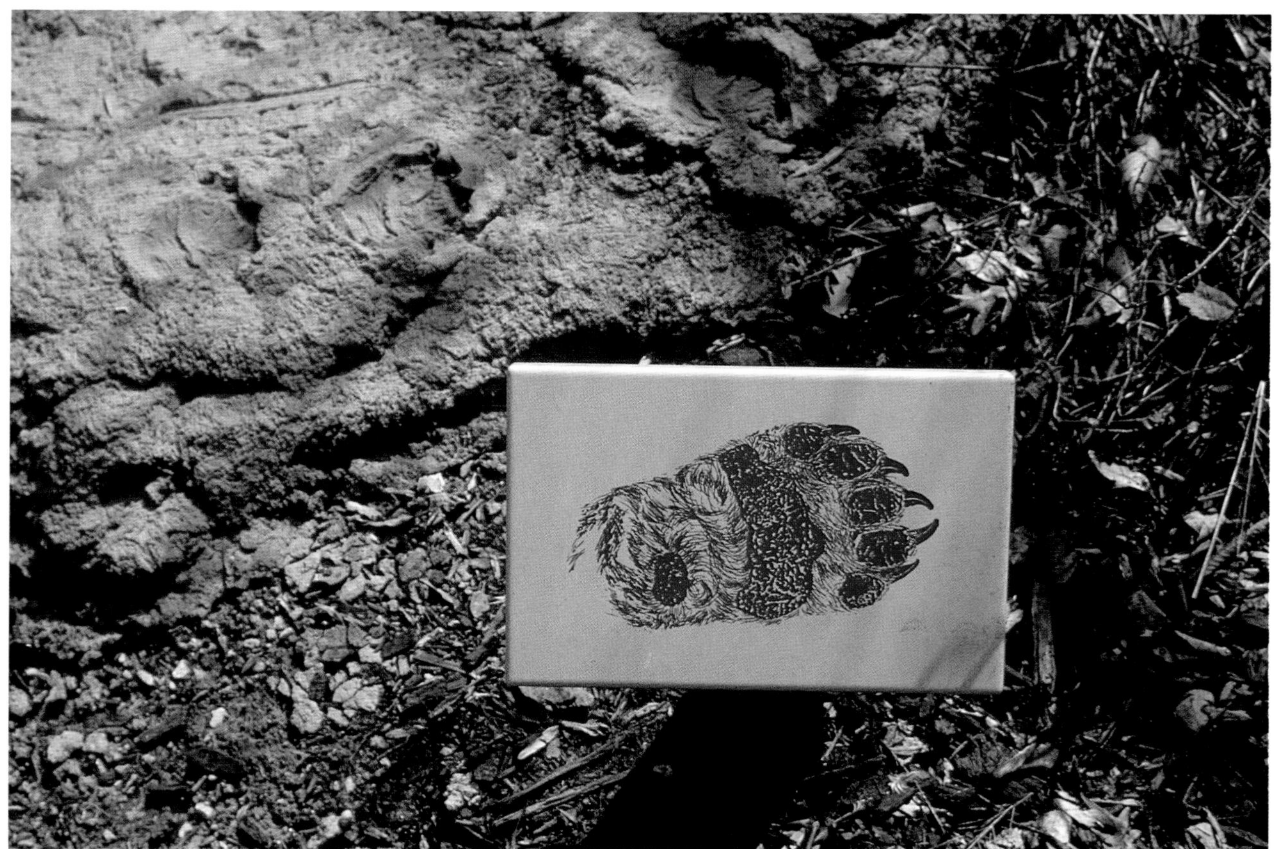

In addition to porcelain enamel, natural slate and cedar are used for signs in the farmstead area

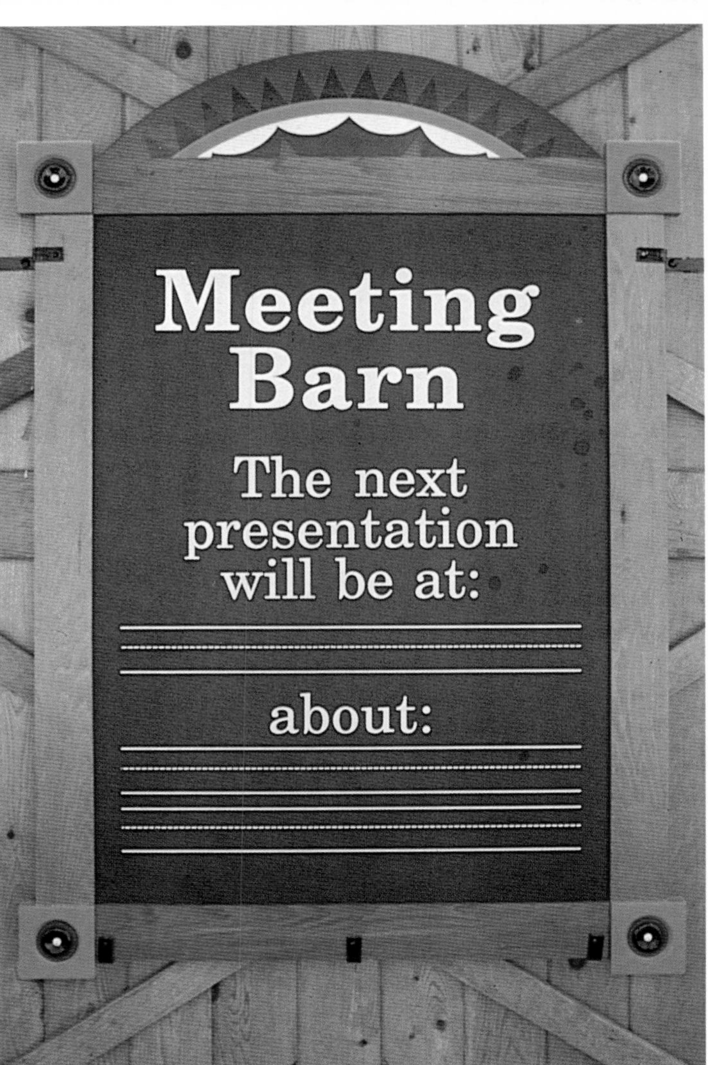

Graphics screened directly on the split viewing windows leave a clear view for otters and kids

Wayne Lynch/Masterfile

The New York Zoological Society's Bronx Zoo was founded in 1895. Americas' largest urban zoological park now contains more than 4000 animals of 650 species on 265 acres of temperate forest. Naturalistic habitats and interactive environmental graphics are designed to instill an awareness of wildlife and wild habitats.

In addition to the Bronx Zoo, The New York Zoological Society operates New York Aquarium, Central Park Zoo, Osborn Laboratories of Marine Sciences, St. Catherines Island Wildlife Survival Centre, and Wildlife Conservation International. The Society is unique in its dynamic approach to animal and habitat conservation through the

Silk-screened interpretive graphic panel in the Ethiopian Reserve

Interactive graphic devices in the Ethiopian Reserve field station. Each asks a question with the answer revealed upon lifting the cover. Silk-screened on 6mm formed aluminium

Designers
John Gwynne, Charlie Beier, Sharon Kramer, Stephen Clauson, Gail Tarkan
Illustrator
Deborah Ross

integrated efforts of these facilities. The Society's zoological parks and international field conservation scientists collaborate in formulating plans for the protection of habitats and the breeding of endangered species. Award-winning programs and exhibits in this field continue to provide a valuable resource for other zoological parks worldwide.

The fossil dig site within the Ethiopian Reserve demonstrating the co-evolution of the Gelada baboon and man. Cast epoxy skulls and bone fragments in conjunction with interpretive graphics silk-screened on 6mm aluminium sheet.

African market interpretive graphic panel, silk-screened on 6mm aluminium supported by hand-made brass brackets attached to black locust poles

Entrance pylon to Himalayan Highlands exhibit with hand-painted Tibetan capitals and silk-screened graphic on aluminium

Interactive graphic panel in the Himalayan Highlands conservation garden

Art Directors
Charlie Beier, Sharon Kramer
Designer
Kurt Tow

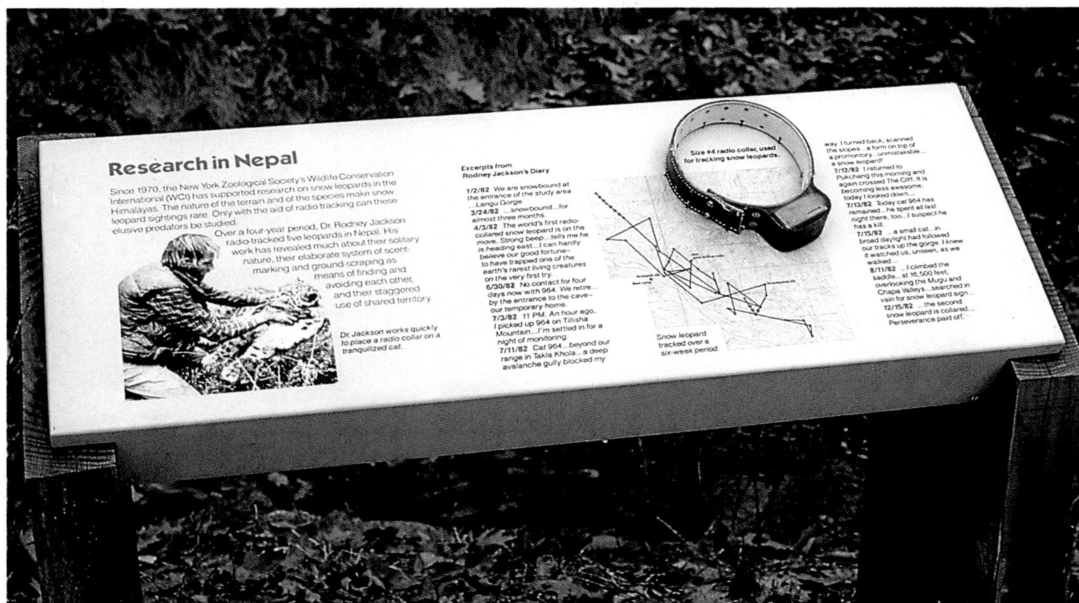

Actual radio tracking collar mounted on interactive graphic panel

Interpretive graphic pylon with hand-painted Tibetan capitals at the entrance to the White-naped Crane

Entrance pylon for Wildfowl Marsh exhibit. Water cut decorative mouldings with silk-screened graphics on 6mm aluminium

Colour porcelain photographs mounted on interpretive graphic panel

Art Directors
John Gwynne, Charlie Beier
Designer
Ron Davis

WILDFOWL
MARSH

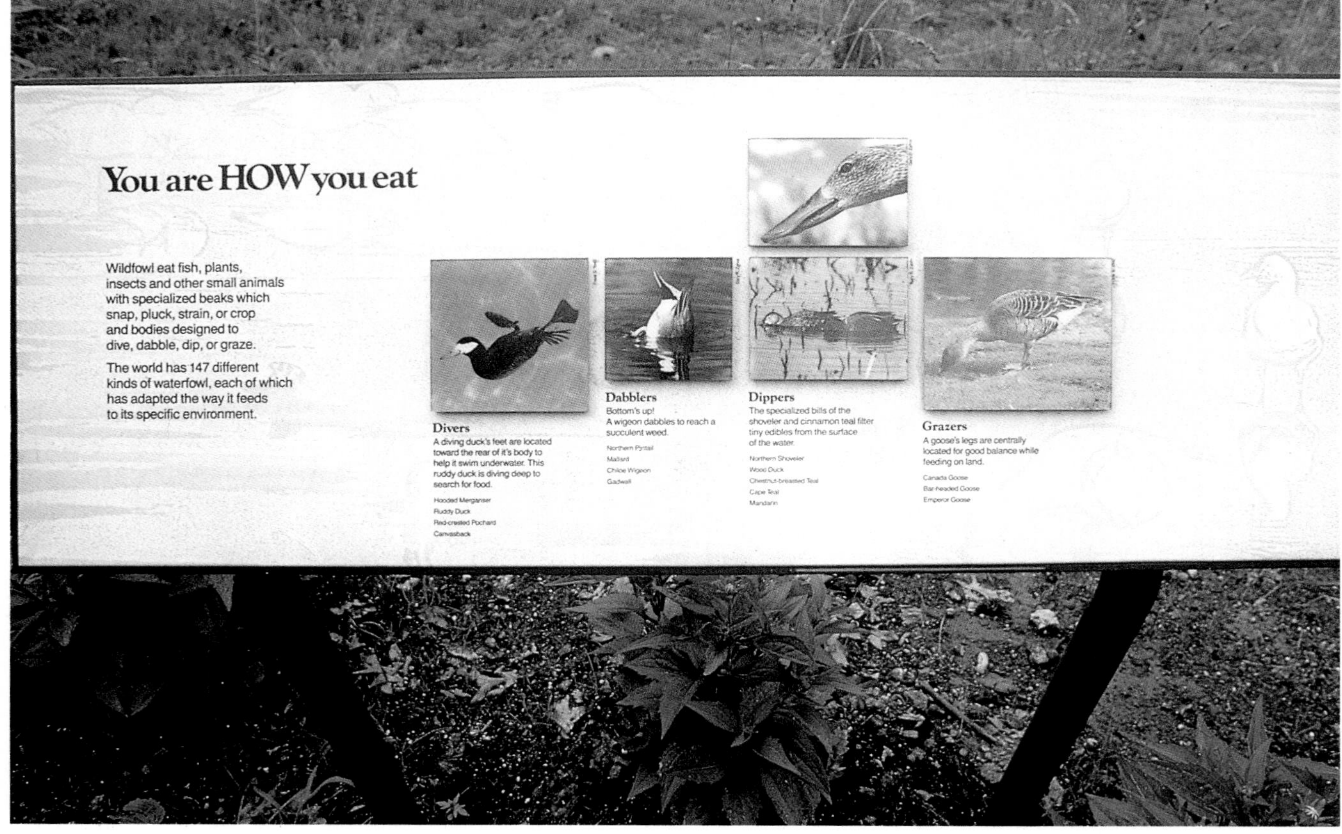
You are HOW you eat
Wildfowl eat fish, plants, insects and other small animals with specialized beaks which snap, pluck, strain, or crop and bodies designed to dive, dabble, dip, or graze.
The world has 147 different kinds of waterfowl, each of which has adapted the way it feeds to its specific environment.
Divers
A diving duck's feet are located toward the rear of it's body to help it swim underwater. This ruddy duck is diving deep to search for food.
Hooded Merganser
Ruddy Duck
Red-crested Pochard
Canvasback
Dabblers
Bottom's up!
A wigeon dabbles to reach a succulent weed.
Northern Pyntail
Mallard
Chiloe Wigeon
Gadwall
Dippers
The specialized bills of the shoveler and cinnamon teal filter tiny edibles from the surface of the water.
Northern Showeler
Wood Duck
Chestnut-breasted Teal
Cape Teal
Mandarin
Grazers
A goose's legs are centrally located for good balance while feeding on land.
Canada Goose
Bar-headed Goose
Emperor Goose

Identifier for the new Birds of Paradise exhibit in the World of Birds. Silk-screened with hand tipped colour on aluminium sheet

Art Directors
John Gwynne, Charlie Beier
Designer
Sharon Kramer
Illustrators
Deborah Ross, Sharon Kramer

White-Crested Laughing Thrush
Garrulax leucolophus

More often heard than seen, this bird is famous for its laughlike calls—a common sound in southeast Asian teak forests and bamboo thickets.

lifts its crest
when excited
or calling

Flowering Maple
Abutilon hybridum

The first monsoons of the rainy season stimulate lush new growth and blooming of the yellow-flowered abutilon. Its hibiscus-like blossoms reveal its membership in the mallow family.

protective hairs on leaves shade tissue, radiate heat, buffer dry wind

Red-Whiskered Bulbul
Pycnonotus jocosus

Bold and noisy, red-whiskered bulbuls enliven forest edges, farms, gardens, and city parks with their constant chatter as they dart after insects and scurry through the trees looking for ripe fruit.

together, male and female
build a cup nest
woven of grass, moss,
and leaves

Temporary construction sign silk-screened on aluminium sheet

Semi-permanent signage wrapping on exterior cages of an old zoo building. Hand-painted graphics and silk-screened text on Sunbrella awning fabric

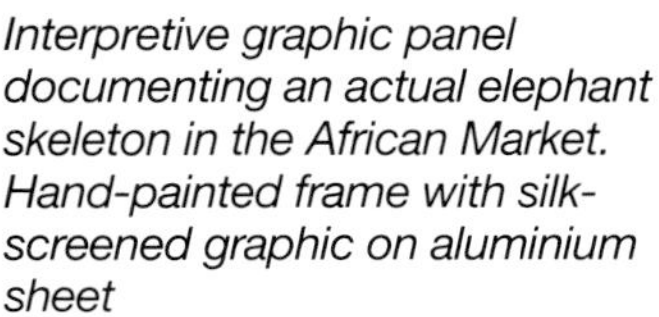

Interpretive graphic panel documenting an actual elephant skeleton in the African Market. Hand-painted frame with silk-screened graphic on aluminium sheet

Porcelain enamel interpretive panel in verdigris copper frame for elephant exhibit at Zoo Centre

Designer
Charlie Beier
Illustrator
Deborah Ross

Commemorative poster for the opening of Zoo Centre – a year round viewing of Asian elephants and a Sumatran rhino – at the Bronx Zoo

Art Director
Ed Curran
Designer
Ken Kneitel
Illustrator
James McMullen

Graphics panels

Designer
Elie Aliman
Illustrator
Tomi Ungerer
Copywriter
Dr. William G. Conway

Hand-applied and hand-screened poster

Art Director
John Gwynne
Designer
Ron Davis
Illustrator
Deborah Ross

what is a bird?
If an animal has feathers, it's a bird; if it hasn't, it isn't.
Birds are warm-blooded, egg-laying, toothless vertebrates specialized for flight. From condor to cardinal, their anatomy is remarkably uniform but they have adapted to life on every part of the earth except the polar wastes.
Birds – the class Aves – evolved at least 150,000,000 years ago and there are 8,600 species of birds alive today.

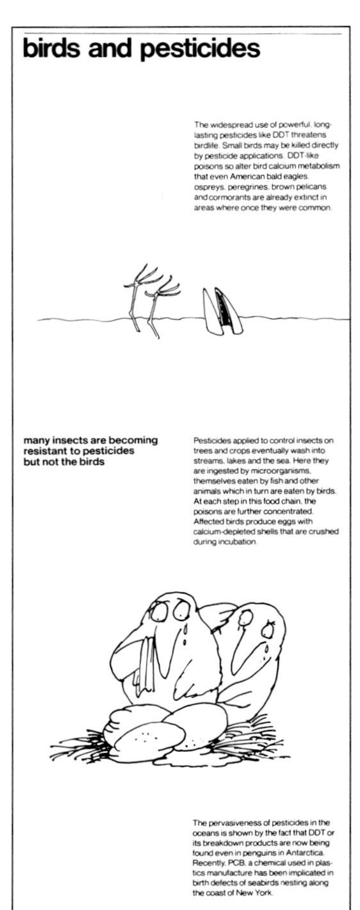

birds and pesticides
The widespread use of powerful, long-lasting pesticides like DDT threatens birdlife. Small birds may be killed directly by pesticide applications. DDT-like poisons so alter bird calcium metabolism that even American bald eagles, ospreys, peregrines, brown pelicans and cormorants are already extinct in areas where once they were common.
many insects are becoming resistant to pesticides but not the birds
Pesticides applied to control insects on trees and crops eventually wash into streams, lakes and the sea. Here they are ingested by microorganisms, themselves eaten by fish and other animals which in turn are eaten by birds. At each step in this food chain, the poisons are further concentrated. Affected birds produce eggs with calcium-depleted shells that are crushed during incubation.
The pervasiveness of pesticides in the oceans is shown by the fact that DDT or its breakdown products are now being found even in penguins in Antarctica. Recently, PCB, a chemical used in plastics manufacture has been implicated in birth defects of seabirds nesting along the coast of New York.

birds and birders in new york
pigeons aren't the only birds in gotham
410 kinds of birds have been identified in New York State
257 have been identified in Central Park
Today, bird watchers are the most productive group of amateur environmentalists in the United States. Getting back to nature in their own back yards, New York birders take part in regular wildlife lectures, field trips and special events like the exciting "Christmas Count" and "Spring Census."
40,000 people are serious field observers of birds in new york.
A visit to the World of Birds is a start, now consider joining the New York Zoological Society or one of the following groups:
National Audubon Society
950 Third Avenue
New York, N.Y. 10022
Local chapters of Audubon in New Jersey, Connecticut, Massachusetts, Pennsylvania
Hawk Mountain Sanctuary
Kempton, Pennsylvania
Zoological Society membership information is available at the World of Birds shop and the Safari Shop.

Birds of Paradise
NOW ON EXHIBIT AT THE WORLD OF BIRDS

Zoological Society of San Diego

The Central Park Zoo occupies 5.5 acres of Central Park in Manhattan. The Zoo features nearly 1000 animals in naturalistic exhibits representing the earth's three major climatic zones: the Tropic Zone, the Temperate Territory and the Polar Circle.

The Tropic Zone building is home to animals representing the diversity of life in the world's rainforests. A mezzanine level displays the jewels of the rainforest: tiny tamarins, poison dart frogs and other colourful, small birds, reptiles and amphibians.

The outdoor Temperate Territory features animals from the temperate zones including Lesser pandas, North American river otters and a troop of Japanese snow monkeys on their own island.

Exhibit area identification sign in Central Garden near sea lion pool

Exterior porcelain enamel interpretive graphic panel marking entrance to Polar Zone exhibit: "The Poles of The Earth"

Art Director
David Gibson
Designer
Tracy Cameron
Design Firm
Two Twelve Associates, Inc.
Photographer
Peter Aaron

The Polar circle hosts a large polar bear exhibit where the bears can be observed swimming underwater; a mixed exhibit of Harbour seals and Arctic foxes and a special building featuring birds from opposite poles: Gentoo and Chinstrap penguins from the Antarctic and puffins from the north pole region.

A central garden of four landscaped corner beds circles the glass-enclosed California sea lion pool. The Zoo also features a Conservation Centre with changing displays and videos produced by the Zoo's Education Department.

Visitors using porcelain enamel directory map of zoo and global climate zones

Interior porcelain enamel interpretive graphic panel in Tropic Zone Building, "The School of Ill Repute"

Locomotion

Kuhl's Gecko	Chameleon	Tokay Gecko	Red-eyed Treefrog
Ptychozoon kuhli	*Chameleo deveurensis*	*Gekko gecko*	*Agalychnis callidryas*
	Foot detail	Foot detail	

Many arboreal animals exhibit specialized shapes adapted for movement through the rain-forest canopy.

Narrow bodies balance more easily on thin branches. A prehensile tail aids in grasping branches and tree trunks. Toes tipped with suction cups, treaded pads, or long claws are wonderful adaptations for climbing.

Some species can even glide or parachute through the forest using expandable flaps of skin that open up along the sides of the body.

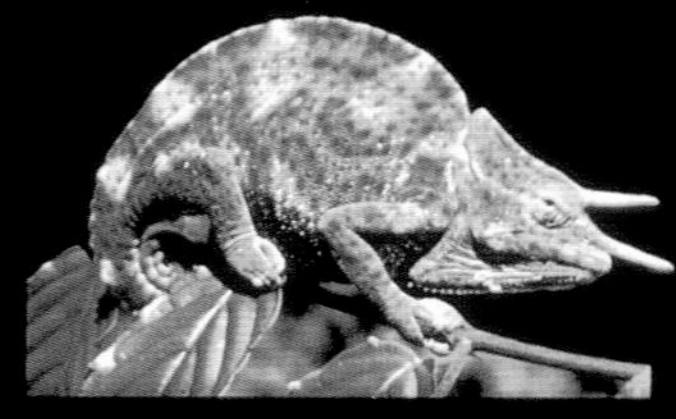

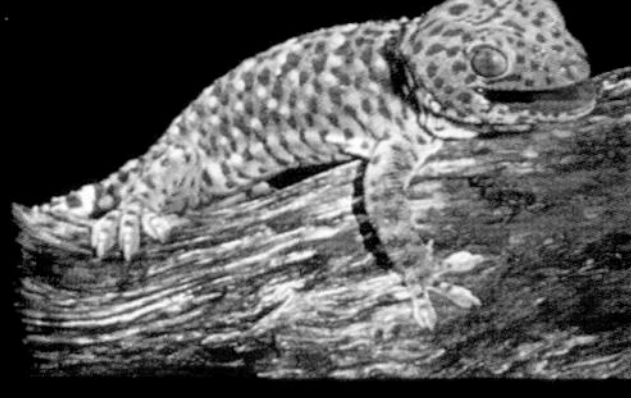

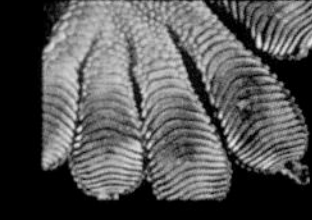

Rear-illuminated interpretive graphic panel transparencies

Life on the Edge

Antarctica is the coldest place on earth. Winter temperatures may reach -120°f and wind speeds 100 miles per hour. Terrestrial life is possible only at the continent's edges, where the climate is moderated by the surrounding Southern Ocean.

Even there, only a few simple plants and insects endure year round, though some seal and penguin species continue to occupy the ice shelf.

Along the northern rim of Eurasia and North America, however, at the southern edges of the Arctic, temperatures rise well above freezing in summer, and a surprisingly diverse community of plants and animals abides.

The warmth of summer's midnight sun stimulates a brief but intense burst of productivity before the long, bitter winter months.

Spring

In late spring, as day length and temperatures increase, the earth thaws, and meltwater from the light snow that covered the tundra during winter nourishes a rich mosaic of lichens, grasses, herbs, and shrubs.

Caribou follow the flush of new growth northward to their summer calving grounds in the high Arctic. In turn, fattened caribou sustain the packs of Arctic wolves which shadow the movement of the herds.

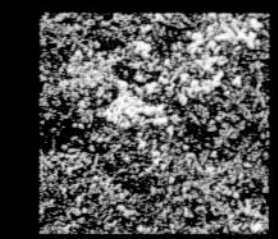

Summer

As summer progresses, vast numbers of migratory birds arrive from the south to nest, and swarms of biting insects fill the air.

Multitudes of small rodents—Arctic lemmings and tundra voles—harvest the abundant summer grasses.

Arctic foxes and snowy owls search out these prolific rodents in order to nourish their young, which must grow rapidly to survive the sudden onset of winter.

Autumn

As summer wanes, caribou leave the open tundra for the protection of the boreal forest to the south. Fat reserves accumulated during lush summer grazing sustain the herds as the weather grows colder.

Arctic ground squirrels and brown bears, also fat from gluttonous summer feeding, begin their long winter hibernation.

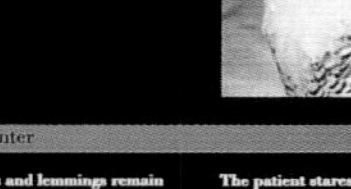

Winter

Voles and lemmings remain active beneath the snowcover, feeding on roots and caches of grass but still vulnerable to Arctic foxes, with their extraordinarily sensitive hearing.

The patient stares of snowy owls focus on the furtive movements of Arctic hares and willow ptarmigan, which forage winterlong on windswept tundra slopes. Life endures only in anticipation of the sun's return.

Current Effects

The South Pole is twice as cold as the North Pole though each receives the same amount of solar energy.

Ocean currents constantly move warm water, and therefore additional heat, from the tropics into the Arctic Ocean, which comprises two-thirds of the North Polar region.

In contrast, two-thirds of the South Polar region is occupied by land, which blocks the flow of warm currents. The climate is consequently colder, and life on the continent is greatly impoverished.

Lemming Limits

At three-to-four-year intervals, lemmings die off in large numbers, after depleting the tundra plants that nourish them. When lemmings are scarce, female Arctic foxes and snowy owls are less likely to breed, their litters and clutches are small, and very few young survive.

As the vegetation gradually recovers, lemmings increase in number. More female owls and foxes reproduce, and more young survive until the cycle repeats itself.

A Desert Swamp

Less precipitation falls on the Arctic tundra than in the Mohave Desert. Yet each summer, when the thin snow cover melts, the tundra becomes an impassable quagmire.

Permafrost, the permanently frozen soil underlying the tundra, prevents meltwater from seeping away. Instead, it remains at the surface, alternately freezing and thawing as the seasons change but available each summer to nourish a lush plant community.

Rear-illuminated interpretive graphic panel transparencies

Seasons in the Cold

At opposite ends of the earth's axis of rotation, the North and South Poles are fixed in the exact center of the two polar regions—the Arctic and the Antarctic.

These regions are defined in precise astronomical terms as the areas enclosed by the Arctic Circle (66° 30′ north latitude) and the Antarctic Circle (66° 30′ south latitude), the northernmost and southernmost points from which the sun can be seen, respectively, at the winter and summer solstices (December 22 and June 21).

In more subtle biological terms, the polar zones are defined by the response of organisms to intense cold. The Arctic's boundary lies in the gradual transition from forest to treeless tundra, the Antarctic's in the sudden change of plankton species off the Antarctic coast.

Both definitions are based on the effects of the earth's relationship with the sun.

Sunlight in the Polar Regions

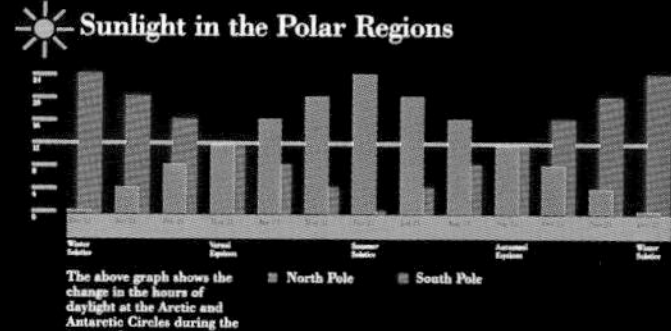
North Pole
South Pole

The above graph shows the change in the hours of daylight at the Arctic and Antarctic Circles during the course of a year.

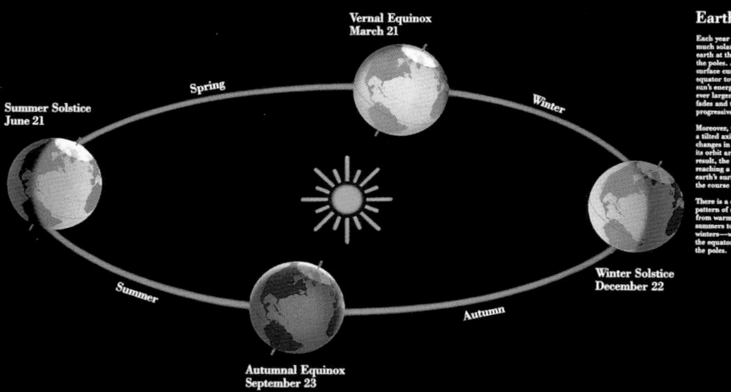
Vernal Equinox
March 21
Spring
Winter
Summer Solstice
June 21
Summer
Autumn
Winter Solstice
December 22
Autumnal Equinox
September 23

Earth's Orbit Around the Sun

Each year more than twice as much solar energy reaches the earth at the equator than at the poles. As the earth's surface curves away from the equator toward the poles, the sun's energy is dispersed over ever larger areas. Its warmth fades and the climate becomes progressively colder.

Moreover, the earth rotates on a tilted axis and therefore changes in orientation during its orbit around the sun. As a result, the amount of energy reaching a given place on the earth's surface varies through the course of a year.

There is a corresponding pattern of seasonal change—from warmer, brighter summers to darker, colder winters—which is subtle at the equator but dramatic at the poles.

Within the Arctic and Antarctic circles, the sun never rises above the horizon in the depth of winter, and never sets at the height of summer, when for a brief period as much solar energy reaches the poles as the equator. This seasonal climatic change makes life possible in the polar regions.

If the earth's axis were not tilted, temperatures would remain relatively constant throughout the year—not as cold in winter but never as warm in summer—and life would withdraw from the polar regions toward the equator.

A Desert of Ice

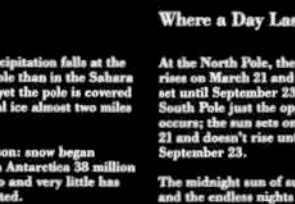

Less precipitation falls at the South Pole than in the Sahara Desert, yet the pole is covered by glacial ice almost two miles thick.

The reason: snow began falling in Antarctica 38 million years ago and very little has ever melted.

Where a Day Lasts a Year

At the North Pole, the sun rises on March 21 and doesn't set until September 23. At the South Pole just the opposite occurs; the sun sets on March 21 and doesn't rise until September 23.

The midnight sun of summer and the endless nights of winter profoundly influence the patterns of polar life.

A World Kept Warm by Ice

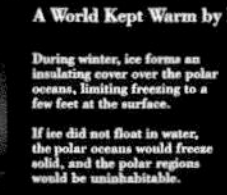

During winter, ice forms an insulating cover over the polar oceans, limiting freezing to a few feet at the surface.

If ice did not float in water, the polar oceans would freeze solid, and the polar regions would be uninhabitable.

Coping with Cold

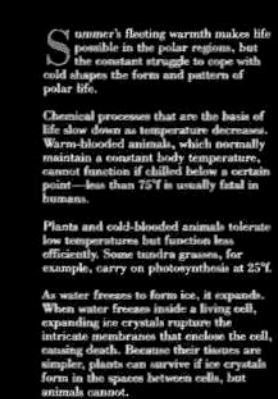

Summer's fleeting warmth makes life possible in the polar regions, but the constant struggle to cope with cold shapes the form and pattern of polar life.

Chemical processes that are the basis of life slow down as temperature decreases. Warm-blooded animals, which normally maintain a constant body temperature, cannot function if chilled below a certain point—less than 75°F is usually fatal in humans.

Plants and cold-blooded animals tolerate low temperatures but function less efficiently. Some tundra grasses, for example, carry on photosynthesis at 25°F.

As water freezes to form ice, it expands. When water freezes inside a living cell, expanding ice crystals rupture the intricate membranes that enclose the cell, causing death. Because their tissues are simpler, plants can survive if ice crystals form in the spaces between cells, but animals cannot.

Some Remarkable Adaptations

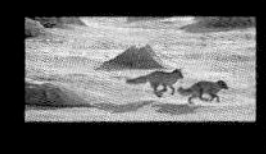

Warm Heart, Cold Feet

Secret of a Long Life

Survival of the Fattest

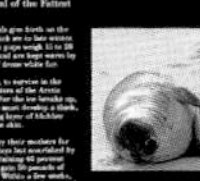

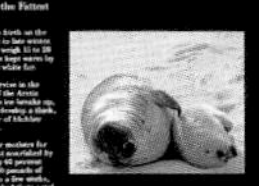

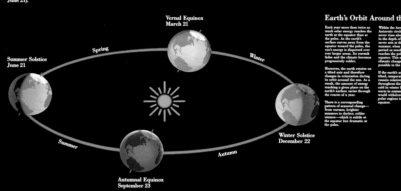

Exterior porcelain enamel interpretive graphic panels at polar bear exhibit

Lee Kuhn – FPG/Masterfile

Although Carl Hagenbecks Tierpark was opened in 1907 in Stellingen, Carl's father, a fishmonger, bought exotic animals from sailors to start a small menagerie in 1848. He patented his concept of the "zoo of the future" with open enclosures and without bars. Just two years after the second world war that destroyed most of the Tierpark, Carl successfully re-built and enlarged it. For more than 140 years, it has been a family enterprise receiving no subsidies from the city.

Today, with 2100 animals residing in 25 hectares of land, Carl Hagenbecks Tierpark has the largest elephant collection in Europe.

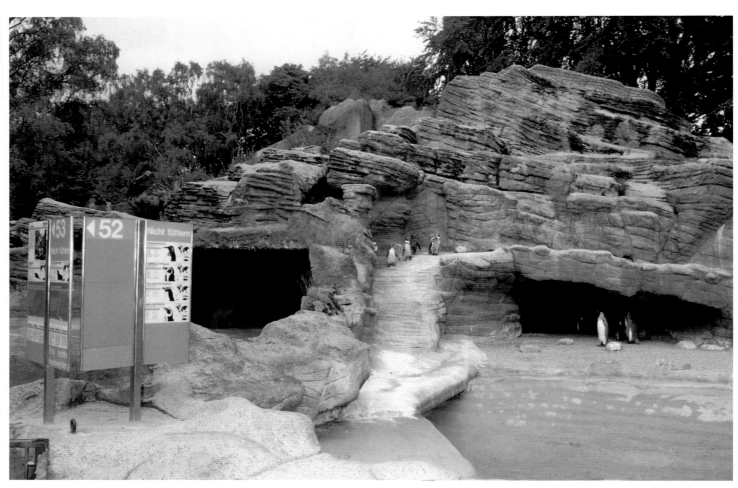

Interpretive panels

Entrance banners

Designer
Hans-Gerhard Meyer

EISBÄR
Ursus maritimus
Polar bear
Gewicht : ♂ bis 450 kg
♀ bis 350 kg
Länge : ♂ bis 2,50 m
♀ bis 2,00 m
Lebens-
erwartung : 30 - 40 Jahre
Tragzeit : 8 - 9 Monate
Geburts-
gewicht : nur ca. 500 g
Nördliche Meeresküsten
Nahrung

Nicht füttern
54
MÄHNENROBBE
KALIFORNISCHER SEELÖWE
Seebären - Bären, die im Wasser leben?
Die Akrobaten unter den Robben
Dicksein ist kein Schönheitsfehler
Merkmale
Vermehrung
Besonderes
Bewegung
Lebensraum
Merkmale
Besonderes
EISBÄR

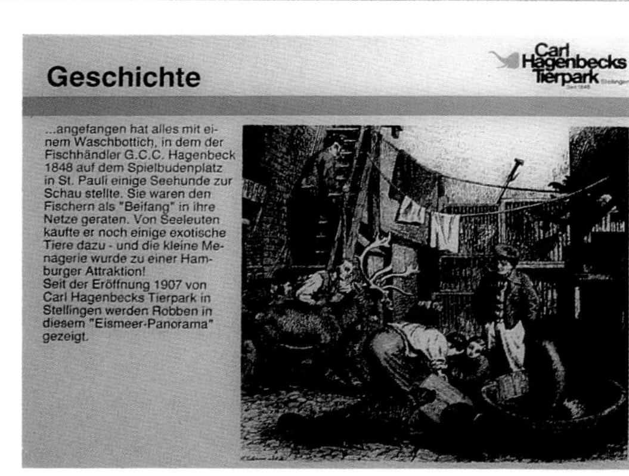
Geschichte
Carl Hagenbecks Tierpark
...angefangen hat alles mit einem Waschbottich, in dem der Fischhändler G.C.C. Hagenbeck 1848 auf dem Spielbudenplatz in St. Pauli einige Seehunde zur Schau stellte. Sie waren den Fischern als "Beifang" in ihre Netze geraten. Von Seeleuten kaufte er noch einige exotische Tiere dazu - und die kleine Menagerie wurde zu einer Hamburger Attraktion!
Seit der Eröffnung 1907 von Carl Hagenbecks Tierpark in Stellingen werden Robben in diesem "Eismeer-Panorama" gezeigt.

Posters and vehicle graphics

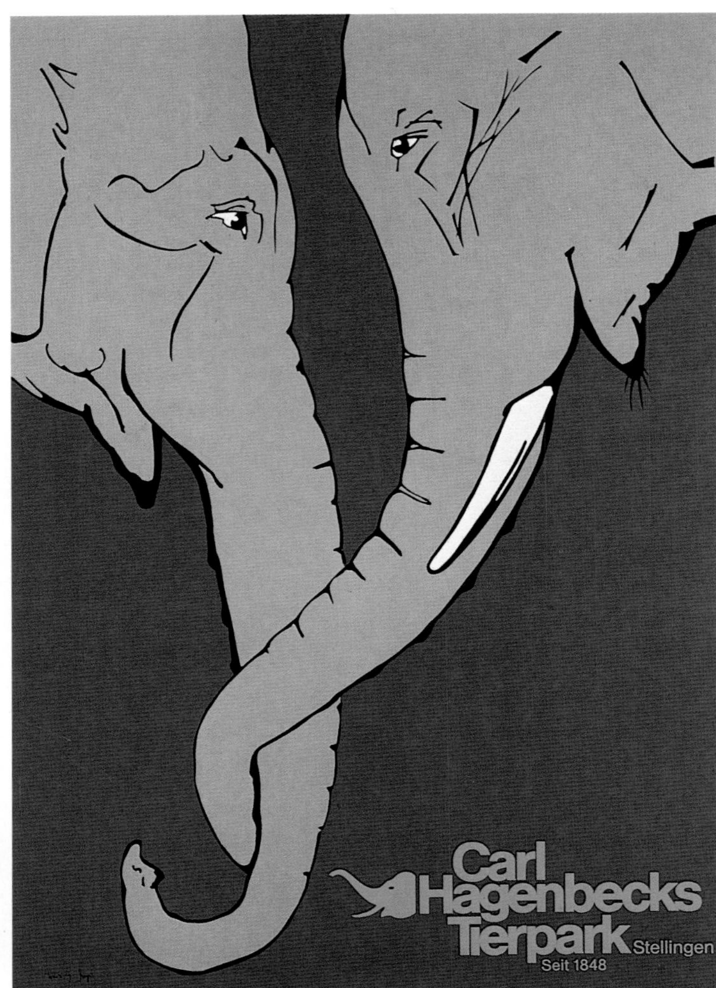

Carl
Hagenbecks
Tierpark Stellingen

Seit 1848

Brochures

Tom Bean/Masterfile

The Dallas Zoo opened in 1888 with two deer and two mountain lions. It has grown to a 70-acre zoo of approximately 1500 animals representing more than 320 species, including many that are rare or endangered.

In April 1990, the Zoo introduced a new 25-acre exhibit called the Wilds of Africa, where some 60 species of animals roam free of bars and cages in simulated natural environments. This is the first zoo exhibit in the world to include every major habitat of an entire continent - in this case, the desert, bush, river, mountain, woodland, and forest habitats of Africa. The focus is on habitats in order to show how animals are suited to their particular surroundings and to highlight the fragile bond between man, animals, and the environment.

Environmental Sculpture – metal rib cage of 30" diameter rings, 4" apart and covered with fibreglass

Art Director
Michael Morris
Design Firm
Michael Morris Design

Poster – Wilds of Africa

Art Director
Marianne Pomeroy

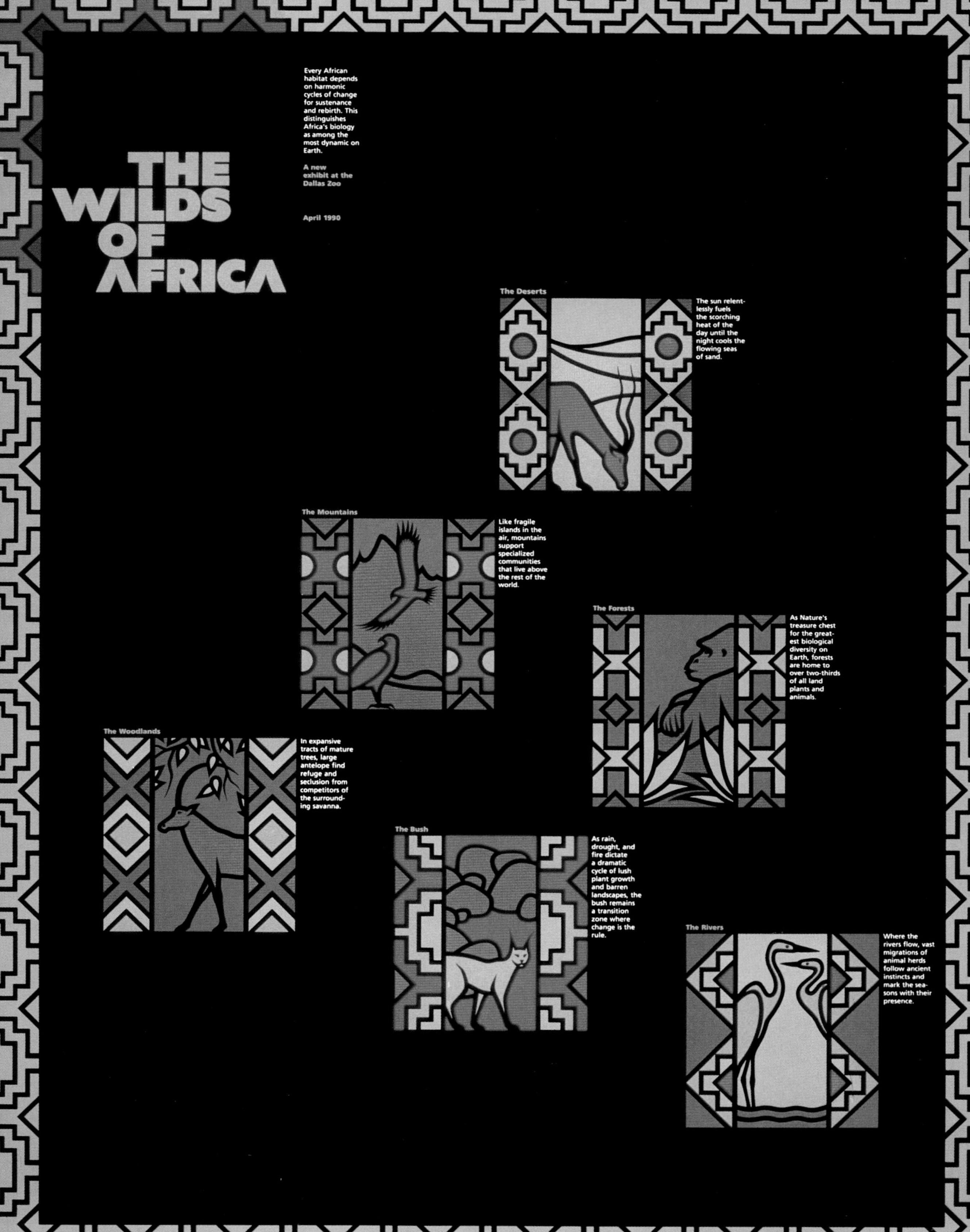
THE WILDS OF AFRICA
Every African habitat depends on harmonic cycles of change for sustenance and rebirth. This distinguishes Africa's biology as among the most dynamic on Earth.
A new exhibit at the Dallas Zoo
April 1990
The Deserts
The sun relentlessly fuels the scorching heat of the day until the night cools the flowing seas of sand.
The Mountains
Like fragile islands in the air, mountains support specialized communities that live above the rest of the world.
The Forests
As Nature's treasure chest for the greatest biological diversity on Earth, forests are home to over two-thirds of all land plants and animals.
The Woodlands
In expansive tracts of mature trees, large antelope find refuge and seclusion from competitors of the surrounding savanna.
The Bush
As rain, drought, and fire dictate a dramatic cycle of lush plant growth and barren landscapes, the bush remains a transition zone where change is the rule.
The Rivers
Where the rivers flow, vast migrations of animal herds follow ancient instincts and mark the seasons with their presence.

Parking lot directional signs with a special feature of rotating arrows

Art Director
Michael Morris
Design Firm
Michael Morris Design

Plywood banners depicting 6 habitats of the Wilds of Africa exhibit

Art Director
Marianne Pomeroy

General Admission – featuring a porcelain enameled steel panel with steel snake-like pipe

Art Director
Michael Morris
Design Firm
Michael Morris Design

Porcelain enameled steel logo pin-mounted on rock

The Ndebele Cafe – motif adapted from traditional designs of the Ndebele tribe of southern Africa

Art Director
Marianne Pomeroy

Orientation map of porcelain enameled steel for the Wilds of Africa

Visitor directional sign

Art Director
Michael Morris
Design Firm
Michael Morris Design

Gorilla interpretive book located in the Gorilla Research Centre

Art Director
Michael Morris
Design Firm
Michael Morris Design
Photographer
Robert Cabello

Nature trail guide – placed at the beginning of the self-guided trail

Art Director
Marianne Pomeroy

Introductory sign made of porcelain enameled steel

Art Director
Michael Morris
Design Firm
Michael Morris Design

Nature Trail numbering system corresponding with the guide. Number locations vary from rock to trees

Art Director
Michael Morris
Design Firm
Michael Morris Design

Collateral pieces – unique designs for T-shirts and greeting cards depicting the 6 habitats found in the Wilds of Africa: the desert, woodlands, forest, river, mountain, and bush.

Art Director
Marianne Pomeroy

3 of 6 billboards produced for the grand opening of Wilds of Africa exhibit

Art Director/Designer
Alan Lidji
Design Firm
Lidji Design, Inc.
Illustrator
C. F. Payne

3 of 6 newspaper ads for the opening of the Wilds of Africa

Art Director
Alan Lidji
Designer
Alan Lidji
Design Firm
Lidji Design, Inc.
Illustrator
Deborah Ross
Copywriter
David Martin

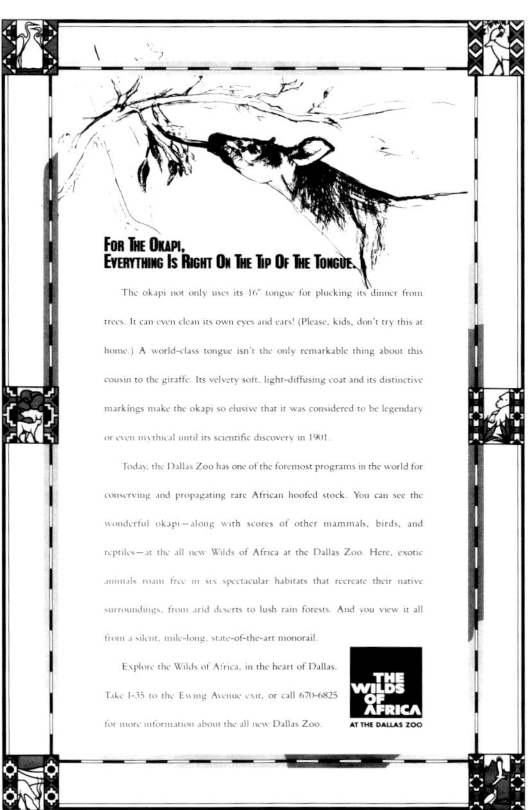

For The Okapi,
Everything Is Right On The Tip Of The Tongue.
The okapi not only uses its 16" tongue for plucking its dinner from trees. It can even clean its own eyes and ears! (Please, kids, don't try this at home.) A world-class tongue isn't the only remarkable thing about this cousin to the giraffe. Its velvety soft, light-diffusing coat and its distinctive markings make the okapi so elusive that it was considered to be legendary or even mythical until its scientific discovery in 1901.
Today, the Dallas Zoo has one of the foremost programs in the world for conserving and propagating rare African hoofed stock. You can see the wonderful okapi—along with scores of other mammals, birds, and reptiles—at the all new Wilds of Africa at the Dallas Zoo. Here, exotic animals roam free in six spectacular habitats that recreate their native surroundings, from arid deserts to lush rain forests. And you view it all from a silent, mile-long, state-of-the-art monorail.
Explore the Wilds of Africa, in the heart of Dallas. Take I-35 to the Ewing Avenue exit, or call 670-6825 for more information about the all new Dallas Zoo.
THE WILDS OF AFRICA
AT THE DALLAS ZOO

For The Egyptian Vulture,
A Well-rounded Meal Is Just A Stone's Throw Away.
It's one of the smallest members of the vulture family, and one of the most resourceful. Take one Egyptian vulture, one unattended ostrich nest, some small rocks, and in a few minutes you've got Serengeti Surprise. This bizarre-looking bird of prey feasts on its culinary creation—at least until the mother ostrich returns. Then the Egyptian vulture must demonstrate another of its attributes: the ability to flee!
It won't be dining on any ostrich eggs, but you can see the strange and wonderful behavior of the Egyptian vulture—along with scores of other mammals, birds, and reptiles—at the all new Wilds of Africa at the Dallas Zoo. Here, exotic animals roam free in six spectacular habitats that recreate their native surroundings, from arid deserts to lush rain forests. And you view it all from a silent, state-of-the-art monorail.
Explore the Wilds of Africa, in the heart of Dallas. Take I-35 to the Ewing Avenue exit, or call 670-6825 for more information about the all new Dallas Zoo.
THE WILDS OF AFRICA
AT THE DALLAS ZOO

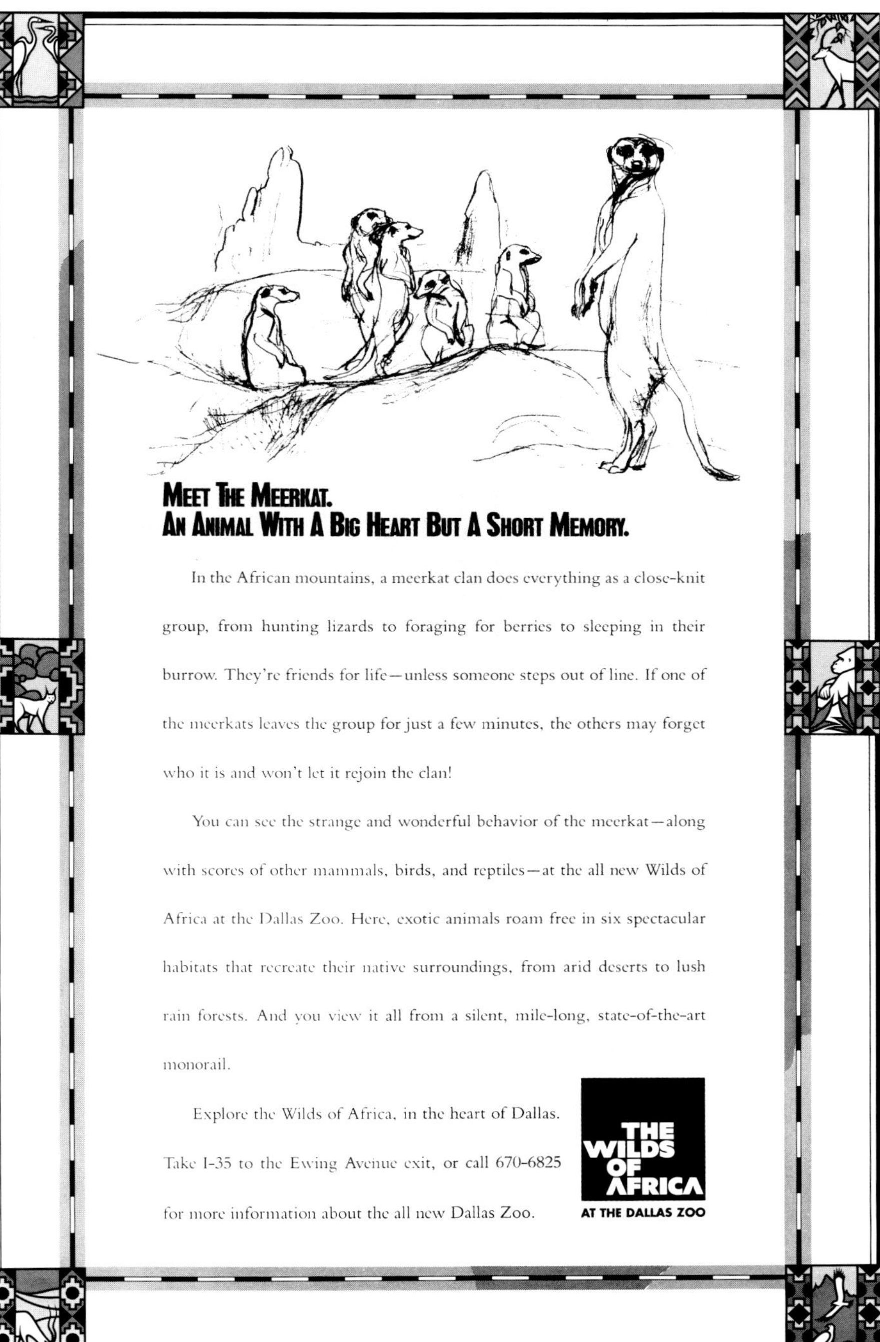

Meet The Meerkat.
An Animal With A Big Heart But A Short Memory.
In the African mountains, a meerkat clan does everything as a close-knit group, from hunting lizards to foraging for berries to sleeping in their burrow. They're friends for life—unless someone steps out of line. If one of the meerkats leaves the group for just a few minutes, the others may forget who it is and won't let it rejoin the clan!
You can see the strange and wonderful behavior of the meerkat—along with scores of other mammals, birds, and reptiles—at the all new Wilds of Africa at the Dallas Zoo. Here, exotic animals roam free in six spectacular habitats that recreate their native surroundings, from arid deserts to lush rain forests. And you view it all from a silent, mile-long, state-of-the-art monorail.
Explore the Wilds of Africa, in the heart of Dallas. Take I-35 to the Ewing Avenue exit, or call 670-6825 for more information about the all new Dallas Zoo.
THE WILDS OF AFRICA
AT THE DALLAS ZOO

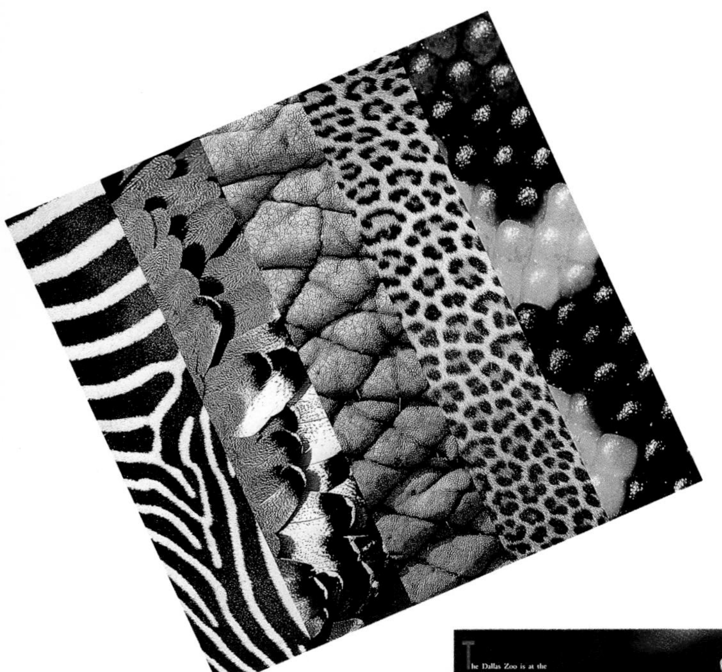

Brochure

Art Director
Alan Lidji
Designer
Alan Lidji
Design Firm
Lidji Design, Inc.
Photographer
Robert Cabello
Copywriter
David Martin

Annual report

Art Director
Scott Ray
Designer
Scott Ray
Design Firm
Peterson & Company
Illustrators
Jack Unruh, James N. Smith, Bryan Peterson, Greg King, Cathie Bleck
Copywriter
Kathleen Crist

Barrett & MacKay/Masterfile

Jurong Birdpark Singapore

The Jurong Bird Park of Singapore opened in 1971 on 20.2 hectares of land. It is home to 4500 birds of 450 species - the largest collection of Southeast Asian birds in the world.

Exhibits are landscaped to reflect the habitat of the various species. An enormous walk-in aviary contains a tropical rain forest where birds fly freely. Other birds are viewed in open areas such as the Crane Paddock, Flamingo Pool, and Cockatoo and Macaw Courtyards.

Entrance directory & signage

Tram graphics

Art Director
Ken Cato
Design Firm
Cato Design Inc.

The Jurong Bird Park has successfully bred rare and endangered species such as the Scarlet Ibis and Bali Mynah. It has established the world's largest captive breeding colony of the endangered Humboldt Penguin.

A monorail guides visitors through the extensive grounds. An amphitheatre stages exciting bird shows.

Staff uniform

Shopping bag and invitation card

Wayne Lynch/Masterfile

The Smithsonian Institution's National Zoological Park is located on a 165-acre tract in Rock Creek Park, Washington, D.C. Here, over 3000 animals representing 800 different species are seen by more than 3.5 million visitors each year.

In 1974 the zoo design concept featured a system of trails, with the central path, Olmsted Walk, traversing the entire zoo area. A prominent system of animal pictographs enable visitors, especially small children, to easily locate the exhibits that interest them.

Although the signage system is now long gone, it remains as one of the classics in zoo graphics.

The symbol was developed using the national symbol of the bald eagle and combining it with the eagle chick to represent the zoo's purpose – the continuation of the species. The National Zoo program was designed the firm of Wyman & Cannan in 1976.

Art Directors
Bill Cannan, Lance Wyman
Designers
Bill Cannan, Lance Wyman, Brian Flahive, Tucker Veimiester, Tom Demonse
Project Coordinator
Robert Mulcahy

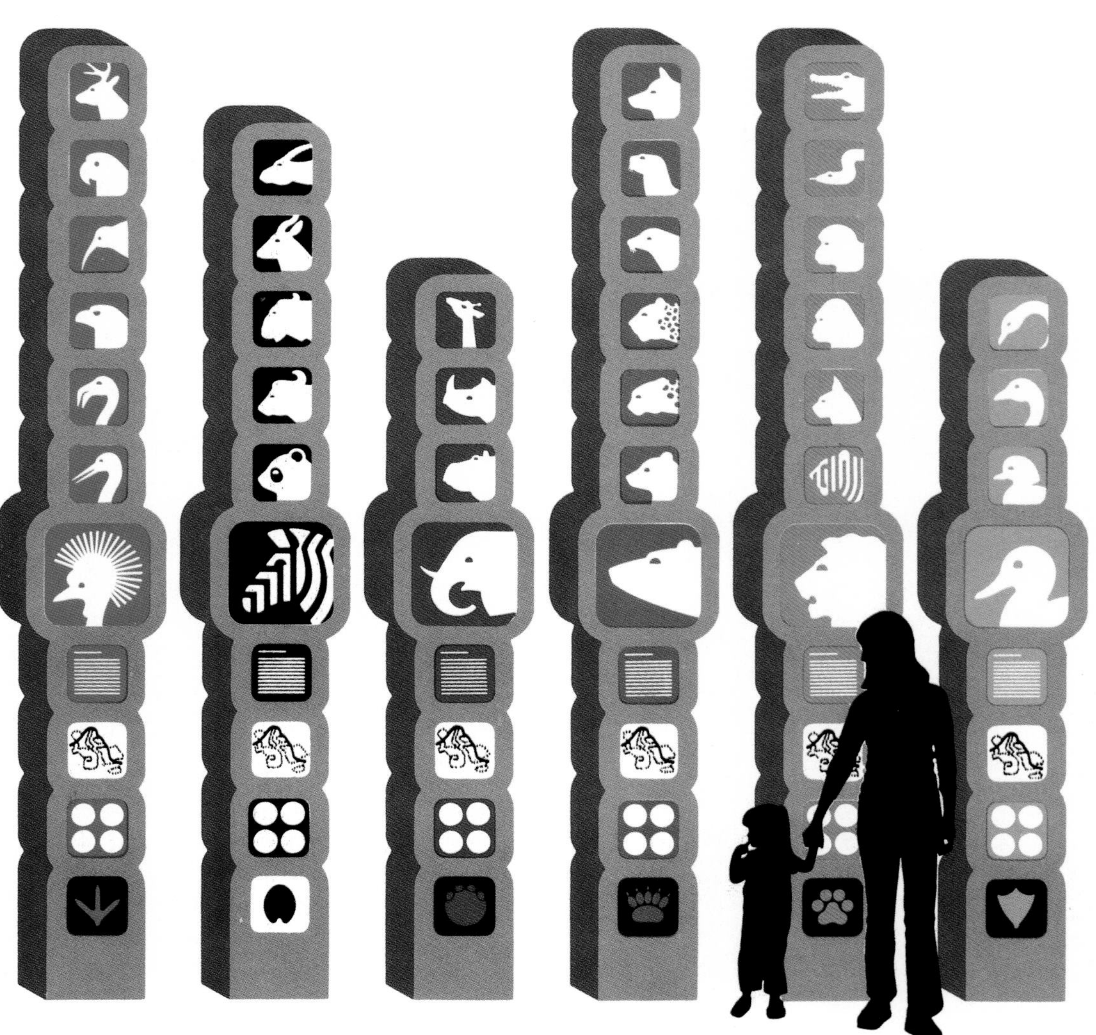

Developing a trail system by dividing the zoo experience into manageable segments – using a totem to represent the major animal exhibits found on that trail. It included such information as trail length, time to complete, services available, etc. Totems also marked the beginning and end of each trail.

The rounded corner forms found in the street furniture inspired the basic geometry of the zoo alphabet.

A B C D E F G H I J
K L M N O P Q R S
T U V W X Y Z 1 2 3
4 5 6 7 8 9 0

Secondary elements to the 12 totems were 6 freestanding map structures and 52 trash receptacles designed to accommodate all secondary service signs into precast configuration.

The use of trail blazers based on the animal featured on that trail. Following these blazers, the visitors always found their way back to the main artery of the zoo, Olmsted Walk. The hilly terrain and numerous paths in the park prompted the use of trail blazing devices implanted directly on the pavement.

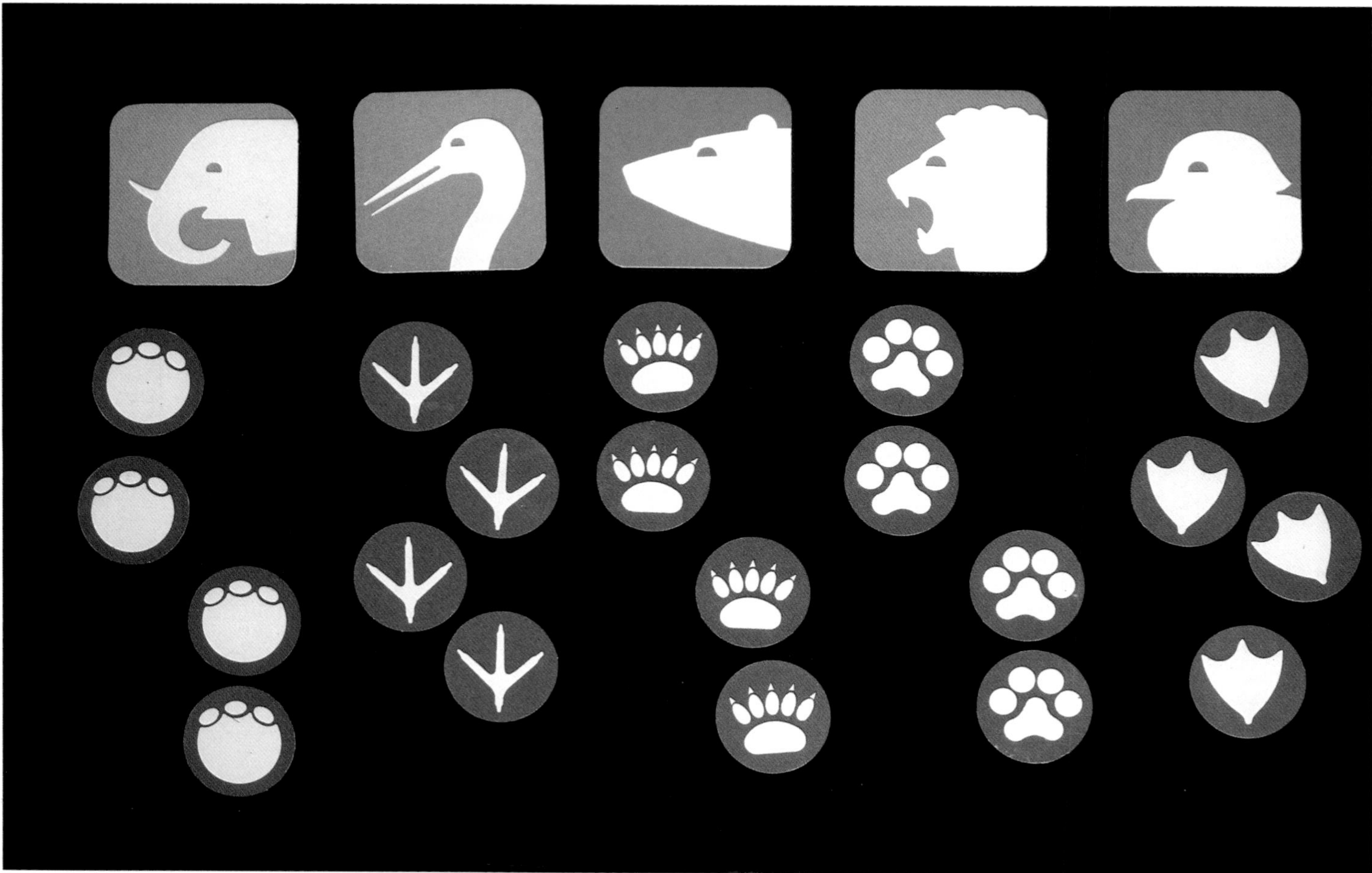

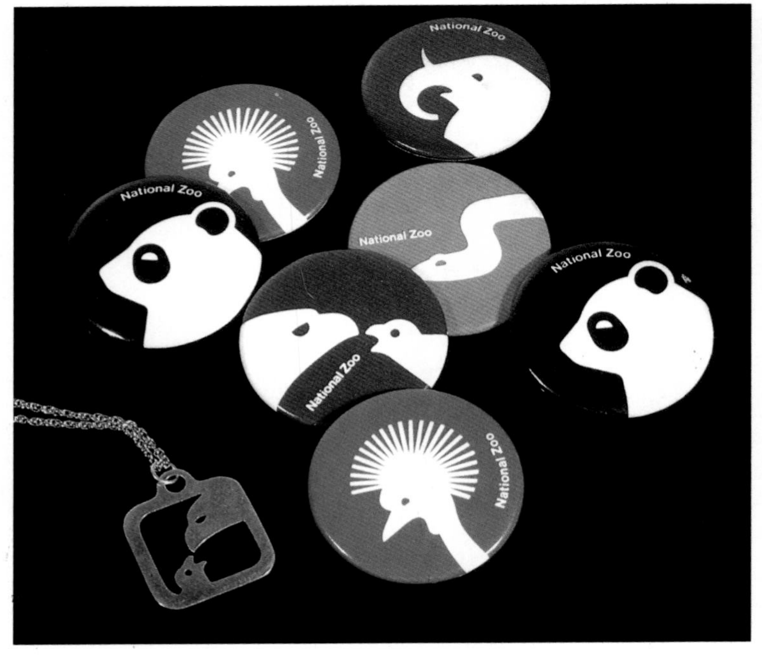

A series of 37 pictograms were developed to identify the major exhibits in the zoo. These were used in a variety of applications such as these buttons.

The National Zoo went through substantial physical changes in its landscape and exhibitory. The original six trails were reduced to two, thereby requiring a new wayfinding system.

The new signage system was designed so that it could be made by the in-house production unit. It was important for the signs to reflect the Zoo's new direction as a BioPark that emphasizes the interconnections of all life on earth.

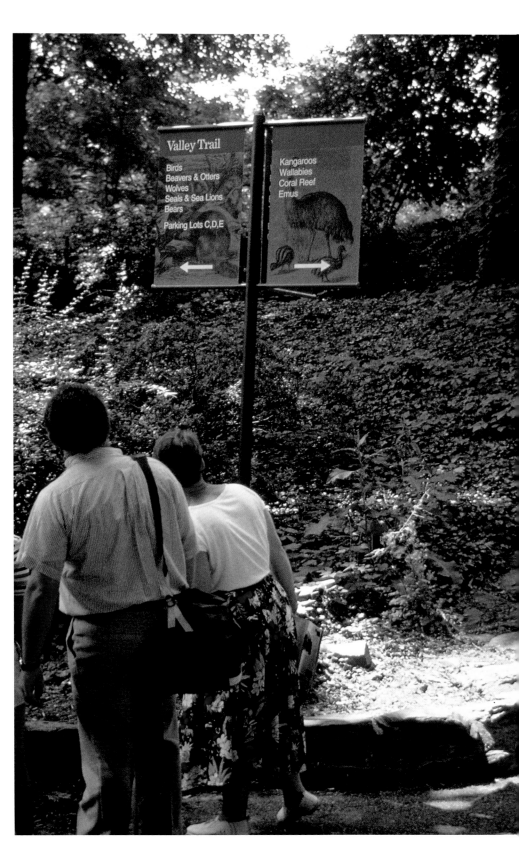

The new wayfinding system includes numbered trail markers, map stand/directories, sign posts and a printed map. The system is based on 2 trails that run through the zoo – Olmsted Walk (coded red) and Valley trail (coded blue). Numbers on the map relate to actual trail markers with corresponding numbers. Sign posts identify the path you are on and the closest animal and service locations to you.

Designer
Larry Matthews
Project Manager
Virginia Mahoney

3 panel display about the Golden Lion Tamarin conservation program

Trail markers & map

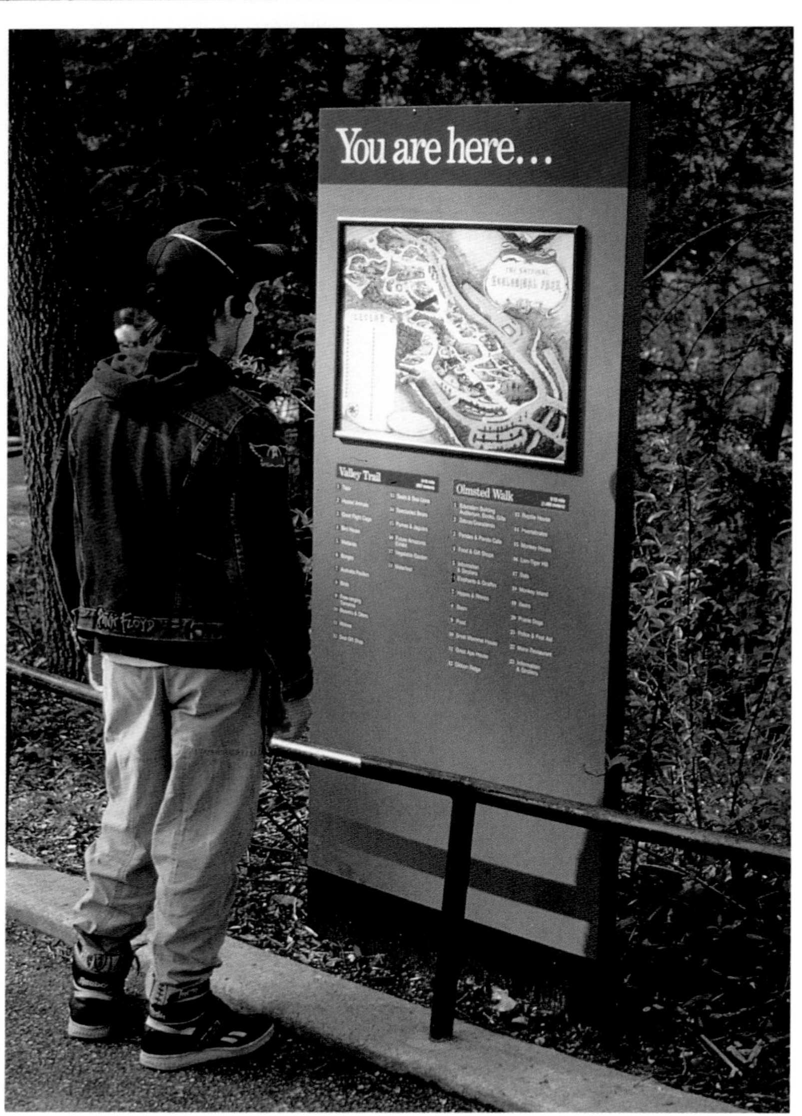

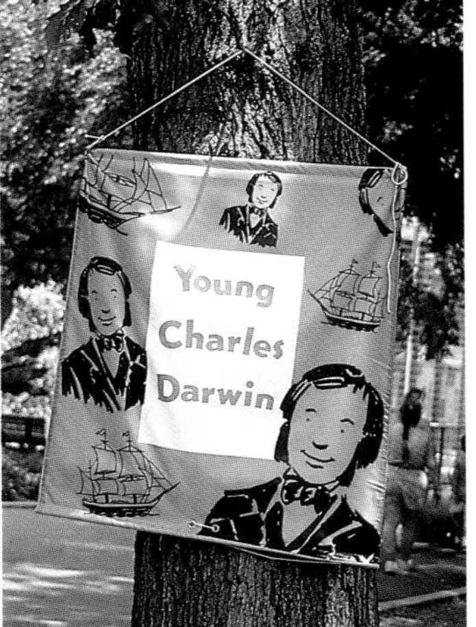

Improving Exhibit Interpretation Project – banner designs to identify interactive educational activities locations

Designer
Larry Matthews
Illustrator
Charles Beyl

Educational panel and exhibit for the honey bee

"Tombstone" sign for the now extinct Tasmanian wolf

Designer
Larry Matthews
Illustrator
Jeff Boyd

Educational sign panel for the Red Panda Yard

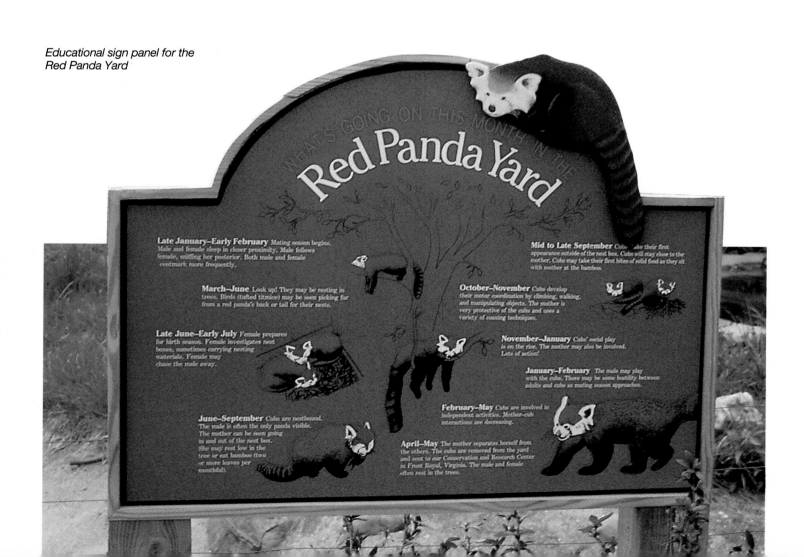

Outdoor mini exhibits during the centennial year

The large Victoria Water Lily sign panel

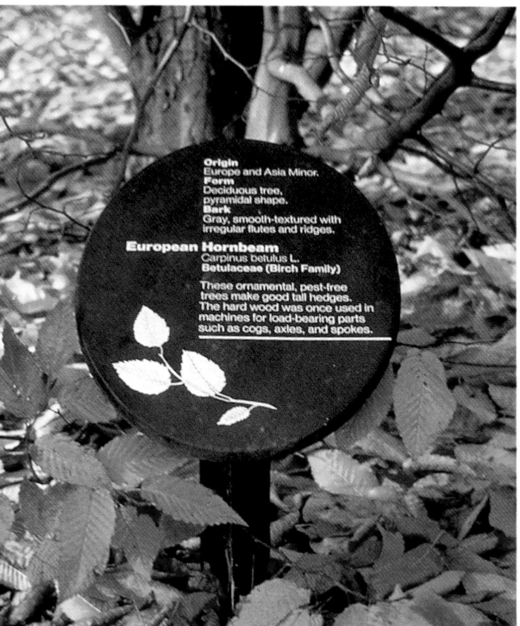

Interpretive graphics trialon at Monkey Island

Plant identification label

Symbol and sign for employee picnic area

Designers
Larry Matthews, Herman Krebs, Bob Bischoff, Ramona Hutko
Illustrator
Warren Cutler

endangered (in dān′jərd)

adj. 1. exposed to danger, harm or loss; in peril. 2. threatened with extinction.

Rare and Endangered Species at the National Zoo

These are just a few of the threatened and endangered species in the National Zoo's breeding program. Some are being kept at our 3000-acre Conservation and Research Center in Front Royal, Virginia.

Poster

Designer
Herman Krebs
Illustrator
Warren Cutler

Posters

Art Directors
Robert Mulcahy, Ramona Hutko
Designer
Ramona Hutko

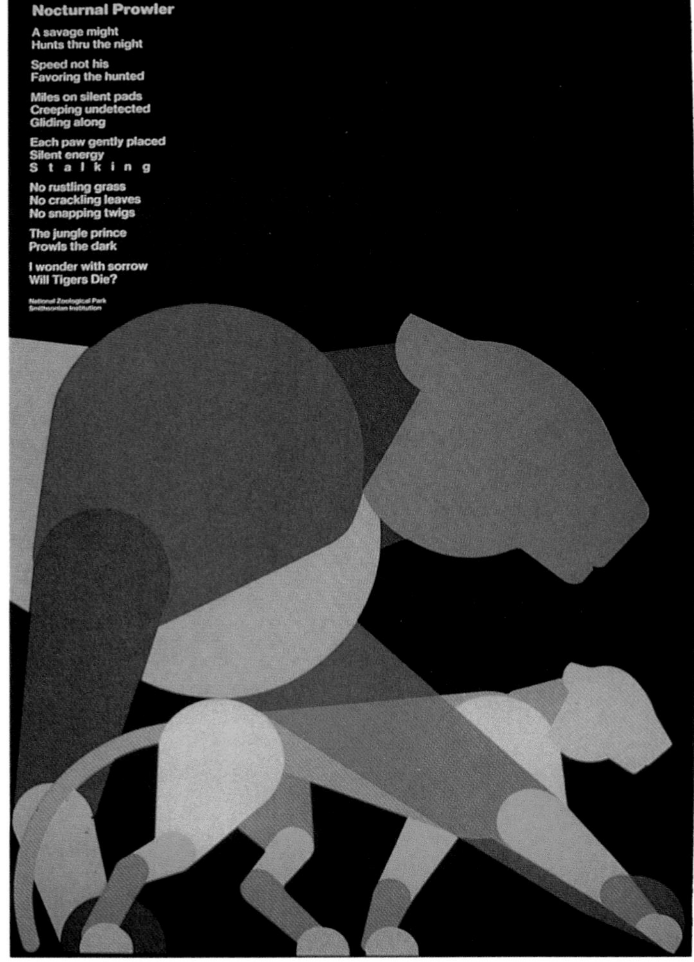

Large backlit poster in Metro stations

Art Director
Robert Mulcahy
Designer
Ramona Hutko
Photographer
Jessie Cohen

The
Mating
Game

Backlit poster in the Metro stations

Large outdoor poster (made in sections) containing schedule and information on Summerfest

Poster – National Zoo Symposium, "The Mating Game"

Designer
Herman Krebs
Photographer
Jordan Ross

Freeman Patterson/Masterfile

New England Aquarium Boston, Massachusetts, USA

The New England Aquarium, a private, non-profit organization, has been "Making Known the World of Water" at its Central Wharf facility for over 22 years. When the Aquarium opened in 1969, it set a national standard for aquariums.

The centrepiece of the Aquarium's existing facility is a 4-storey Giant Ocean Tank which features a Caribbean coral reef replica. The exhibit offers authentic views of the diverse tropical marine life that inhabits this environment. There are five galleries of exhibits: Tropical Gallery, Rivers of the Americans, Northern Waters of the World, Thinking Gallery, and Special Exhibit Gallery (site of the current Rain Forest exhibit).

Logo & signage

Designer
Tom Geismar
Design Firm
Chermayeff & Geismar Associates

Exterior of Building showing Stars banner 32' x 8'

Designers
Debbie Silke, Richard Duggan
Illustrator
Richard Duggan

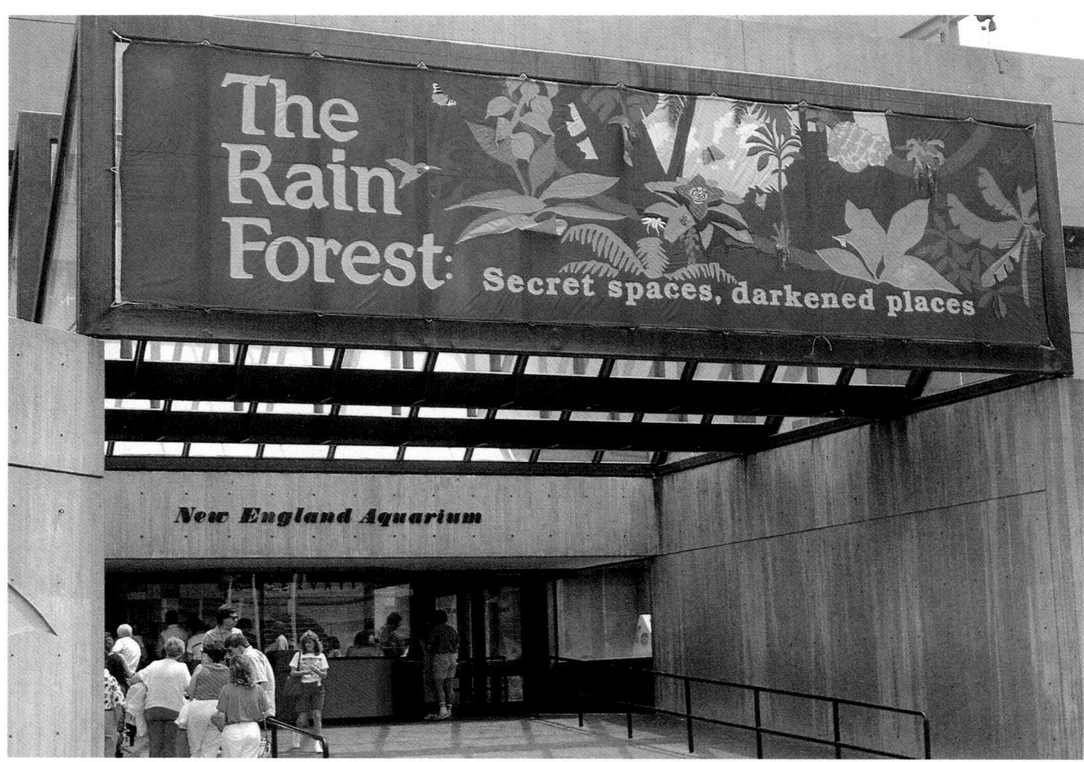

Banner for Rain Forest exhibit 32' x 8'

Designer
John Wrench
Illustrator
John Wrench

There are also penguins, dolphins, seals, sea lions, and the occasional stranded whale. The latest inventory includes 785 species and 17,469 specimens.

The budget for the Exhibits and Graphic Design Department is $400,000/year. All graphics, environments, and designs are produced in-house.

4' x 4' rearlit graphic panels used throughout the Aquarium to provide information about the exhibits

Designers
John Wrench, Richard Duggan
Illustrator
John Wrench
Photographers
Various
Copywriters
S. Duggan, M. Filisky, & others

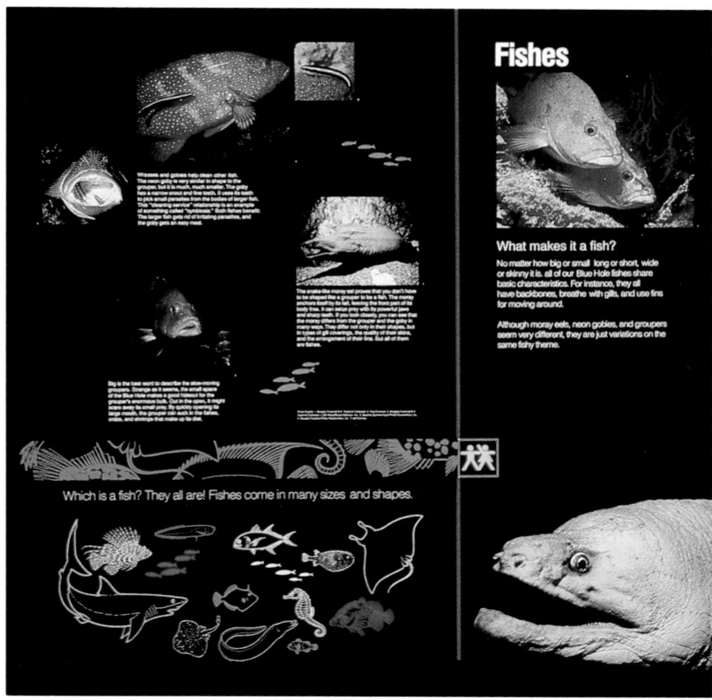

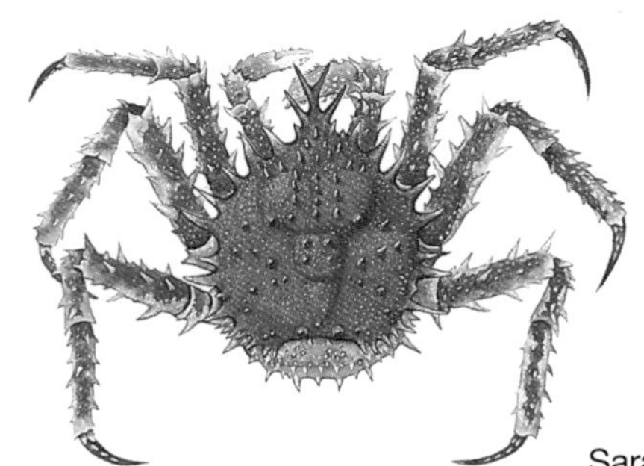

Sarah Landry

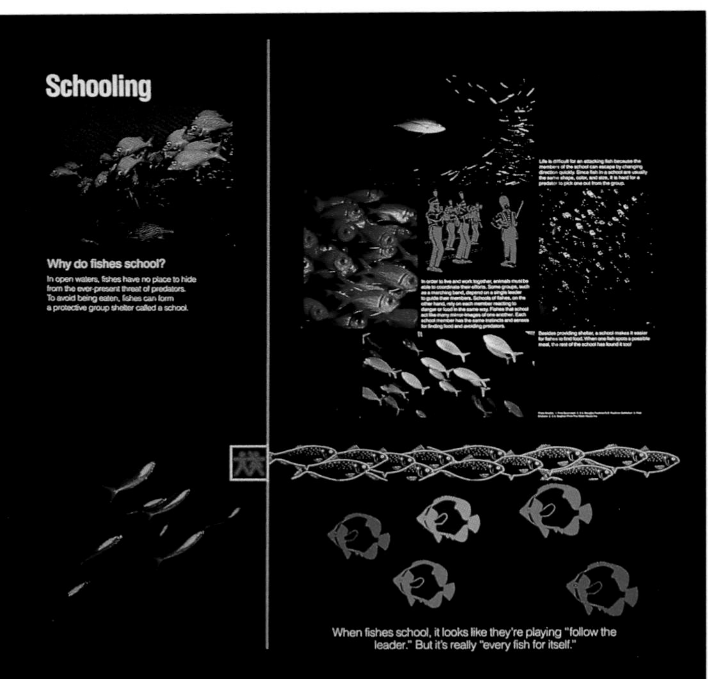

Schooling
Why do fishes school?
In open waters, fishes have no place to hide from the ever-present threat of predators. To avoid being eaten, fishes can form a protective group shelter called a school.
When fishes school, it looks like they're playing "follow the leader." But it's really "every fish for itself."

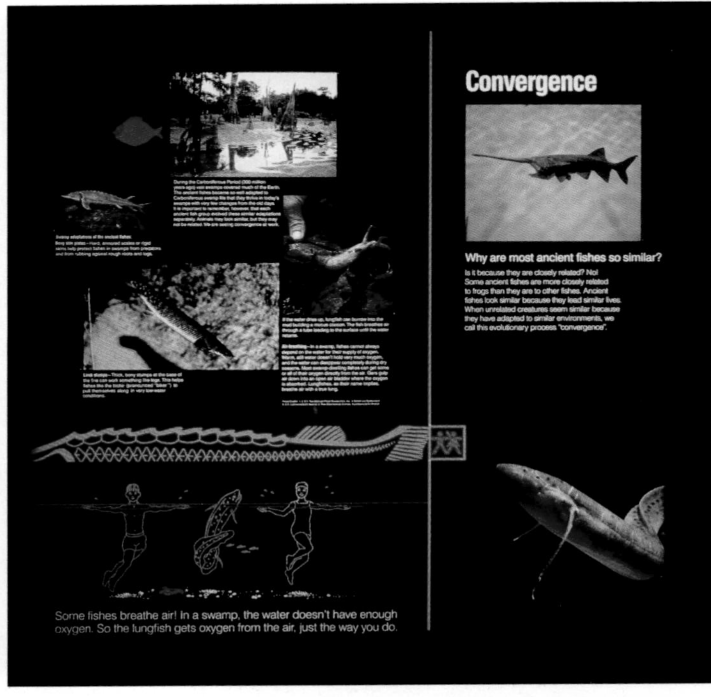

Convergence
Why are most ancient fishes so similar?
Is it because they are closely related? No! Some ancient fishes are more closely related to frogs than they are to other fishes. Ancient fishes look similar because they lead similar lives. When unrelated creatures seem similar because they have adapted to similar environments, we call this evolutionary process "convergence".
Some fishes breathe air! In a swamp, the water doesn't have enough oxygen. So the lungfish gets oxygen from the air, just the way you do.

Ancient Fishes
What pattern does evolution follow?
The old idea was that new species of animals and plants were better than their ancestors. Each new species was seen as a higher rung on the "evolutionary ladder" than the one before. Today, the evidence of science tells a different story. The family history of fishes, for instance, takes many twists and turns. It is much more like an intricate tree than a simple ladder.
A Family Tree of Fishes.

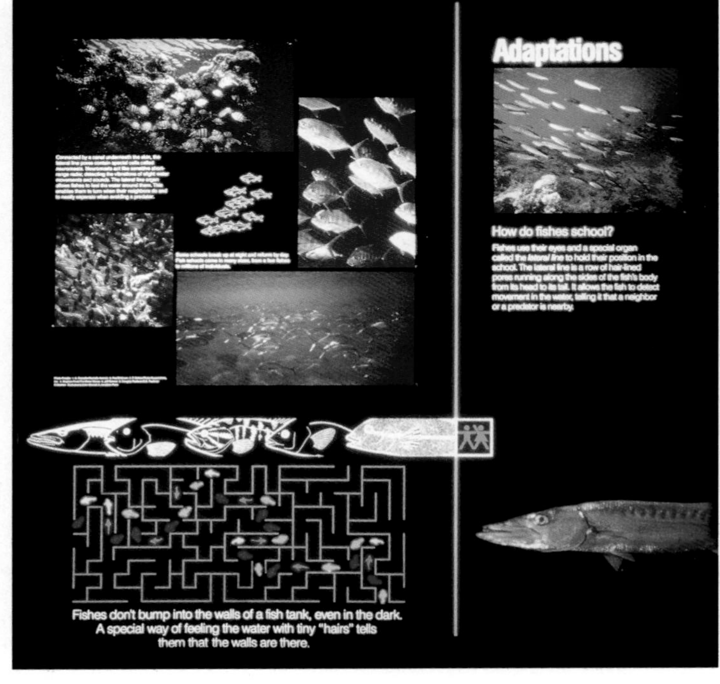

Adaptations
How do fishes school?
Fishes use their eyes and a special organ called the lateral line to hold their position in the school. The lateral line is a row of hair-lined pores running along the sides of the fish's body from its head to its tail. It allows the fish to detect movement in the water, telling it that a neighbor or a predator is nearby.
Fishes don't bump into the walls of a fish tank, even in the dark. A special way of feeling the water with tiny "hairs" tells them that the walls are there.

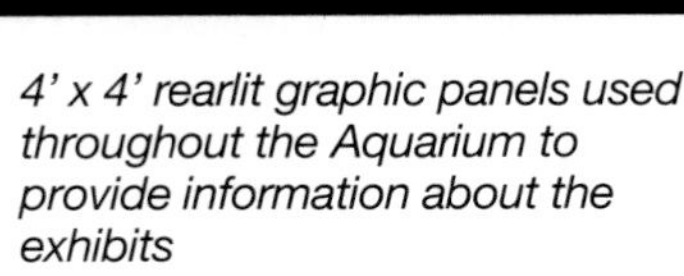

4' x 4' rearlit graphic panels used throughout the Aquarium to provide information about the exhibits

Designers
John Wrench, Richard Duggan
Illustrator
John Wrench
Photographers
Various
Copywriters
S. Duggan, M. Filisky, & others

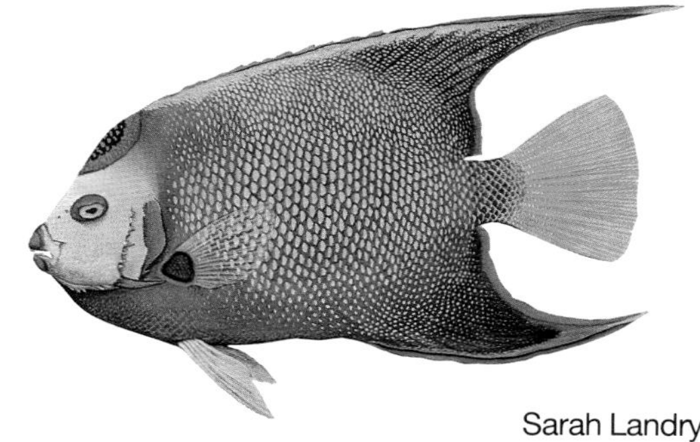

Sarah Landry

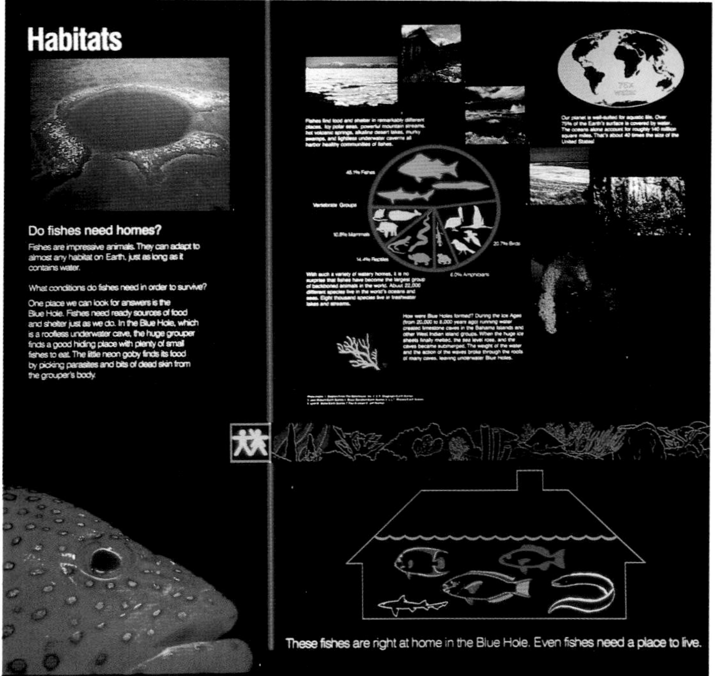
Habitats
Do fishes need homes?
Fishes are impressive animals. They can adapt to almost any habitat on Earth, just as long as it contains water.
What conditions do fishes need in order to survive?
One place we can look for answers is the Blue Hole. Fishes need ready sources of food and shelter just as we do. In the Blue Hole, which is a roofless underwater cave, the huge grouper finds a good hiding place with plenty of small fishes to eat. The little neon goby finds its food by picking parasites and bits of dead skin from the grouper's body.
These fishes are right at home in the Blue Hole. Even fishes need a place to live.

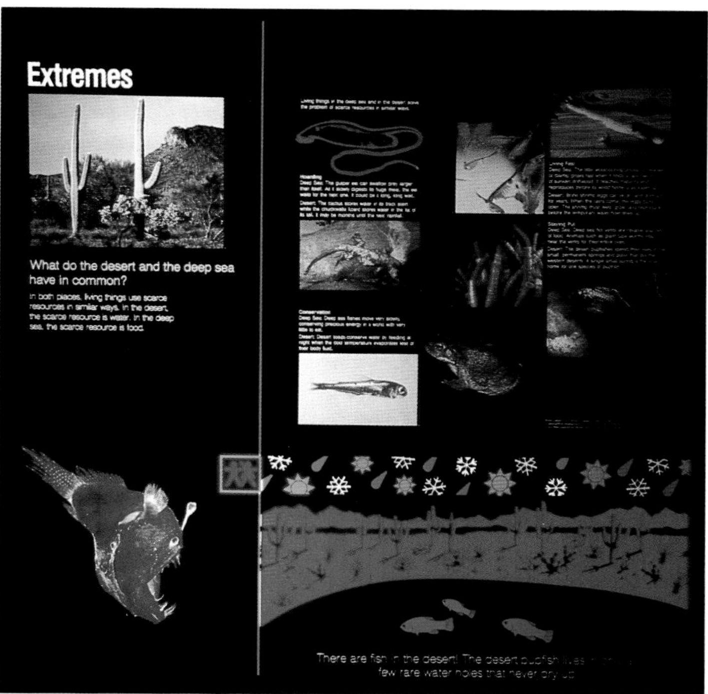
Extremes
What do the desert and the deep sea have in common?
In both places, living things use scarce resources in similar ways. In the desert, the scarce resource is water. In the deep sea, the scarce resource is food.

flooded amazon forest

Information label track installed over Amazon tank has some of over 250 marinelife illustrations produced by Sarah Landry

Designers
Richard Duggan
Illustrator
Sarah Landry
Copywriter
Aquarium education department

Annual report

Designers
Jonathan Place, Denise Bazinet
Photographer
Macy Lawrence
Editor
Andrea Conley

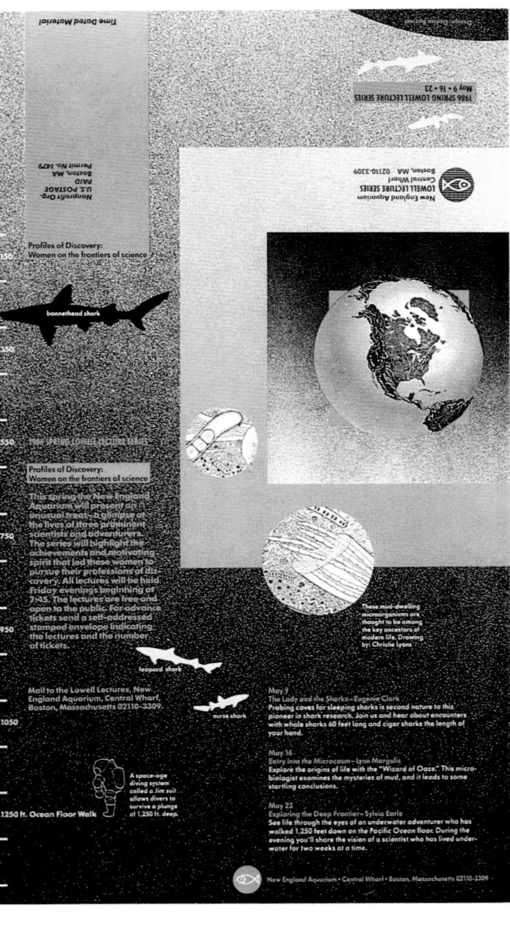

Poster/Brochure

Designer
Denise Bazinet
Illustrator
Christie Lyons
Copywriter
Kenneth Mallory

Poster

Designer
Denise Bazinet
Illustrators
Denise Bazinet, Robert Foley

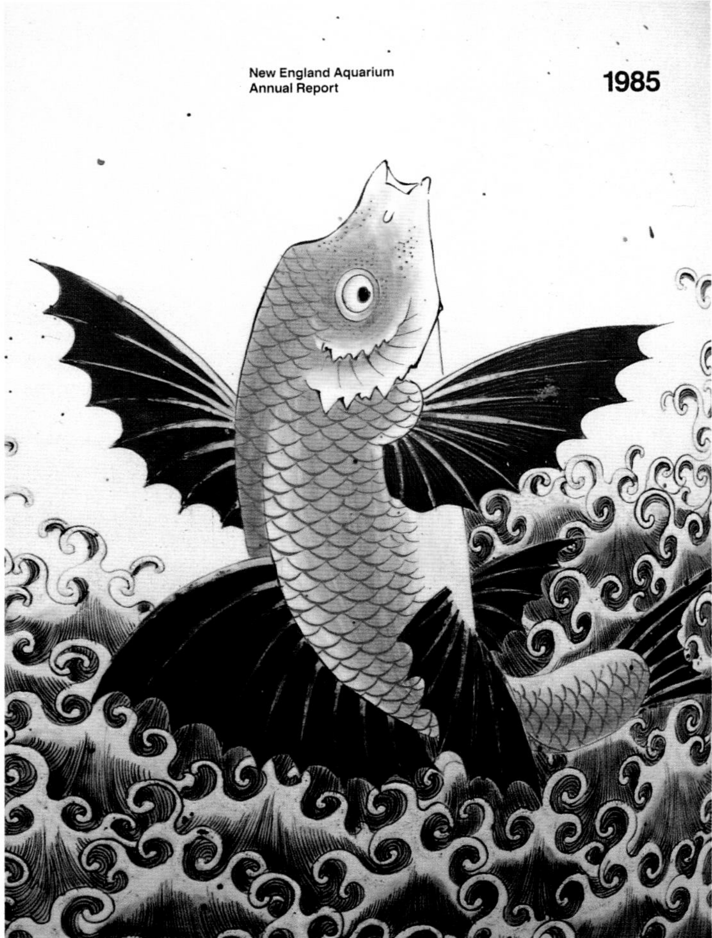

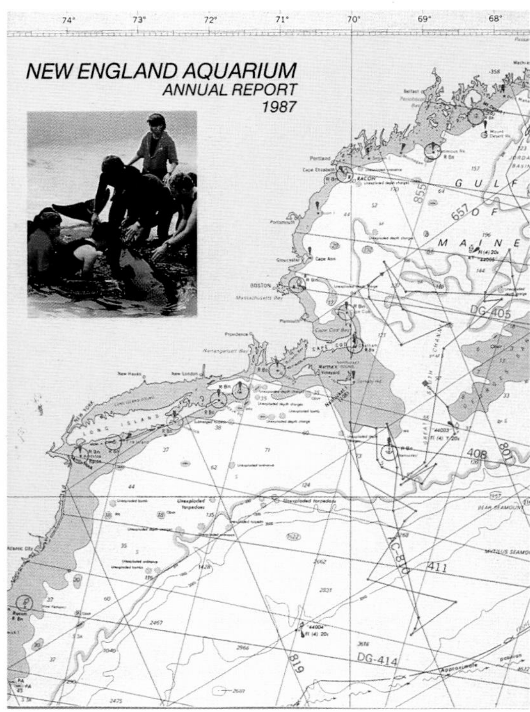

Annual report

Designers
Jonathan Place, David Vergara
Photographer
Bill Wasserman
Editor
Andrea Conley

Annual report

Designers
Jonathan Place, Denise Bazinet
Photographers
Dennis Stierer, Bill Wasserman
Editor
Andrea Conley

Brochure

Designer
Jonathan Place
Illustrator
Andrew Konnerth
Copywriter
Rosalyn Ridgway

Poster

Designer
Jonathan Place
Photographer
Bill Wasserman
Copywriter
Steve Lenox

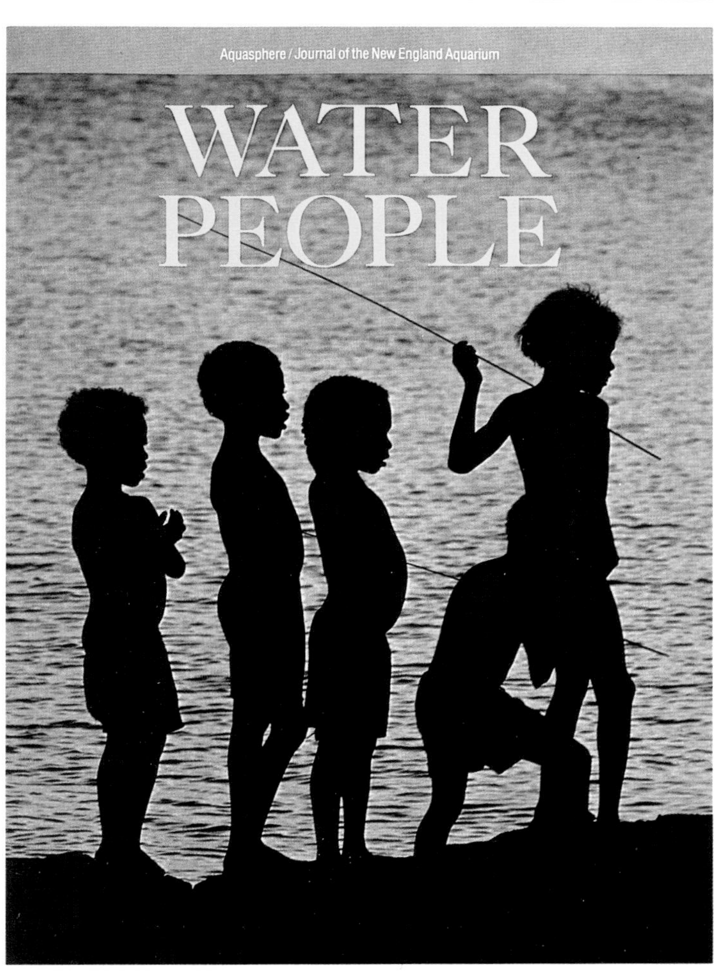

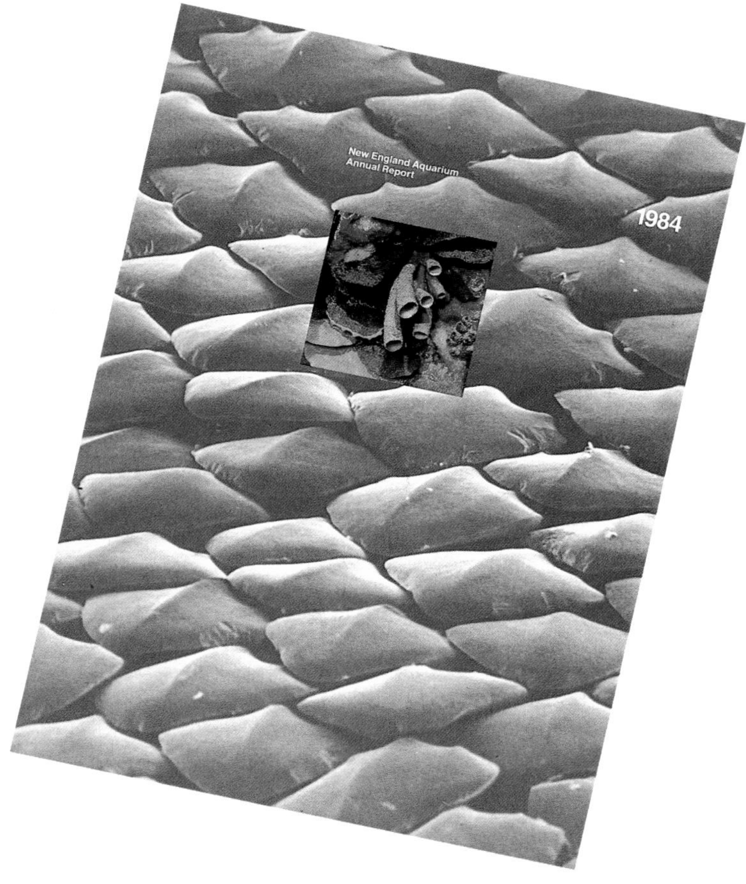

Magazine

Designers
Jonathan Place, David Vergara
Photographer
Douglas Faulkner
Editors
Kenneth Mallory, Louise Berliner

Annual report

Designers
Jonathan Place, David Vergara
Photographer
Bill Wasserman
Editor
Marion Brown

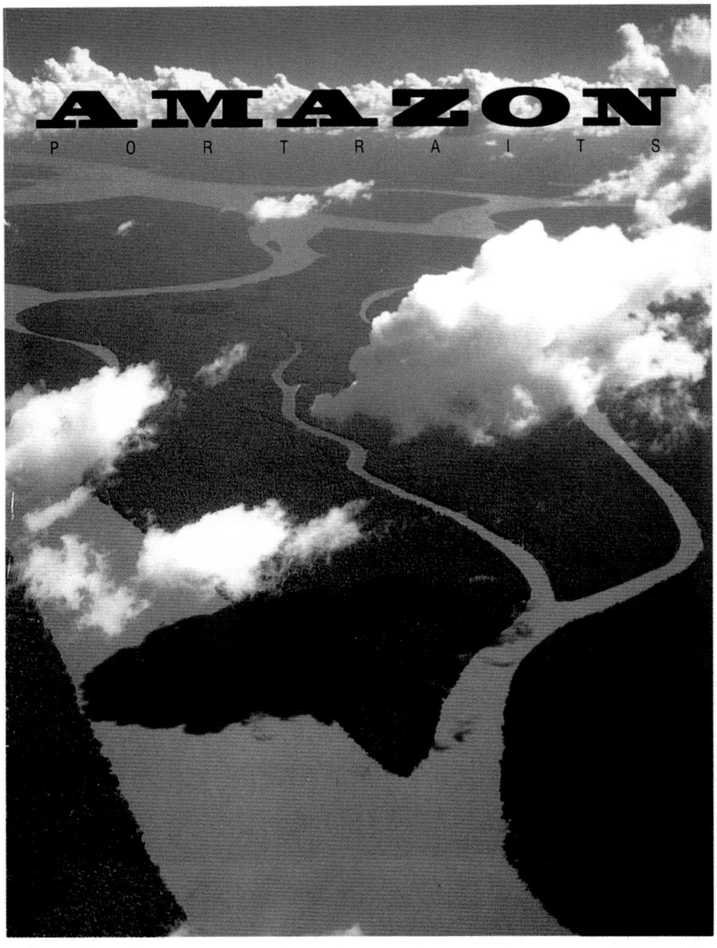

Magazine

Designers
Jonathan Place, David Vergara
Photographer
Loren Alezander McIntyre
Editor
Kenneth Mallory

Magazine

Designer
Jonathan Place
Photographer
Paul Erickson
Editor
Kenneth Mallory

Aquasphere / Journal of the New England Aquarium
The New England Aquarium
20th Anniversary Issue
An eye on the future – A view to the past

Magazine

Designers
Jonathan Place, Denise Bazinet
Photographers
Chris Newbert, Bill Wasserman
Copywriters
Kenneth Mallory, Les Kaufman

Brochure

Designer
Jonathan Place
Illustrator
Andrew Konnerth
Copywriter
Rosalyn Ridgway

Poster

Designer
Jonathan Place
Photographer
Bill Wasserman
Copywriter
Steve Lenox

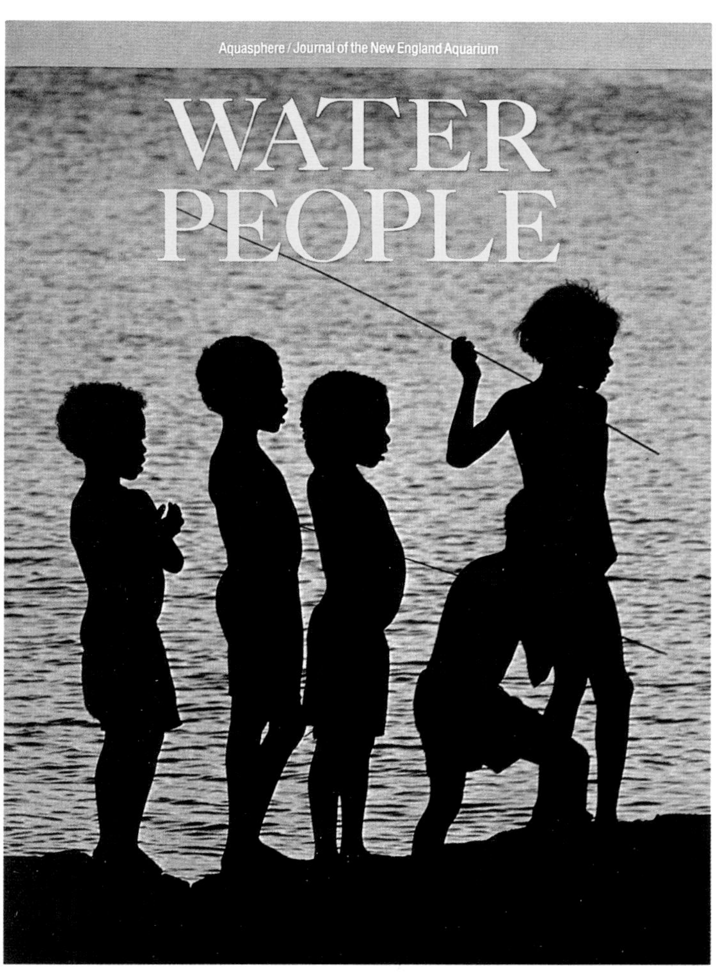

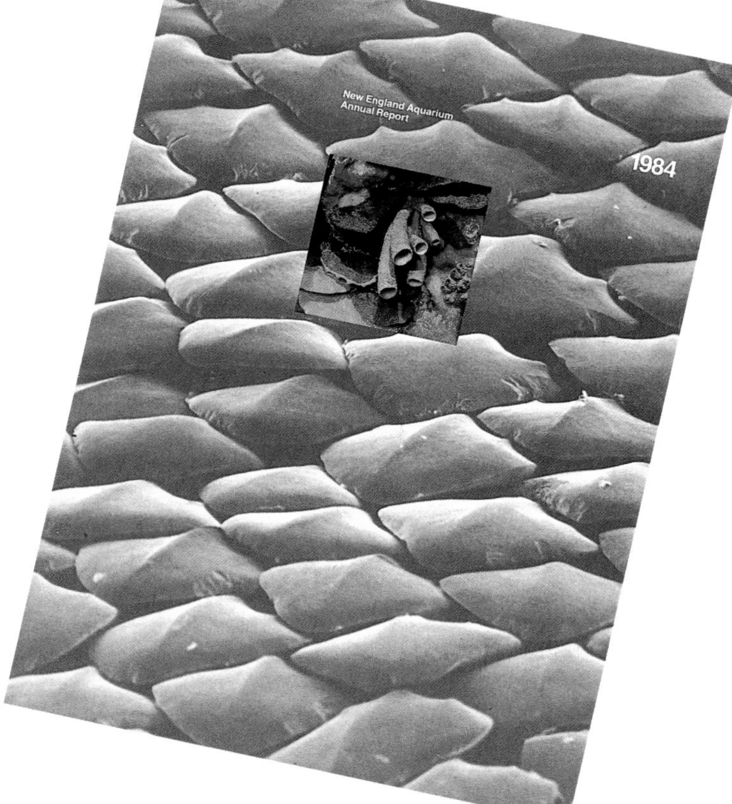

Magazine

Designers
Jonathan Place, David Vergara
Photographer
Douglas Faulkner
Editors
Kenneth Mallory, Louise Berliner

Annual report

Designers
Jonathan Place, David Vergara
Photographer
Bill Wasserman
Editor
Marion Brown

Magazine

Designers
Jonathan Place, David Vergara
Photographer
Loren Alezander McIntyre
Editor
Kenneth Mallory

Magazine

Designer
Jonathan Place
Photographer
Paul Erickson
Editor
Kenneth Mallory

Magazine

Designers
Jonathan Place, Denise Bazinet
Photographers
Chris Newbert, Bill Wasserman
Copywriters
Kenneth Mallory, Les Kaufman

Zoological Society of San Diego

Located in Tempozan, at the inner entrance to Osaka Harbour, the 286,000 square foot Osaka Aquarium is one of the largest in the world. Built at a cost of US$107 million, it contains over 16,000 fish, marine mammals, birds, reptiles, amphibians and invertebrates that live in the Pacific Ocean and along its volcanic perimeter, known as the Ring of Fire.

Osaka Aquarium

Architects
Peter Chermayeff
Cambridge Seven Associates
Designer
Ivan Chermayeff
Design Firm
Chermayeff & Geismar Inc.

Aquarium entrance – canopy with "Ring of Fire" symbol

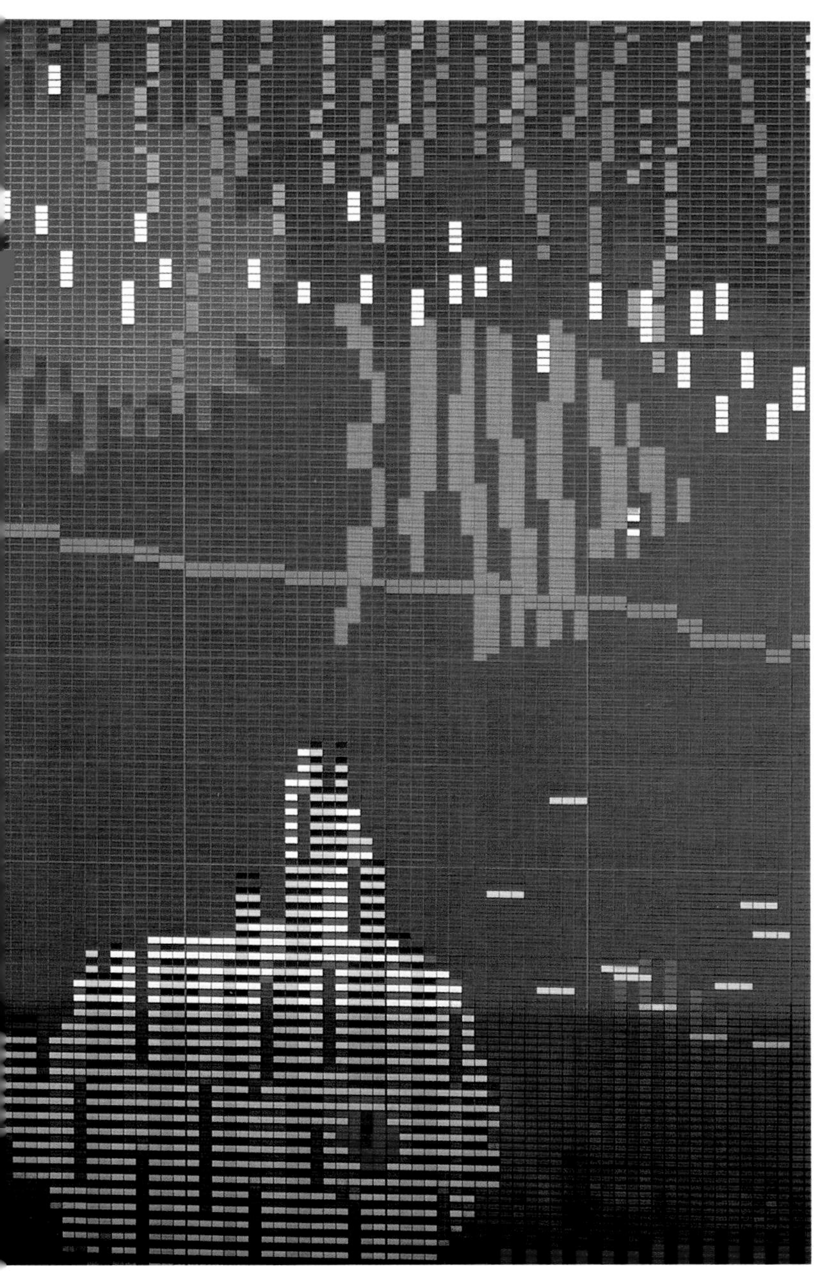

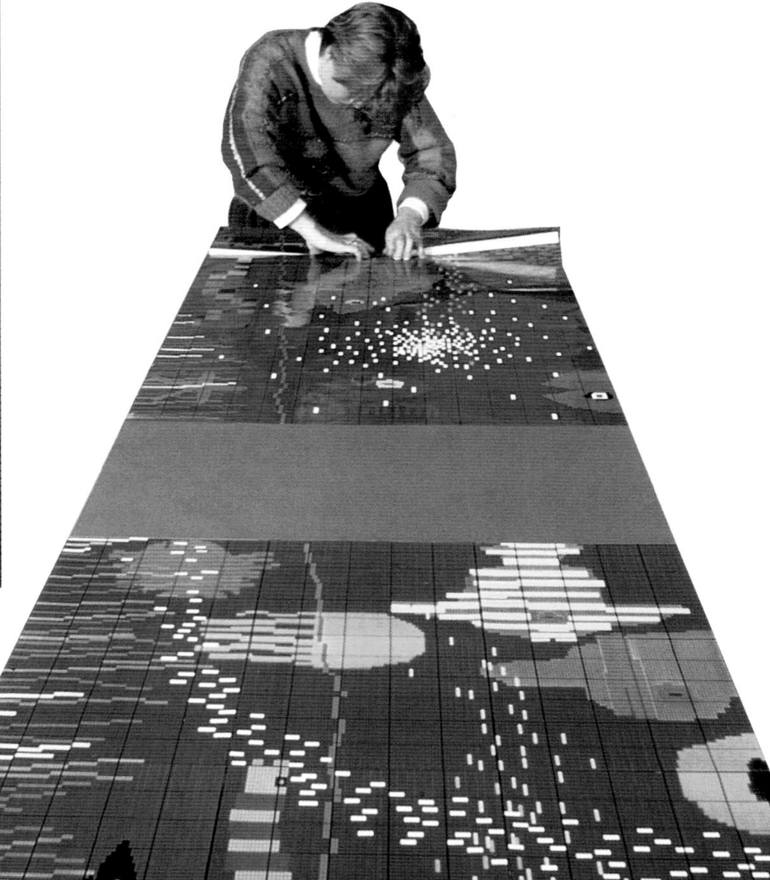

Tile mural details

Preparation of the tile layouts by computer

Sreet entrance canopy

Designer
Chermayeff & Geismar Inc.

Windmills

Designer
Peter Chermayeff

Mural with banner theme

Designer
Chermayeff & Geismar Inc.

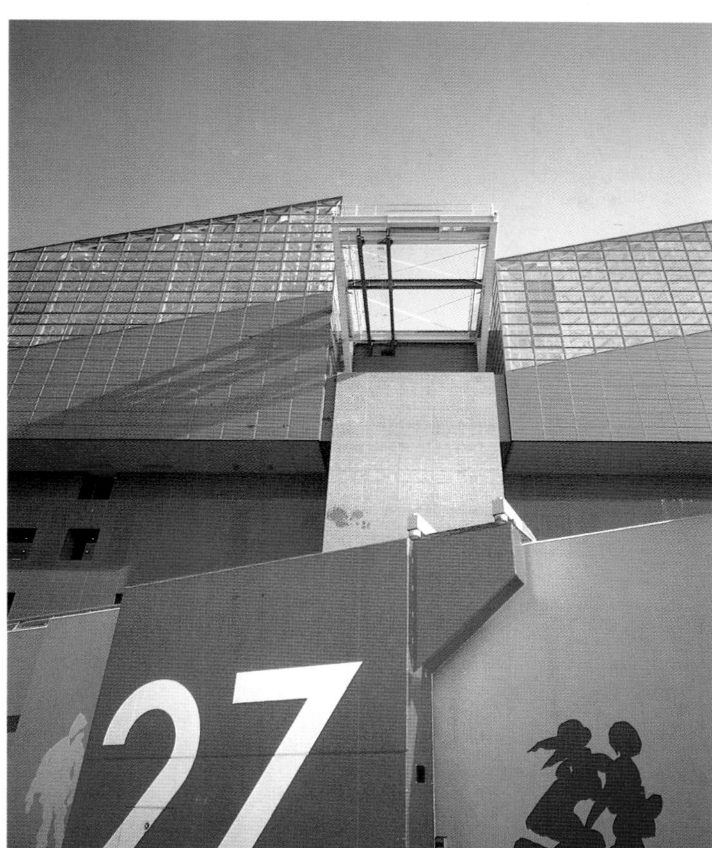

Life-size figures against boardwalk bulkhead door, yellow gantry

Interior signage

Designer
Chermayeff & Geismar Inc.

Interior Tempozan Marketplace and frieze detail surrounding Daiquiri Bar

Architects
Cambridge Seven Associates
Designer
Ivan Chermayeff

School of fish

Designer
Chermayeff & Geismar Inc.

環太平洋火山帯
RING OF FIRE

太平洋を取り囲み、とぎれずに続く荒々しい海岸線、そこでは生物が生きながらえるのは奇跡と思われるほど火山や地震の活動が烈しく行われています。けれども、自然はその姿を自由に表現しています。豊かな生命体を象徴するかのように、私たちの想像を超えた美しい色彩と形をつくりだし、陸や海、空で破壊が起きている今も、自然は活発な活動を止めてはいません。
太平洋のはるか、遠く、遠くかなたへ、リング・オブ・ファイア（環太平洋火山帯）の海岸へと遠征してください。つま先立ちでそっと火山口のふちへ近づいたり、はるかかなたの大陸の海岸線を散歩してください。深海の冒険のスリルに息をつまらせ、イルカが楽しいダイビングであげる水しぶきを感じてください。
そして、深呼吸をしてから、できるだけ近くに寄ってみてください。波の奥を、岩と岩そしてサンゴ礁の枝々の間までのぞきこんでみましょう。それは陸と海の間にかわされた秘密の数々を共にする不思議な時間です。

A continuous rim of rugged shoreline ... encircling the Pacific ... where the violence of volcanoes and earthquakes makes survival seem a miracle ... but where Nature expresses herself freely ... in the unmatched color and beauty of abundant life ... flourishing amid disruptive changes on the land, in the sea, in the sky.

Come away—far, far away—on an expedition into the Pacific, to the Ring of Fire's farflung shores. Tiptoe to the edge of a volcano. stroll the shoreline of a faroff land. Gasp at the thrills of a deep-sea adventure. Feel the splash of a dolphin's joyful dive.

Then, take a deep breath. Come closer—as close as Man can ever come. Look beneath the waves, between the rocks, through spikes of coral. For a magic moment, share the secrets told between land and sea.

1

まず、太平洋岸の水面の上と下… 高くそびえる山々や太陽の光をあびるサンゴ礁、そして氷河の岩壁をのぞいてみましょう。地震が海底の断層をつくり出し、山に亀裂が入るほど激しく揺り動かしています。そこでは、誰にも予測できない大自然の力がはたらいているのです。活火山の奥底ではいまだに溶岩がたぎり、ペンギンは、流氷の上で遊んでいます。そして、太平洋の水面下では、世界でも珍しい水生植物や魚類が生まれ、育っているのです。

Look for clues first above, then below the water of the Pacific Rim's rugged mountains, sunwashed coral reefs, and icy cliffs. Feel the unpredictability of life where earthquakes split the sea floor and tremble up and down fault-riddled shore mountains. Lava boils deep inside still-active volcanoes. Penguins slide on ice floes broken by a raging sea. Within the rim, the Pacific shelters some of the world's most exotic aquatic plants and fishes.

2

3

5

6

海遊館の中を歩いていると、いろいろなところで生きものたちとの出会いがあります。風のそよぎや波の音、そして、オットセイのほえる声や貝のささやきからも、生きもののみずみずしい生命を感じとることができるでしょう。リング・オブ・ファイア（環太平洋火山帯）の自然に触れ、決して消えることのない強烈な印象を、あなた自身の生命の時間に記していってください。

8

As you travel through Osaka's ocean-life pavilion, you will see life renewed everywhere around you and smell it on the breeze, you will hear it in the lap of the waves, the bark of a seal, the whisper of a shell's echo. Celebrate with Nature its Ring of Fire, and take with you lasting memories to carry through your own changing life.

1. 海中溶岩 2.日本の森 3. ペンギン、南極大陸 4. イグアナ、パナマ湾 5. ラッコ、アリューシャン列島 6. うつぼ、クック海峡 7. かえる、エクアドル熱帯雨林 8. 草花、日本の森 9. じんべえざめ、太平洋 10. グレート・バリア・リーフ 11. ひとで、モンタレー湾

Photo Captions and Credits:
1.Underwater Lava (Sharkbait Productions Hawaii) 2.Japan Forest (Higeta Norizo) 3.Penguins, Antarctica (Comstock/Roger Tory Peterson) 4.Iguana, Gulf of Panama (Loren McIntyre) 5.Sea Otter, Aleutian Islands (Norbert Wu) 6.Moray eel, Cook Strait (Carl Roessler, See & Sea Travel) 7.Frog, Ecuadorean Rainforest (Greg Vigle) 8.Flowers, Japan Forest (Ojiro Akio, Nature Photo Library) 9.Whale Shark, Pacific Ocean (Howard Hall) 10.Great Barrier Reef (Chris Newbert) 11.Starfish, Monterey Bay (Sea Studios, Inc.) Reverse Side: Globe Icon (Paul Souza)

11

9

10

海遊館の外観はリング・オブ・ファイア（環太平洋火山帯）そのものを表現しています。タイル張りの青い壁は、大海のたたえる水の豊かさを連想させます。
建物頂上の大きな赤いガラス部分は、大洋の火山帯のリングを連想させ、ガラスの中の生きものたちが生息している透明な中央部を支えています。建物の中に入ると、人は水の壁にかこまれ、水の中の生きものにとりまかれ、大洋の迷宮を巡遊することになるのです。

The aquarium's exterior architecture expresses the Ring of Fire. Blue walls of tile suggest the large volumes of ocean water within. Red glass volumes at the top suggest the ocean's ring of volcanoes, and support a crystalline crown of habitats under glass. Inside, you will tour the ocean's labyrinth, immersed between walls of water, surrounded by aquatic life.

海遊館 大阪ウォータフロント開発株式会社
大阪・天保山 (06)574-8665

OSAKA AQUARIUM TEMPOZAN OSAKA TEL 06-574-8665

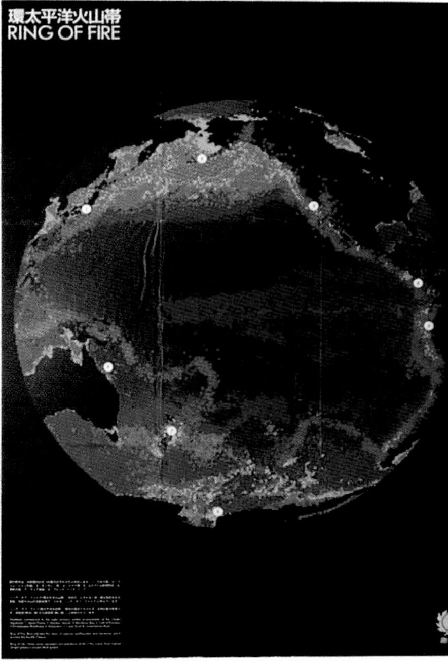

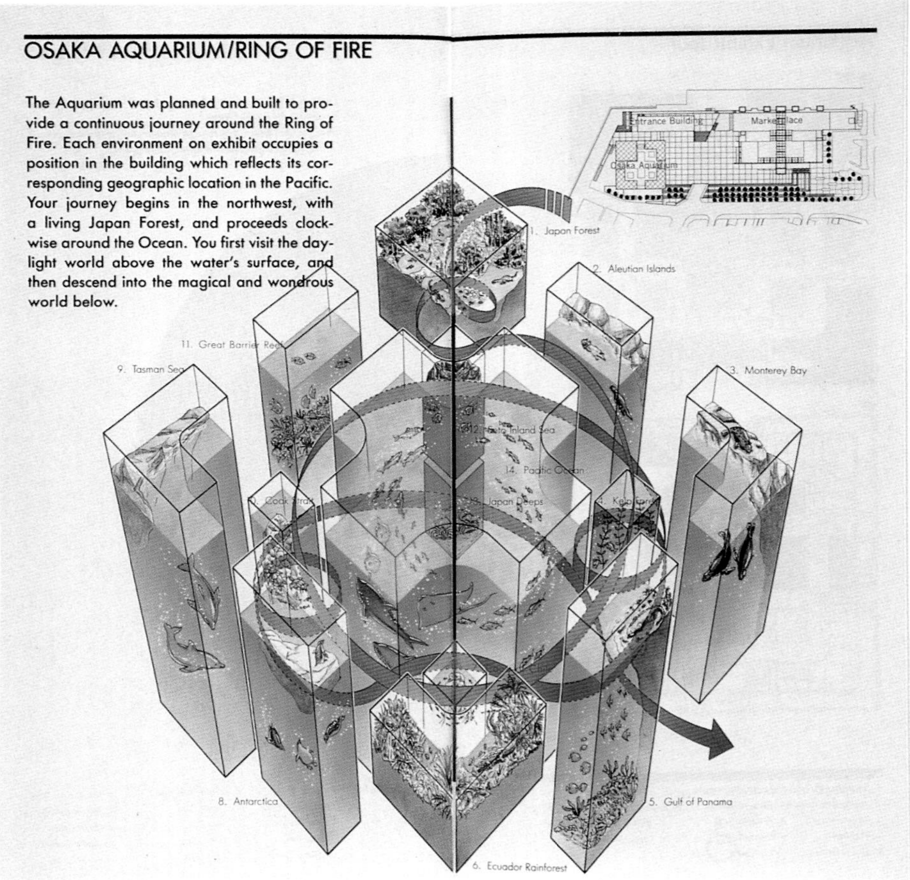

OSAKA AQUARIUM/RING OF FIRE

The Aquarium was planned and built to provide a continuous journey around the Ring of Fire. Each environment on exhibit occupies a position in the building which reflects its corresponding geographic location in the Pacific. Your journey begins in the northwest, with a living Japan Forest, and proceeds clockwise around the Ocean. You first visit the daylight world above the water's surface, and then descend into the magical and wondrous world below.

Entrance Building
Marketplace
Osaka Aquarium
1. Japan Forest
2. Aleutian Islands
3. Monterey Bay
5. Gulf of Panama
6. Ecuador Rainforest
8. Antarctica
9. Tasman Sea
14. Pacific Ocean
Japan Deeps

1 Japan Forest/Northwest Pacific

Begin your trip around the Ring of Fire here in a lush green forest. It is here, in the mists and gentle rains of the mountains, that the water cycle begins. Even on land, every form of life depends on water. Journey with a drop of water, from a misty volcanic peak, down rocky cascades to join a river, and finally reach the sea.

Plants and animals coexist in a delicate balance in the forest. How many kinds of life can you find? Some animals are shy, and hide among the leaves and rocks. Some animals can be heard more easily than seen.

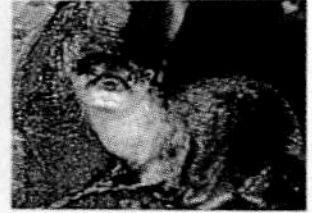

The river otter loves to play in the water. Watch ours closely, so you can compare them to the sea otters in the next exhibit, the Aleutian Islands.

left: Yaku Island／Norizo Higeta
top: Misty mountains, middle: Flowers／Ojiro Akio
above: River otter／Jerry Ferrara

Brochure

海遊館
OSAKA AQUARIUM
RING OF FIRE

Mike Dobel/Masterfile

Philadelphia Zoo Pennsylvania, USA

America's first zoo, opened July 1, 1874, now hosts more than 1.2 million visitors annually. Its 42 acres are filled with exciting flora and fauna, including over 1700 animal specimens. The Philadelphia Zoo also boasts some of the best examples of American architecture, and a sculpture collection which chronicles mankind's perception of the natural world and his relationship to it.

Visitors to the Zoo can go on an expedition through the Jungle Bird Walk, experience the world from a bee's perspective in the Treehouse, or explore the World of Primates, where gorillas, gibbons, orang-utans, and drills live on four beautiful

islands. Among many other features are a children's zoo, the Rare Mammal House, Bear Country, and Penn's Woodland Trail. The Safari Monorail offers a 20-minute ride through the various attractions.

The Zoo's graphics department has an annual budget of over $250,000 for production and/or fabrication of on-site signage, collateral, posters, T-shirts, buttons, advertising, and promotion.

3 of the old posters for this oldest zoo in America

VISIT
THE
GREAT
NEW
LION HOUSE
OPENS APRIL 14th
Philadelphia ZOO

Art Director
Virginia Gehshan
Designer
Jerome Cloud
Design Firm
Cloud and Gehshan
Associates, Inc.
Illustrator
Annette Chang Vander
Copywriter
Kati Sowiak

Signs silk-screened and painted on cedar and Sintra

Meet
the
Keeper
Here
Eagles
Friday at 1:30
Shows
Children's
Zoo
Daily

Meet
the
Keeper
Here
Lions
or
Tigers
Sunday at 12:30

Graphics for the exhibit featuring "Big Pig" The Warthog

Designers
Frank Pileggi, Kati Sowiak
Illustrators
John Emil Cymerman,
Karen Smith

Construction graphics for new carnivore centre

Designers
Kati Sowiak, Frank Pileggi
Copywriter
Kim Gigstead

CATS ON THE MOVE

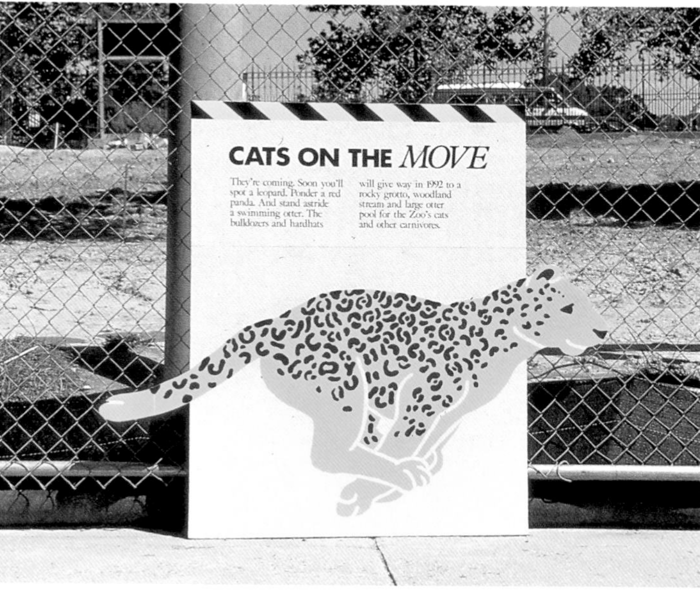
CATS ON THE MOVE
They're coming. Soon you'll spot a leopard. Ponder a red panda. And stand astride a swimming otter. The bulldozers and hardhats
will give way in 1992 to a rocky grotto, woodland stream and large otter pool for the Zoo's cats and other carnivores.

Interpretive display for "Experiences" campaign

Designers
Kati Sowiak, Carolyn Lastick, Frank Pileggi
Illustrator
John Emil Cymerman
Copywriter
Vicky Mehl

Backyard Bugs – exhibit within the children's zoo for ages 4 - 8

Designers
Kati Sowiak, Carol Baxter
Illustrator
John Emil Cymerman
Copywriter
Janet Jackson

Poster

Designer
Ronald Searle
Illustrator
Ronald Searle

Philadelphia

Poster

Designer
Kati Sowiak
Illustrator
Bob Roper

Poster

Designer
Kati Sowiak
Illustrator
Bob Roper

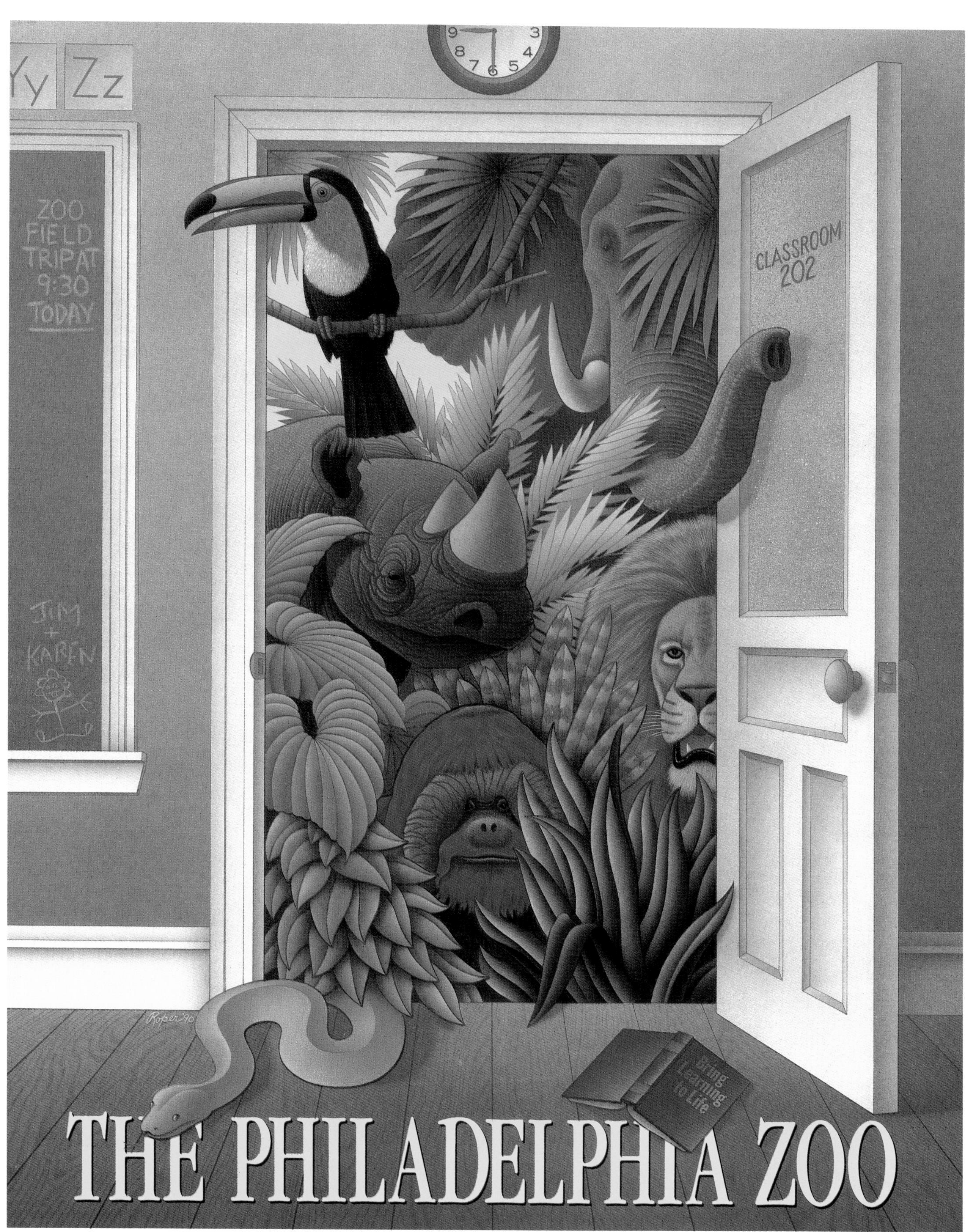

the Philadelphia Zoo for experiences you never outgrow
Experience...
WEIRD

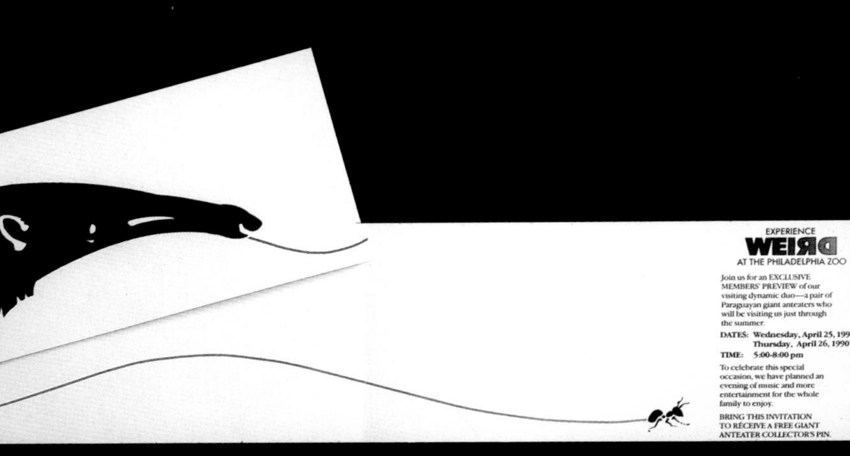
EXPERIENCE
WEIRD
AT THE PHILADELPHIA ZOO
Join us for an EXCLUSIVE MEMBERS' PREVIEW of our visiting dynamic duo—a pair of Paraguayan giant anteaters who will be visiting us just through the summer.
DATES: Wednesday, April 25, 1990
Thursday, April 26, 1990
TIME: 5:00-8:00 pm
To celebrate this special occasion, we have planned an evening of music and more entertainment for the whole family to enjoy.
BRING THIS INVITATION TO RECEIVE A FREE GIANT ANTEATER COLLECTOR'S PIN.

L
I EXPERIENCED
SIL Y
AT THE PHILADELPHIA ZOO

2 buttons for "Experiences" campaign

Designers
Kati Sowiak, Carolyn Lastick, Frank Pileggi
Illustrator
John Emil Cymerman
Copywriter
Vicky Mehl

Member's invitation to preview white tiger exhibit

Designers
Kati Sowiak, Elizabeth Hummer
Illustrator
John Emil Cymerman
Copywriter
Sally Mazor

Greeting card

Designers
Kati Sowiak, Frank Pileggi
Illustrator
John Emil Cymerman

HAPPYHOLIDAYS
from the Philadelphia Zoo

Invitation to members' appreciation day

Designer
Carolyn Lastick
Illustrator
Jessica the Gorilla

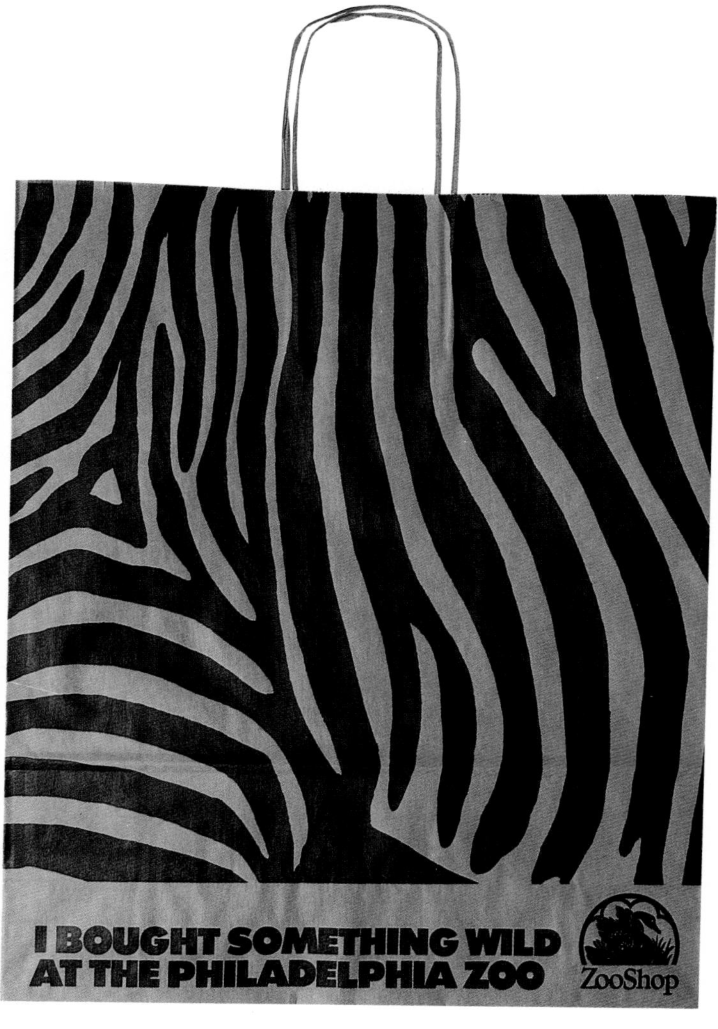

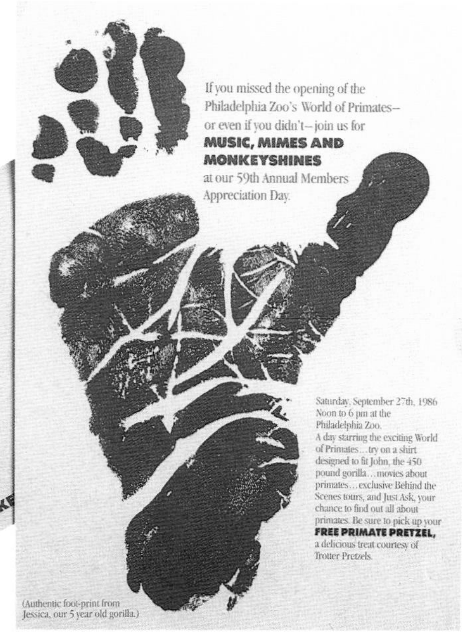

Shopping bag

Designers
Kati Sowiak, Carolyn Lastick

Invitation for 10th Annual Corporate Sponsors Night

Designers
Kati Sowiak, Jill Beidleman

Interpretive display for "Experiences" campaign

Designers
Kati Sowiak, Carolyn Lastick, Frank Pileggi
Illustrator
John Emil Cymerman
Copywriter
Vicky Mehl

Poster commemorating the opening of The World of Primates

Designers
John Emil Cymerman, Kati Sowiak
Illustrator
John Emil Cymerman

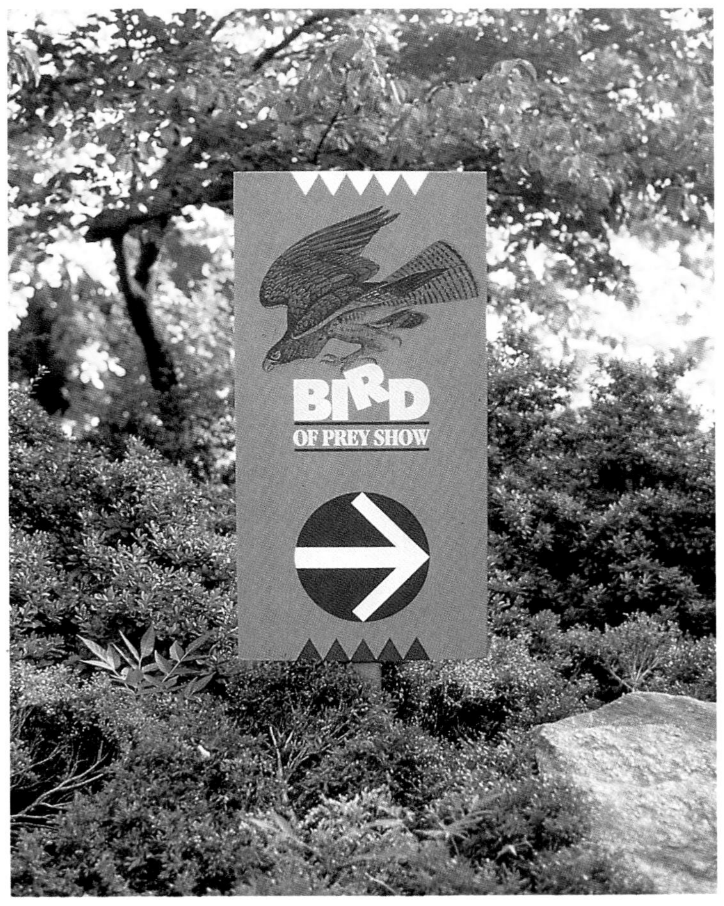

Temporary sign for seasonal show

Designer
Kati Sowiak

Promotional T-shirts

Designer
Kati Sowiak, Carol Baxter
Illustrator
John Emil Cymerman

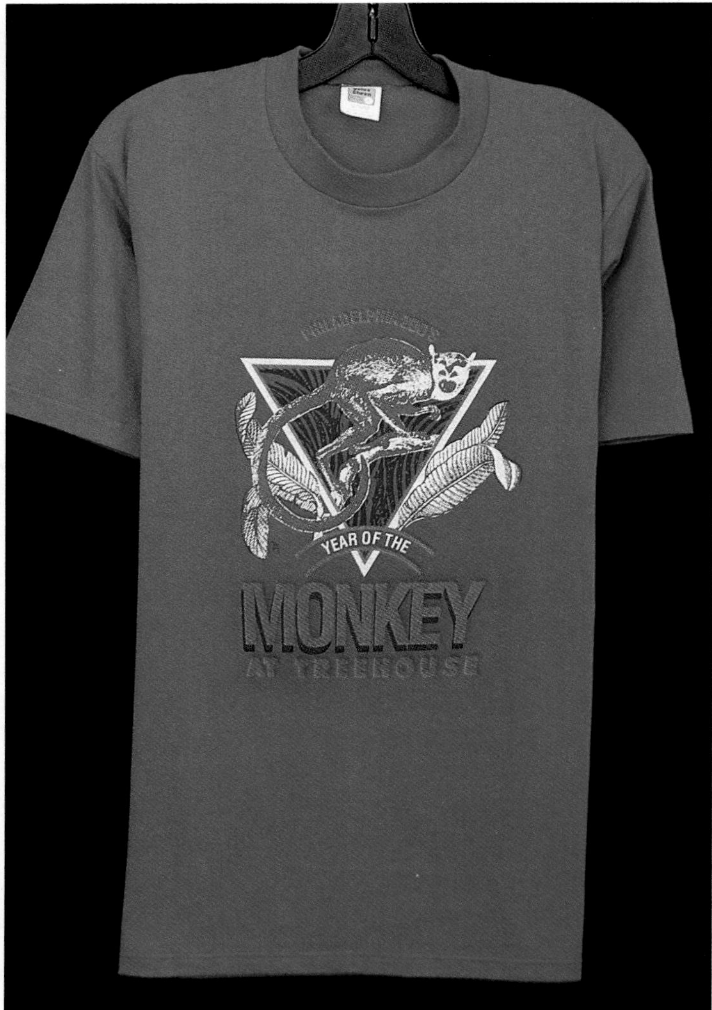

Freeman Patterson/Masterfile

The Phoenix Zoo Arizona, USA

The Phoenix Zoo is the most popular year-round attraction in the metro-Phoenix area, visited by approximately one million people a year. Designed on a habitat theme, it displays more than 1300 animals, of which 200 are endangered. The zoo is located on 125 acres in Papago Park, with approximately half of the acreage developed and the balance covered by a master plan for the future.

The Phoenix Zoo is owned and operated by the Arizona Zoological Society, and governed by a Board of Directors. Opened since 1962, it is the country's leading privately owned, non-profit zoo. It accepts no tax-derived government funds. Admissions, memberships, donations, gift shop sales, and food service sales provide the operating income for the zoo. Additional fund-raising activities supplement the operating budget and provide funds for capital projects.

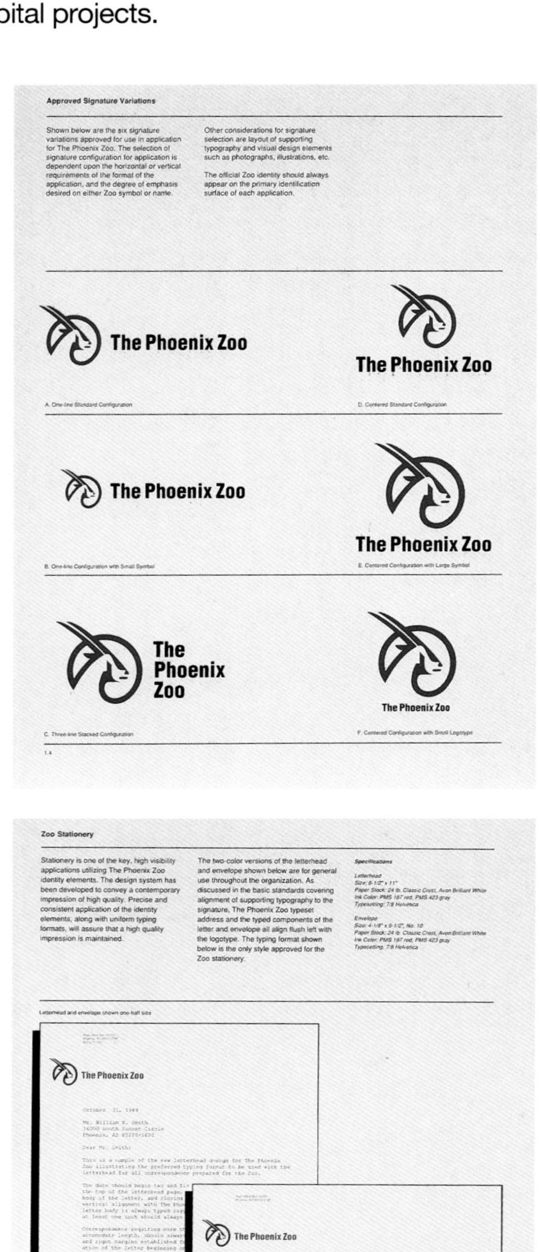

Approved Signature Variations

Shown below are the six signature variations approved for use in application for The Phoenix Zoo. The selection of signature configuration for application is dependent upon the horizontal or vertical requirements of the format of the application, and the degree of emphasis desired on either Zoo symbol or name.

Other considerations for signature selection are layout of supporting typography and visual design elements such as photographs, illustrations, etc.

The official Zoo identity should always appear on the primary identification surface of each application.

A. One-line Standard Configuration

D. Centered Standard Configuration

B. One-line Configuration with Small Symbol

E. Centered Configuration with Large Symbol

C. Three-line Stacked Configuration

F. Centered Configuration with Small Logotype

1.4

Zoo Stationery

Stationery is one of the key, high visibility applications utilizing The Phoenix Zoo identity elements. The design system has been developed to convey a contemporary impression of high quality. Precise and consistent application of the identity elements, along with uniform typing formats, will assure that a high quality impression is maintained.

The two-color versions of the letterhead and envelope shown below are for general use throughout the organization. As discussed in the basic standards covering alignment of supporting typography to the signature, The Phoenix Zoo typeset address and the typed components of the letter and envelope all align flush left with the logotype. The typing format shown below is the only style approved for the Zoo stationery.

Specifications

Letterhead
Size: 8-1/2" x 11"
Paper Stock: 24 lb. Classic Crest, Avon Brilliant White
Ink Color: PMS 187 red, PMS 423 gray
Typesetting: 7/8 Helvetica

Envelope
Size: 4-1/8" x 9-1/2", No. 10
Paper Stock: 24 lb. Classic Crest, Avon Brilliant White
Ink Color: PMS 187 red, PMS 423 gray
Typesetting: 7/8 Helvetica

Letterhead and envelope shown one-half size

2.1

The Phoenix Zoo logo was a collaboration between the Zoo and the Arizona State University senior graphic design program. The logo was developed by student Eric Hornaday. Refinement and graphic standards manual was completed by Rowley & Associates.

Design
The Phoenix Zoo Design Department

Currently the Design Department staff consists of a design curator, two graphic designers, three exhibit technicians and a part-time secretary. The total annual Design Department budget is $207,000. Donations for specific graphic projects are sometimes made.

Use of the Symbol as a Design Element

When the symbol is used alone as a primary graphic device in literature, it may be desirable to crop the Oryx image for visual impact. If the symbol is not shown in its entirety, the complete signature must appear elsewhere on the cover of the application. If the full symbol is displayed, it is acceptable to use the logotype alone as a heading for the particular application.

Separating the logotype for use as a heading in literature is acceptable only if the logotype is completely separated from the symbol, and if its size relates to the supporting typography of the application. The examples shown below demonstrate the guideline.

It is impossible to anticipate all circumstances in which separation of the logotype and symbol is acceptable. Separation of the elements must involve good taste and judgment in preparing the design, and use of the guidelines as a basis for the final design decision.

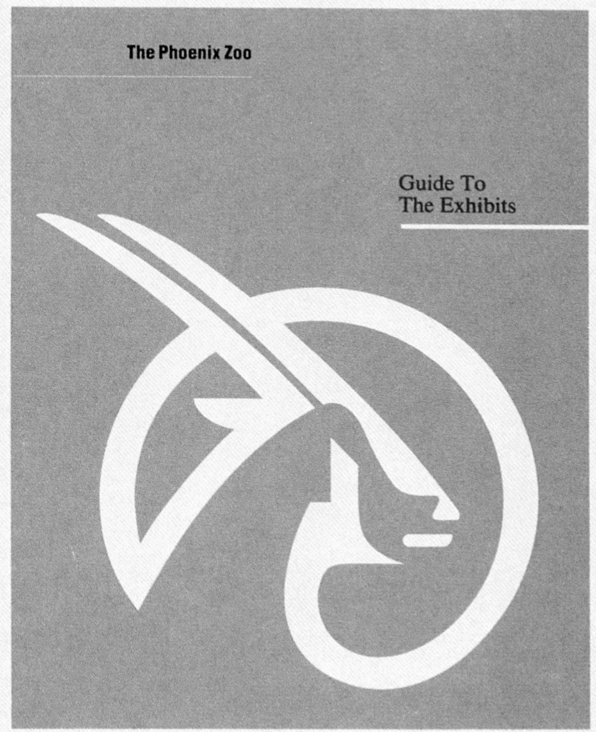

African Savanna Exhibit – interpretive display includes 3 five-sided kiosks with powder coated aluminium boxes. Graphic panels are screen-printed, hand-coloured and weather protected with automotive clear coat.

Plant Life
Man and the Savanna

Termites

Cymothoe
Insects of the Savanna
Precis
Papilionidae

Children's Zoo – aluminium monoliths powder coated, screen-printed with the use of some vinyl letters. Automotive clear coat is used over finished pieces.

Children'sZoo
Entrance

Standard exhibit panels – Redwood posts and backing, hand-coloured and screenprinted with automotive clear coating.

Benjamin Rondel/Masterfile

Founded in 1898, the Pittsburgh Zoo is located only 8 miles from downtown Pittsburgh. It is home to 351 species of animals. Although a relatively small site of 77 acres, the zoo provides diverse, quality exhibits, and has been able to attract some 500,000 people annually.

The Pittsburgh Zoo underwent major renovations in the early 1980's to achieve landscape immersion, allowing animals to roam in a more natural environment. This project provides a more educational setting for visitors, and more importantly encourages natural interaction between animals of the same species and often between different species.

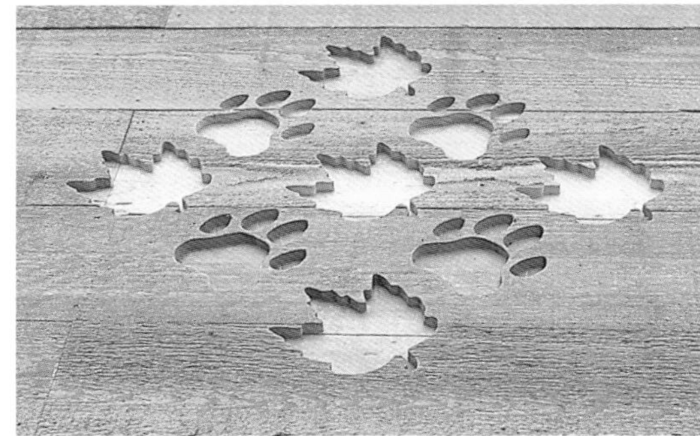

The Pittsburgh Zoo uses an open concept where barriers that separate animal and visitor are concealed in the landscape.

Agnew Moyer Smith Inc. represents this approach with a pawprint-and-leaf symbol which is used on signs, stationery and promotional material.

Agnew Moyer Smith Inc. created interpretive graphics (John Dawson, designer) to help visitors learn about animals. Analogies like "A rhinoceros is like a two-ton lawnmower" stimulate imagination and fun for the visitors.

The program includes supplementary graphics such as specimen identification and directional signs.

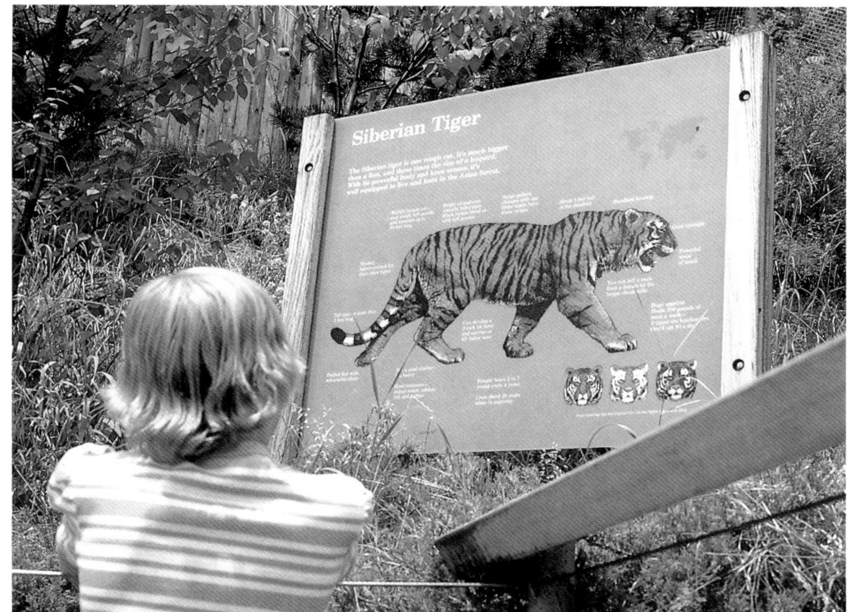

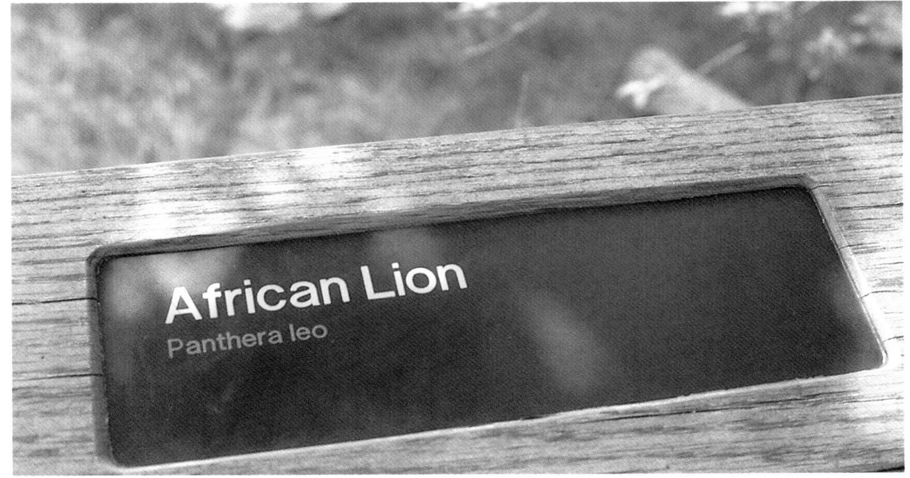

Some examples of illustrated graphic panels that help visitors understand the peculiarities of the animals without long paragraphs of text. A map helps to navigate the visitor through the zoo's network of pathways.

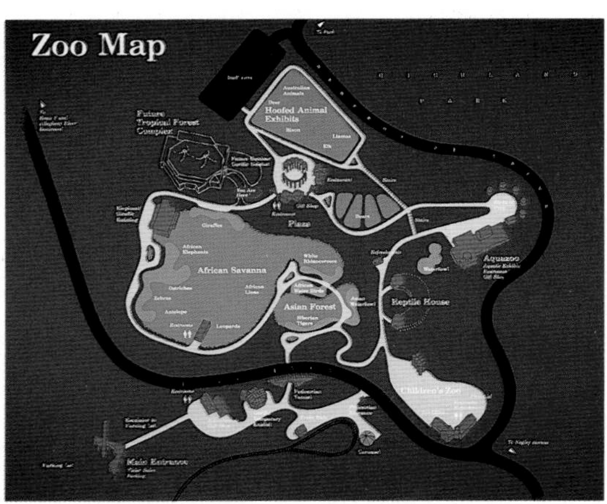

Greg Stott/Masterfile

The Royal Melbourne Zoological Gardens Australia

The Zoological Board of Victoria is Australia's premier zoo organization, operating three major zoos - The Royal Melbourne Zoological Gardens, Healesville Sanctuary, Werribee Zoo. In addition, it provides significant education, conservation and research programs, for the Board's mission is "to create positive attitudes towards wildlife and conservation of the world's natural living resources".

Melbourne Zoo displays a comprehensive collection of over 3000 animals from more than 350 exotic and native species. Highly regarded for its botanic as well as zoological exhibits, it is one of the world's "Top 10" zoos. A master plan for the zoo's 22 hectares organizes exhibits into habitat areas representing bioclimatic zones.

Banners for Panda exhibit

Designers
Margaret Mason, Nigel Triffitt, Brier Gough

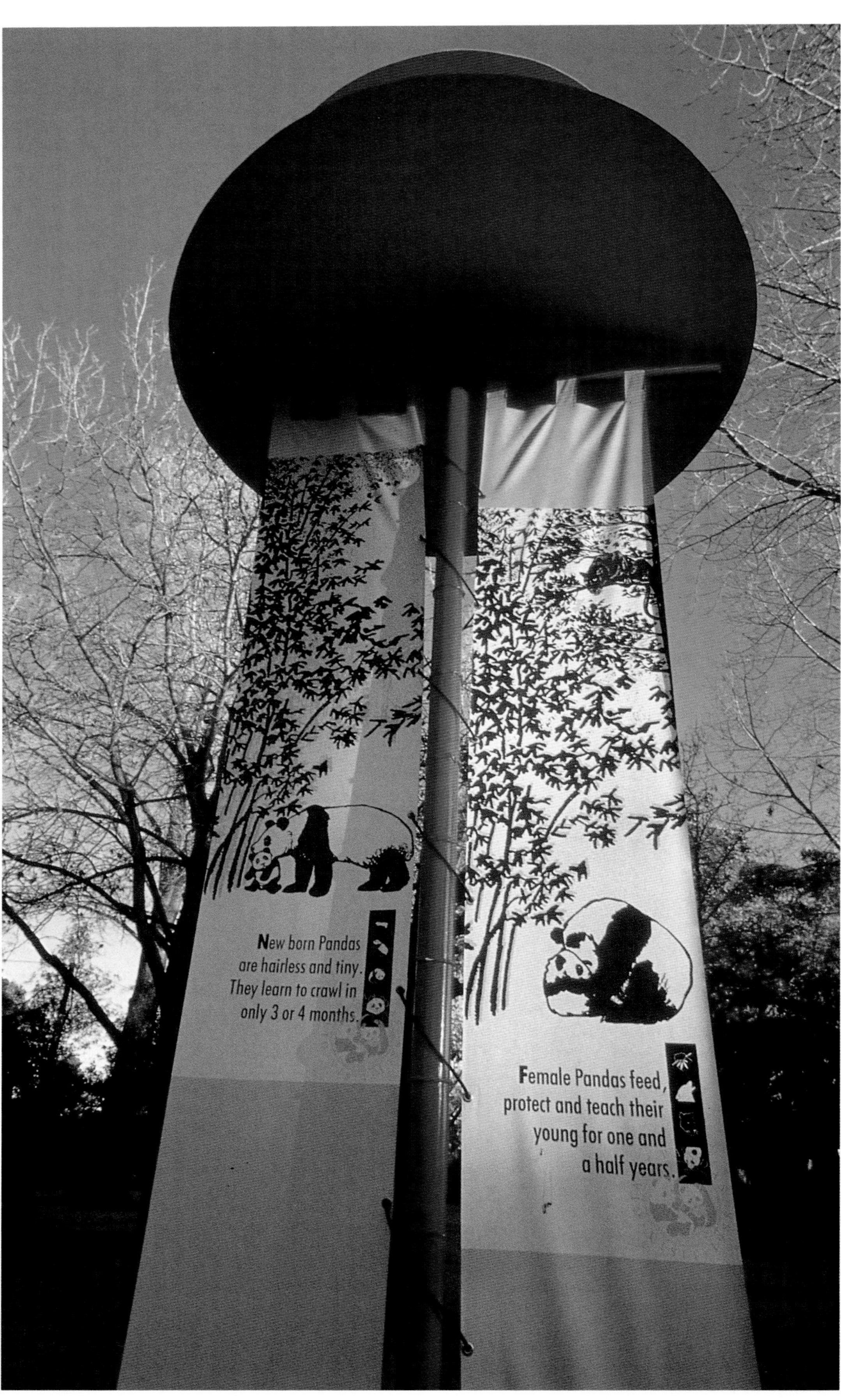

New born Pandas
are hairless and tiny.
They learn to crawl in
only 3 or 4 months.
Female Pandas feed,
protect and teach their
young for one and
a half years.

Hats on long poles to reflect Chinese village

Chinese wall – exhibit entry area

The loan of the Giant Pandas
is a gift from the
Government of the People's Republic of
China to the Australian Government to
mark Australia's Bicentenary.

Logo and promotional material for Panda visit

Designer/Illustrator
David Lancashire
Design Firm
David Lancashire Design

MELBOURNE
1988 · ZOO · 1988

THE GIANT PANDA EXHIBITION
CAAC
Scallywags Socks

1. Australian Birdwing. (Ornithoptera priamus) Largest Australian butterfly. Not uncommon in Qld rain forests. 2. Australian Leafwing. (Doleschallia bisaltide) E. Qld to Clarence River. 3. Orange Lacewing (Cethosia penthesilea) N. Territory. 4. Green-spotted Triangle. (Graphium agamennon) Cape York to Mackay. 5. Canopus Butterfly. (Papilio canopus) N. Territory & n. Western Australia. 6. Common Grass Yellow. (Eurema hecabe) western, northern and eastern Australia, from Geralton to Sydney.

The Royal Melbourne Zoological Gardens

Open 365 Days a Year From 9 am – 5 pm Daily. Elliott Avenue, Parkville. Telephone (03) 347 1522. Calendar Poster No. 17 Series 1988. Design & Artwork by David Lancashire. Insects Depicted: Australian Butterflies.

JULY

S	M	T	W	T	F	S
31					1	2
3	4	5	6	7	8	9
10	11	12	13	14	15	16
17	18	19	20	21	22	23
24	25	26	27	28	29	30

AUGUST

S	M	T	W	T	F	S
	1	2	3	4	5	6
7	8	9	10	11	12	13
14	15	16	17	18	19	20
21	22	23	24	25	26	27
28	29	30	31			

SEPTEMBER

S	M	T	W	T	F	S
				1	2	3
4	5	6	7	8	9	10
11	12	13	14	15	16	17
18	19	20	21	22	23	24
25	26	27	28	29	30	

OCTOBER

S	M	T	W	T	F	S
30	31					1
2	3	4	5	6	7	8
9	10	11	12	13	14	15
16	17	18	19	20	21	22
23	24	25	26	27	28	29

NOVEMBER

S	M	T	W	T	F	S
		1	2	3	4	5
6	7	8	9	10	11	12
13	14	15	16	17	18	19
20	21	22	23	24	25	26
27	28	29	30			

DECEMBER

S	M	T	W	T	F	S
				1	2	3
4	5	6	7	8	9	10
11	12	13	14	15	16	17
18	19	20	21	22	23	24
25	26	27	28	29	30	31

Poster calendar for Butterfly exhibit

Designer/Illustrator
David Lancashire
Design Firm
David Lancashire Design

Endangered
CPI Papers
This graceful antelope, the Scimitar-horned Oryx, is disappearing from its north African habitat. Werribee Zoo is committed to heightening people's awareness of the plight of our world's endangered species.

MELBOURNE ZOO

JULY

AUGUST

SEPTEMBER

OCTOBER

NOVEMBER

DECEMBER

1990

THE ROYAL MELBOURNE ZOOLOGICAL GARDENS ELLIOTT AVE PARKVILLE PH (03) 347 1522 OPEN EVERY DAY OF THE YEAR FROM 9AM TILL 5PM

Poster sponsored by Consolidated Paper Industries

Designers
Brier Gough, Tracey Wylie
Photographer
Max Deliopoulos

Poster calendar

Designer/Illustrator
Brier Gough

Poster

Illustrator
David Higgins

Poster

Designer
Brier Gough

The firm of Emery Vincent Associates was asked to develop a new sign system for the zoo. It was first introduced as a prototype in the Gorilla Rainforest.

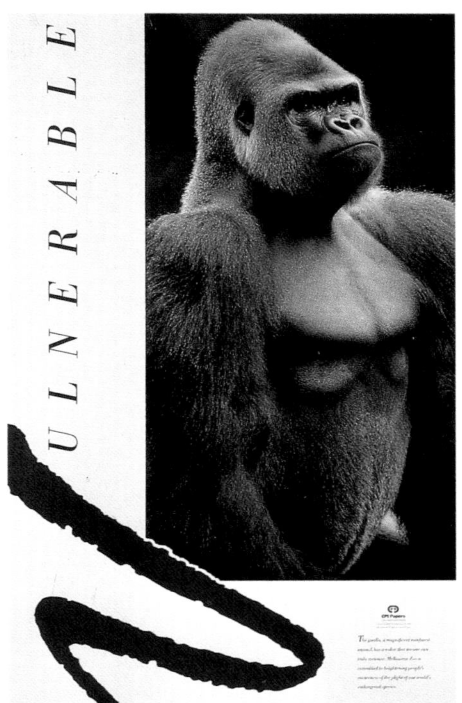

Poster sponsored by Consolidated Paper Industries

Designers
Brier Gough, Tracey Wylie
Photographer
Max Deliopoulos

Various print material

Designers
Errill & Knight Associates
Brier Gough, Tracey Wylie

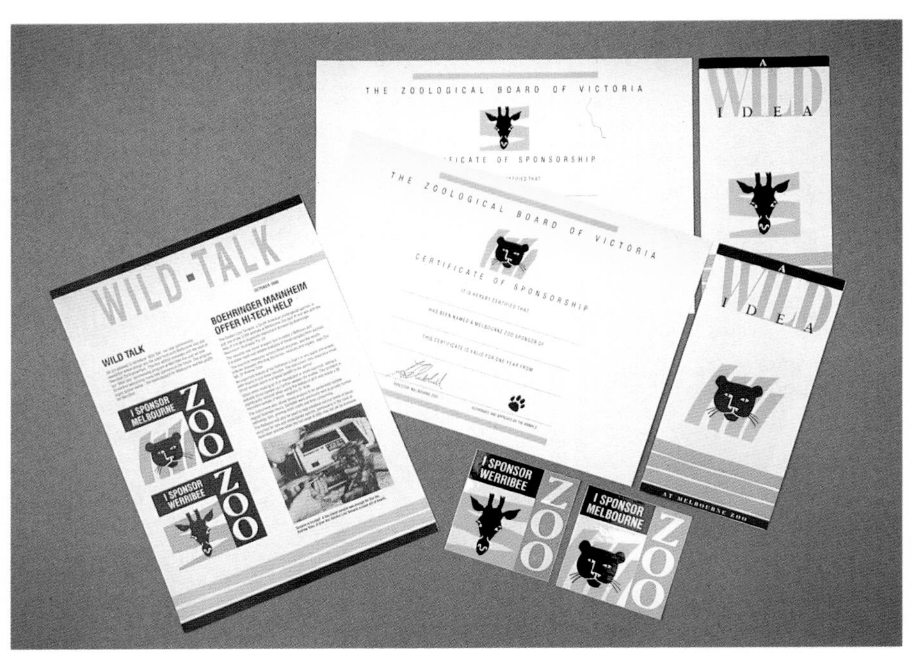

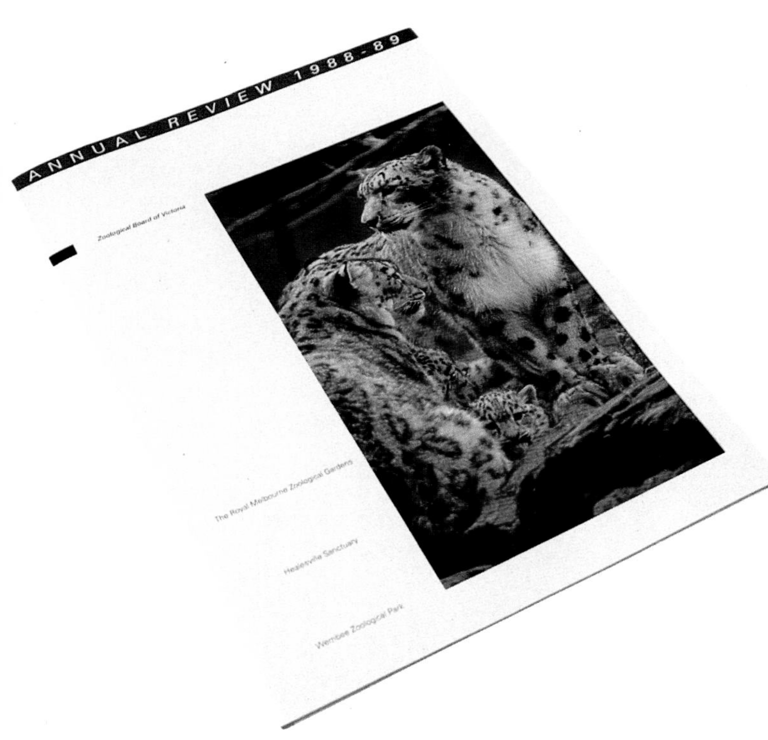

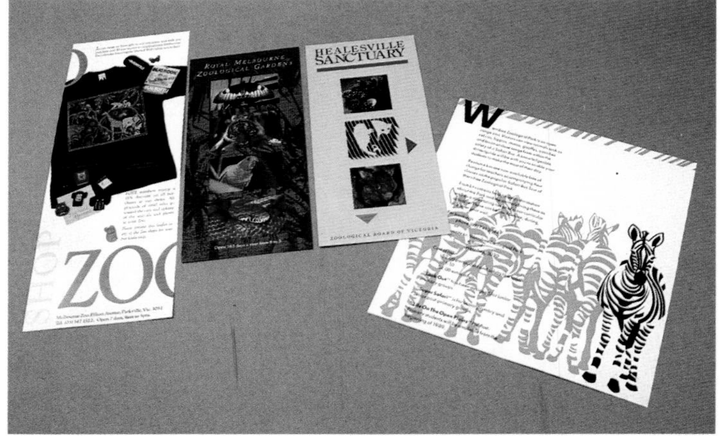

Healesville Sanctuary Melbourne, Australia

Healesville Sanctuary is a leading specialist-collection zoo, displaying Australian fauna and flora in a 31-hectare bushland environment. It is currently undertaking a major re-vegetation program. At present it is home to more than 180 species of animals.

Front entrance signage

Designers
David McCabe Design,
Nuttshell Graphics

Revegetation program signage sponsored by Western Mining Corporation

Designer
Brier Gough

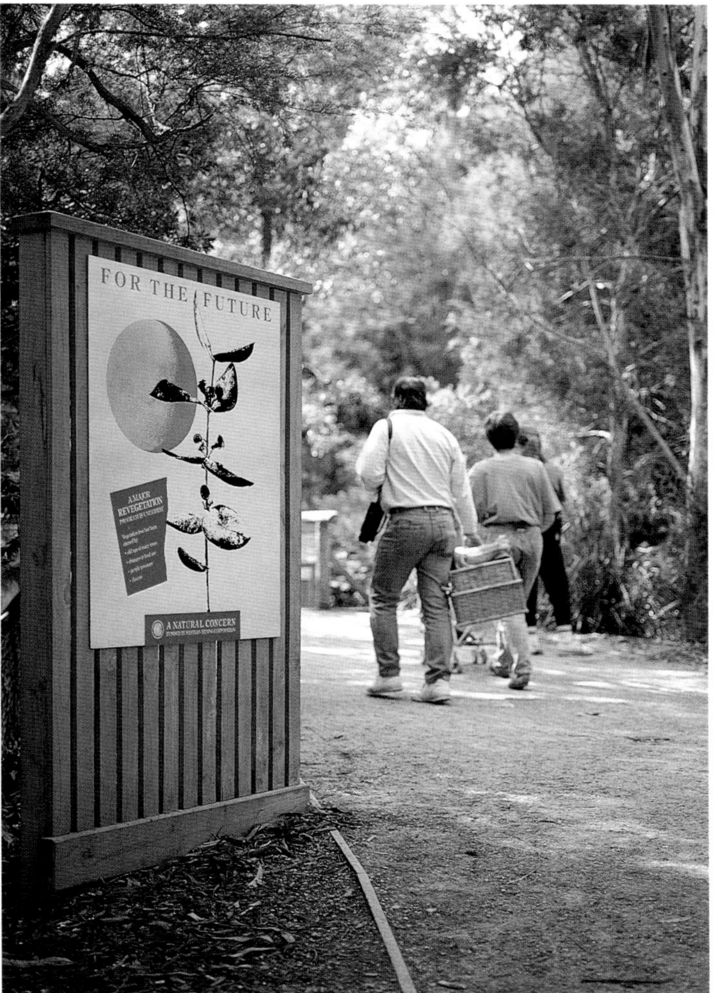

Wetlands entrance identification, revegetation program and way-finding maps

Designer
Brier Gough, Tracey Wylie
Copywriter
Margaret Mason

Revegetation program signage sponsored by Western Mining Corporation

Designer
Brier Gough
Copywriters
Margaret Mason

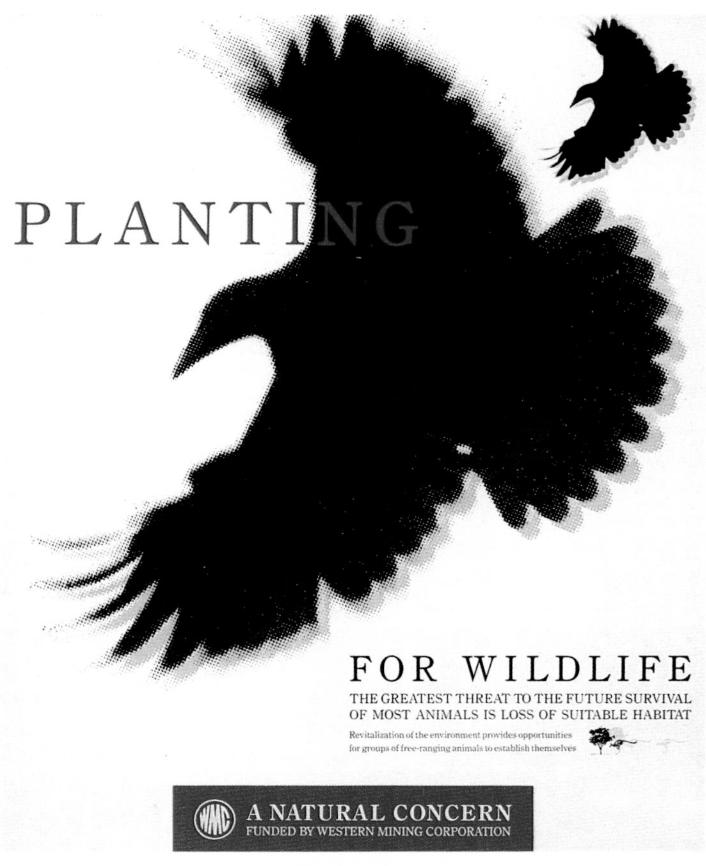

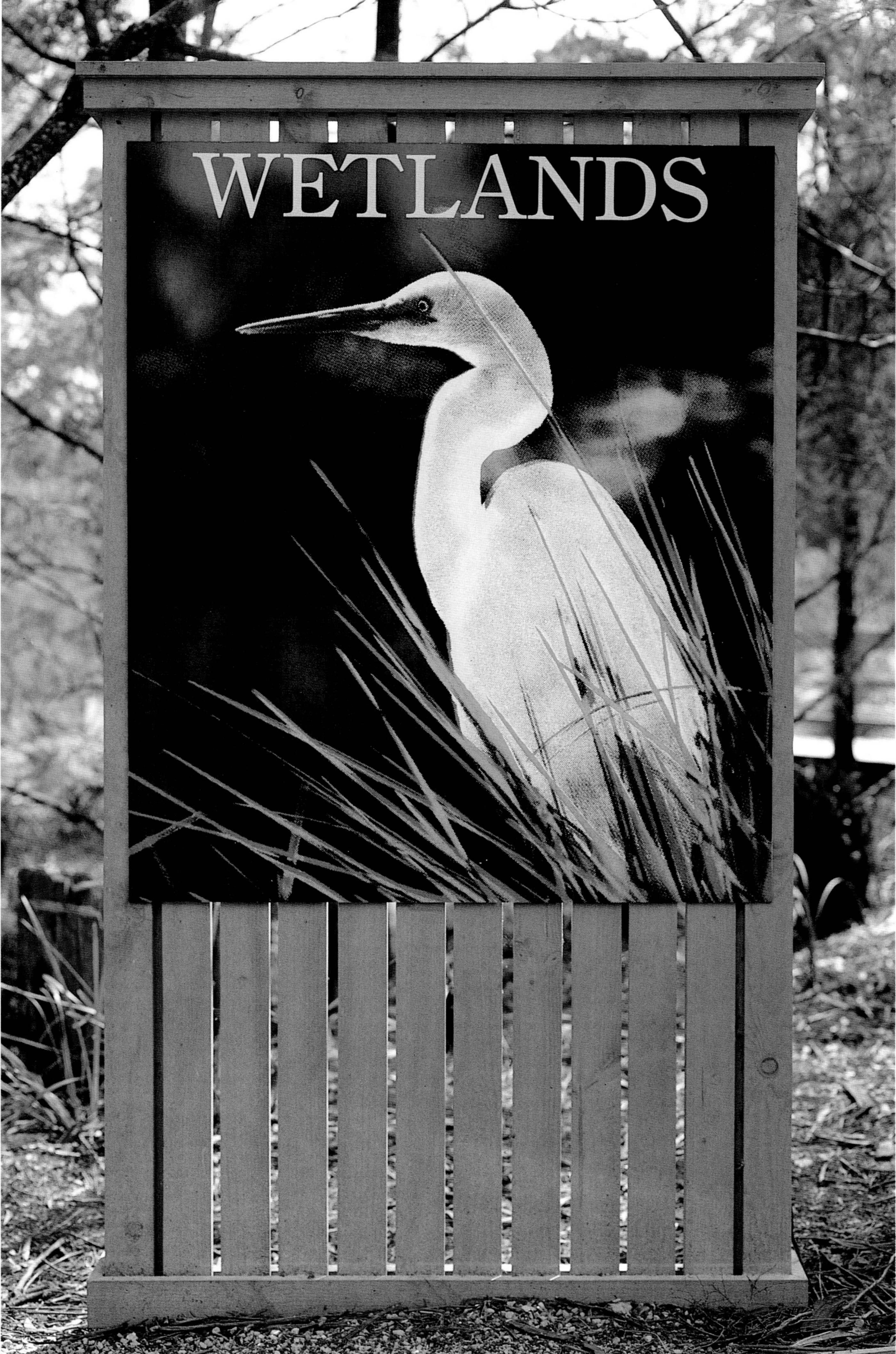
WETLANDS

Calendars, poster & brochure

Designers
Brier Gough, Tracey Wylie
Illustrators
Margaret Towt, David Higgins,
Wendi Henderson

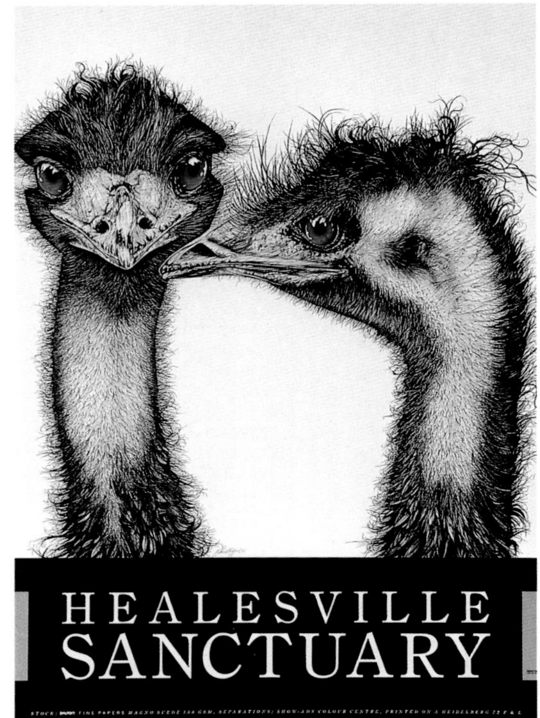

ZEFA/Masterfile

For many San Diegans and Southern Californians, family entertainment can be equated with the San Diego Zoo. The world-famous Zoo is San Diego's leading visitor attraction and will be seen by over three million people this year.

Opened since 1922, the zoo is situated on a 100-acre tract in Balboa Park. The huge animal collection includes many rare and exotic species seldom seen in zoos. Most of the Zoo's inhabitants are exhibited in barless, moated enclosures which resemble the animals' natural homes in the wild. Visitors marvel at the beautiful tropical garden setting - the result of 50 years of careful landscaping. The city's ideal climate makes it possible for the Zoo to exhibit animals outdoors year-round and for visitors to

Pictorial signing in the zoo parking – using 12 different animals and colours for ease of identification

Design Director
William Noonan

have a pleasant visit no matter what the season. Convenient transportation is provided by guided bus tours and an aerial tramway.

Among the highlights of this zoo are an imaginative children's zoo, an educational program ranging from pre-school to college, and the internationally known Center for Reproduction of Endangered Species, unique in its multi-disciplinary approach.

The San Diego Zoo is owned by the city and managed by the Zoological Society of San Diego. Trustees from the community oversee the management. With its 180,000 member households, the Society is the largest zoological association in the world.

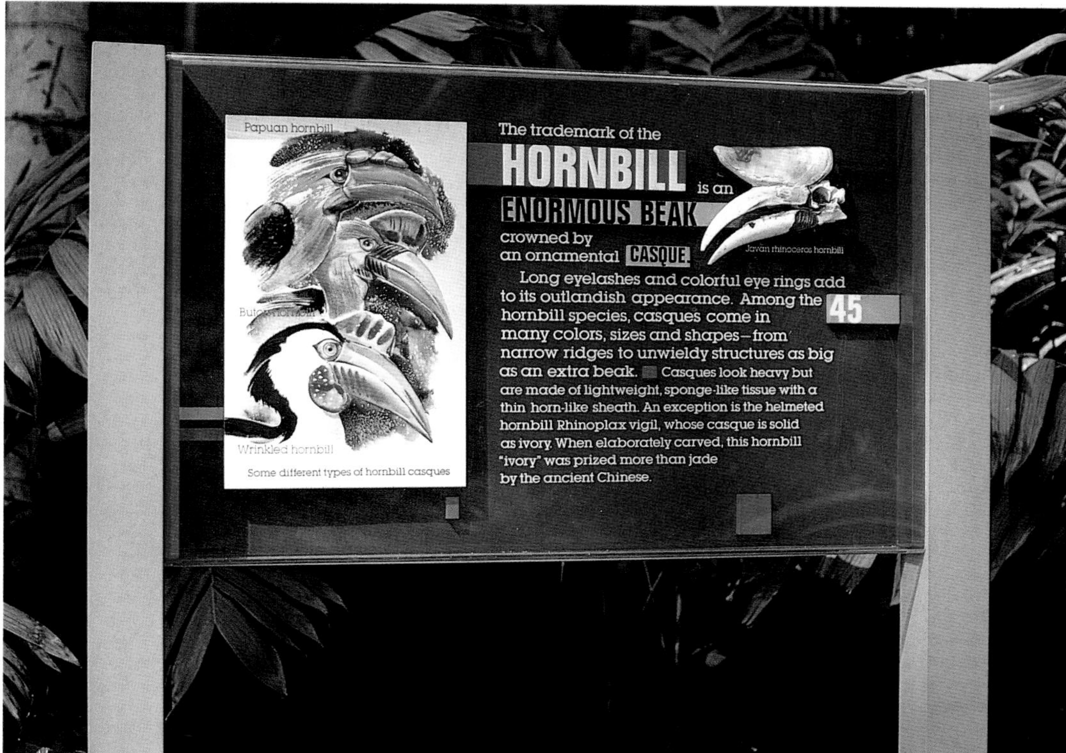

Interpretive graphic panels installed adjacent to animal enclosures

Design Director
William Noonan

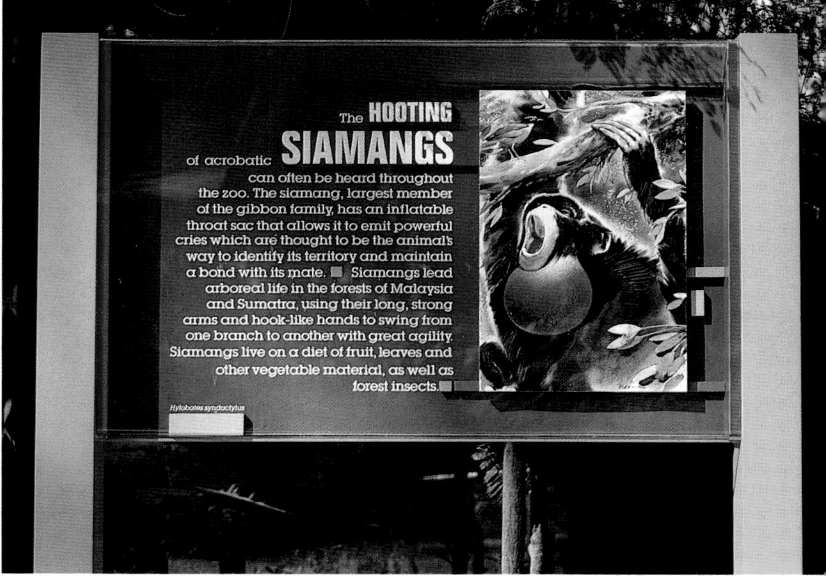

HEART OF THE ZOO
he Zoological Society is implementing the most ambitious adventure of its long and distinguished history. This second phase of the Heart of the Zoo improvements will replicate the African rain forest habitat of the magnificent lowland gorilla and other exceptional animals that dwell in this lush domain: pigmy chimpanzees, hornbills, hammerkops, crowned eagles and many, many more unique and infrequently seen species. We hope you will follow our progress in construction of this major bioclimatic element which is helping to fulfill the Zoological Society's long range plan to present the most authentic and comprehensive simulation of natural animal environment anywhere in the world.

Information panels – painted aluminium and plexiglas – in the renovated Gorilla Tropics

Design Director
William Noonan

Please follow temporary detour route during Heart of the Zoo construction
NEW HOME FOR GORILLAS

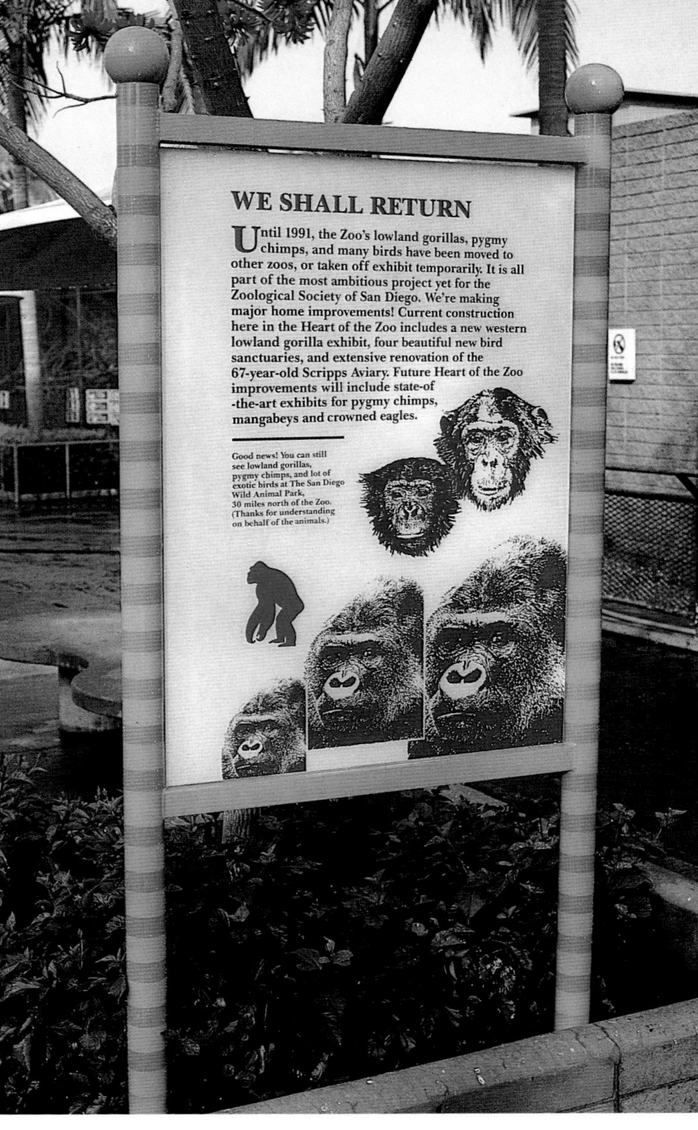
WE SHALL RETURN
Until 1991, the Zoo's lowland gorillas, pygmy chimps, and many birds have been moved to other zoos, or taken off exhibit temporarily. It is all part of the most ambitious project yet for the Zoological Society of San Diego. We're making major home improvements! Current construction here in the Heart of the Zoo includes a new western lowland gorilla exhibit, four beautiful new bird sanctuaries, and extensive renovation of the 67-year-old Scripps Aviary. Future Heart of the Zoo improvements will include state-of -the-art exhibits for pygmy chimps, mangabeys and crowned eagles.
Good news! You can still see lowland gorillas, pygmy chimps, and lot of exotic birds at The San Diego Wild Animal Park, 30 miles north of the Zoo. (Thanks for understanding on behalf of the animals.)

Information panels silk-screened on Sintra

Design Director
William Noonan

Billboard

Art Director
Bob Kwait
Designer
Bob Kwait
Design Agency
Phillips-Ramsey
Illustrator
Darrel Milsap
Copywriters
Bob Kwait, Rich Badami,
Dave Bradley

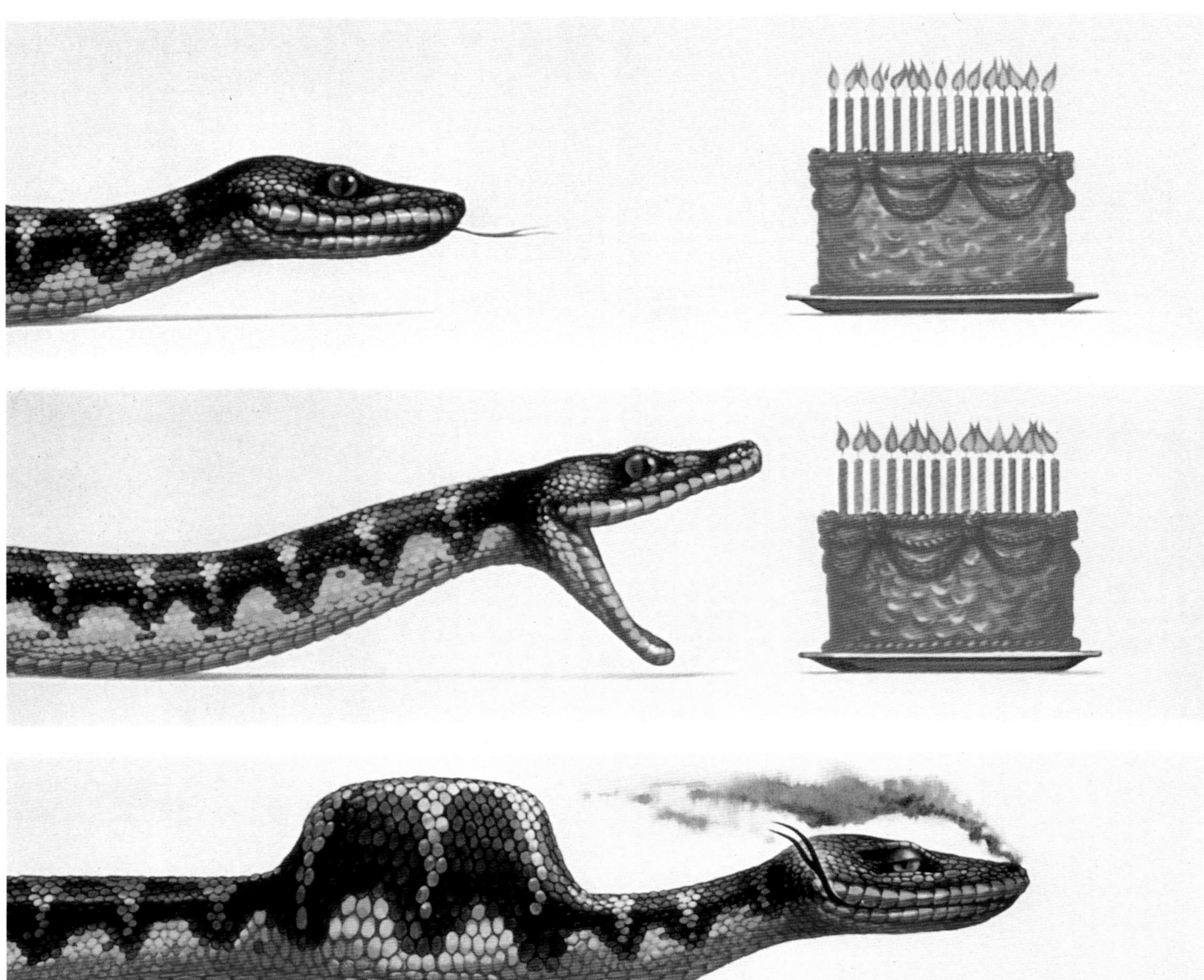
Celebrate the San Diego Zoo's 70th birthday.

Billboard

Art Director
Bob Kwait
Designer
Bob Kwait
Design Agency
Phillips-Ramsey
Illustrator
Darrel Milsap
Copywriter
Lynn Macey

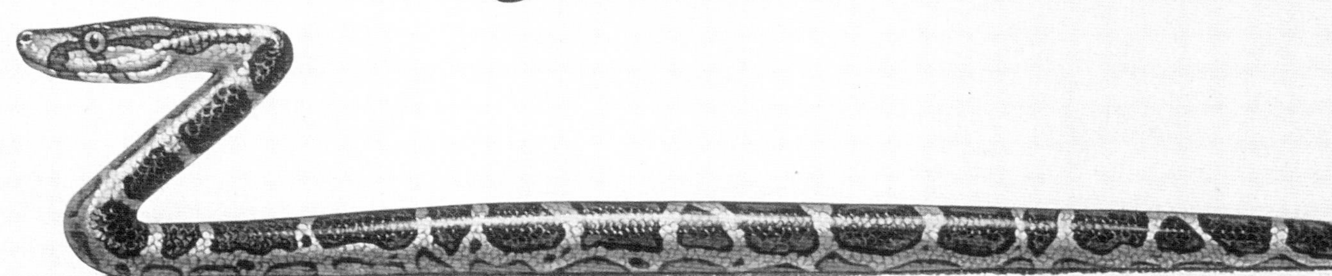
Tiger River.

A new twist.

At the San Diego

Billboard

Art Director
Bob Kwait
Designer
Bob Kwait
Design Agency
Phillips-Ramsey
Illustrator
Darrel Milsap
Copywriter
Bob Kwait

See you later.
The San Diego Zoo

Make my day.
Visit the San Diego Zoo.

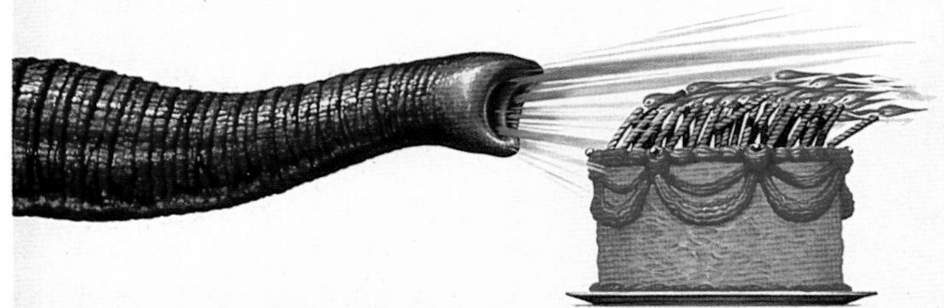

Celebrate the San Diego Zoo's 70th birthday.

Never a dull moment.
The San Diego Zoo

You won't believe your eyes.
Tiger River.
New at the San Diego Zoo

Posters and wine labels which are used on wine bottles sold by the Zoological Society

Design Director
William Noonan

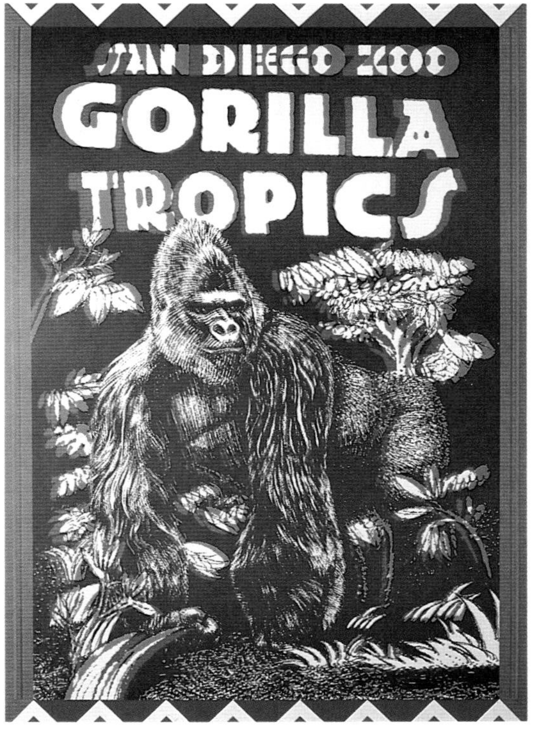

Opened to the public on May 10, 1972, the San Diego Wild Animal Park is a bold experiment - a zoo unlike zoos - in which animals roam in entire herds and flocks, in enclosures measured in acres rather than feet. It is a facility designed first for the animals, and second for the people who come to observe them. It is a sanctuary for 41 endangered animal species, 30 of which have been successfully reproduced here. Completing its second decade of study and preservation, it remains, as dubbed at its birth, "the zoo of the future".

The San Diego Wild Animal Park is the sister facility of the San Diego Zoo; both are owned and operated by the non-profit Zoological Society of San Diego. The Park is

Main Identification

Food concession building in the foreground with clock tower behind

Park hours sign

Designer
John Follis
Design Firm
Follis Design

2150 acres in size, and is located in the San Pasqual Valley, an agricultural preserve 30 miles north of downtown San Diego.

1500 mammals and 1500 birds live here; and another 500-600 arrive by birth or hatch each year. In addition to supplementing its own resident population, the Wild Animal Park provides animals to accredited zoological institutions around the world. The Park also breeds species for release back into the wilds. Nearly half the California condors alive today were hatched at the San Diego Wild Animal Park.

Though they are the best known animals in the Park, the condors have never been exhibited to the public. Their seclusion reflects the original intent of the Wild Animal Park

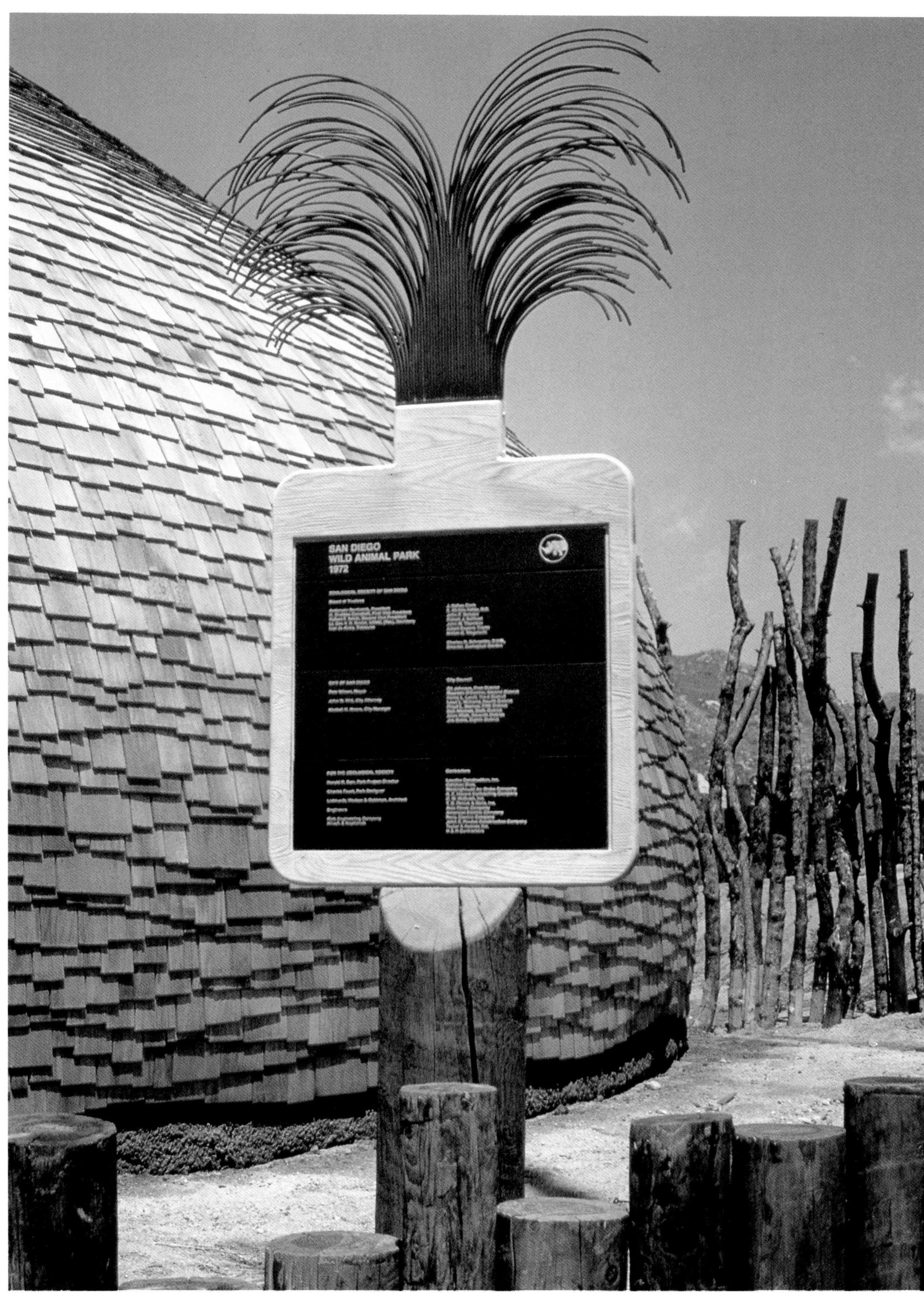

Park statement

The African version of corral with Dutch motif

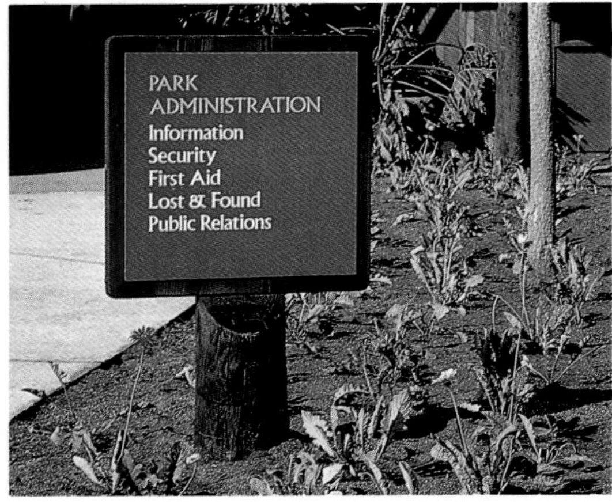

Administration sign – different from the signs for the animals

Painted sign on carved wood

Example of attempt by designer to relate to the Africans

- to establish a breeding facility best suited to animals.

The Wgasa Bush Lino monorail - electric, non-polluting, silent, and run at an elevated position to the animal herds - was specifically designed to allow public viewing with minimal disturbance to the animals. Officials at the Park like to point out that “here we put the people in a moving ‘cage’, and let the animals roam free”.

Education is an important aspect of the Wild Animal Park’s operation. In addition to the daily shows, the Park offers interpretive graphics throughout the grounds, a variety of programs for students, and special tours.

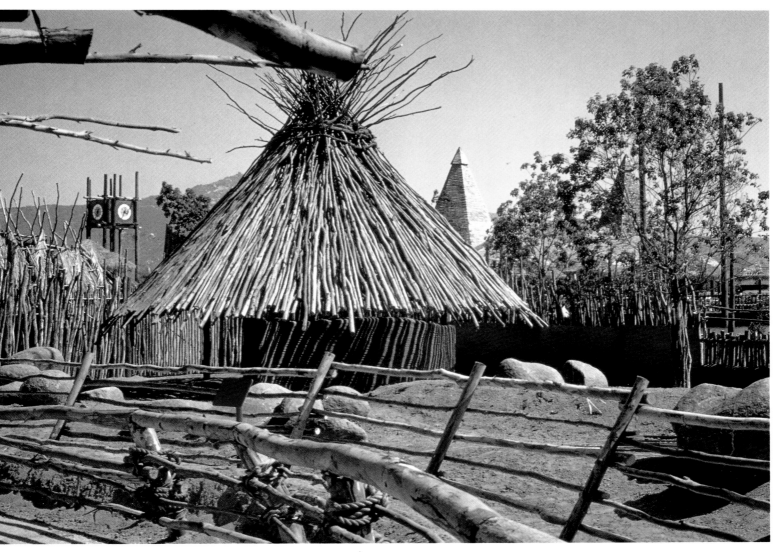

Corral designed by Charles Faust

Uniform symbol patch

Sign painted directly on wood siding

Wood carving by retired San Diego naval officer who worked from a black and white photo of an African carving of a white visitor to Africa. The black carver automatically carved it white but with black ethnic features. The retired naval officer took the carving in the photo to be a black officer and tinted the skin colour brown! By then it was too late to say anything to anybody.

Sandblasted and painted restroom sign

Animal Care Centre

Detail of ticket booth sign

Bird aviary sign – identifying the various birds by actual water-colour illustrations protected by vacuum formed ABS

San Diego Zoo
California, USA

Art Director
Brenda Bodney
Designers
Brenda Bodney, Maurya Siedler
Design Firm
Bodney + Siedler Design
Illustrator
Dale Verzaal

Birds of the Endangered Rain Forests
©Verjeel
SAN DIEGO ZOO

Art Director
Brenda Bodney
Designers
Brenda Bodney, Maurya Siedler
Design Firm
Bodney + Siedler Design
Illustrator
Jennifer Hewitson

Art Director
Brenda Bodney
Designers
Brenda Bodney, Maurya Siedler
Design Firm
Bodney + Siedler Design
Illustrator
Amanda Schaffer

Art Director
Brenda Bodney
Designers
Brenda Bodney, Maurya Siedler
Design Firm
Bodney + Siedler Design
Illustrator
Tracy Sabin

GIANT PANDAS ~ SAN DIEGO ZOO ~ 1987–1988
The Zoological Society of San Diego hopes to help the panda's plight by spreading the message of conservation.

SAN DIEGO ZOO · WILD ANIMAL PARK
The Color of Conservation
SECOND ANNUAL ART COMPETITION
1 9 8 9

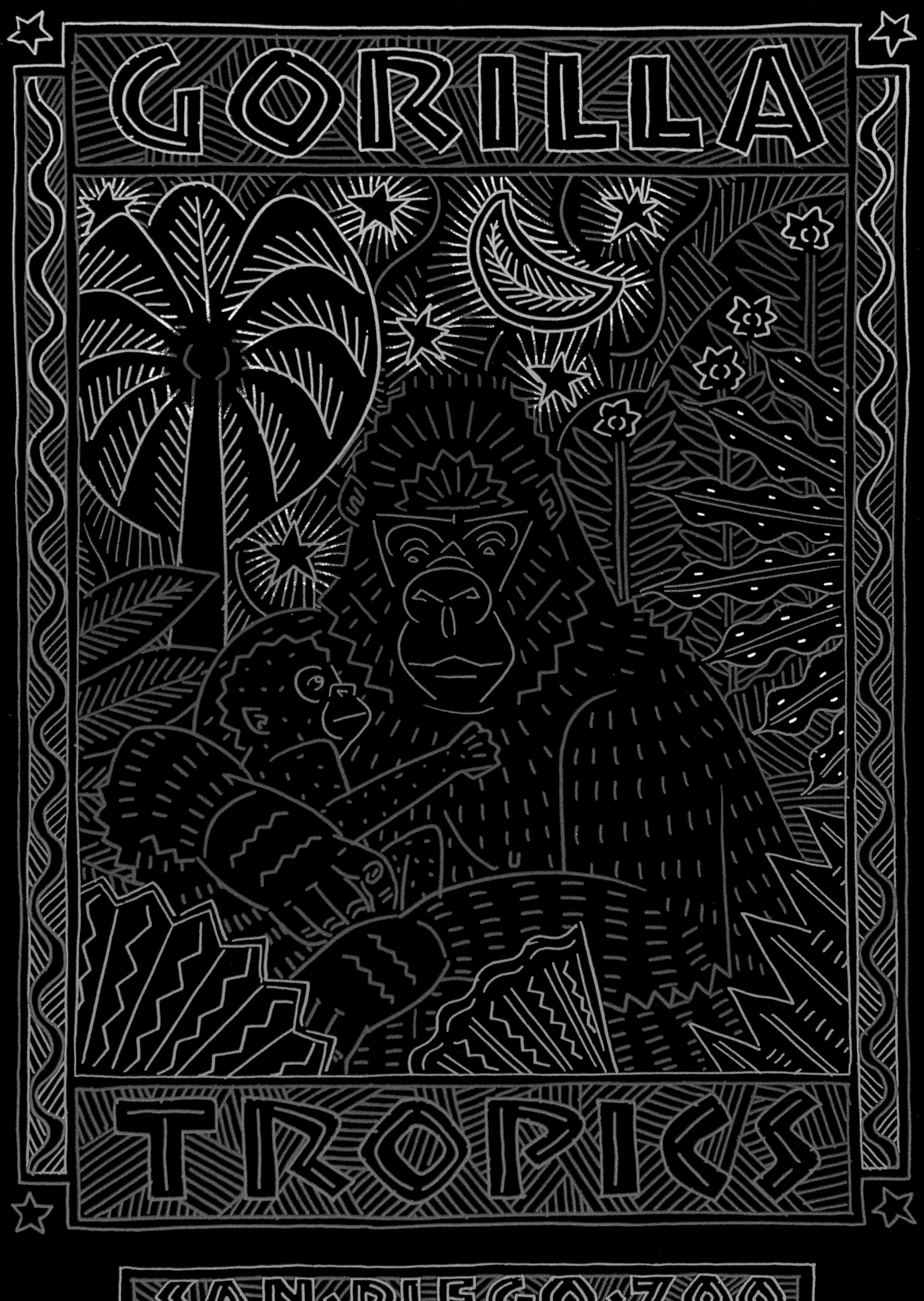
GORILLA
TROPICS
SAN·DIEGO·ZOO

San Diego Zoo
California, USA

Art Director
Brenda Bodney
Designers
Brenda Bodney, Maurya Siedler
Design Firm
Bodney + Siedler Design
Illustrator
Pasqual Ortega – Peru

San Diego Zoo
California, USA

Art Director
Brenda Bodney
Designers
Brenda Bodney, Maurya Siedler
Design Firm
Bodney + Siedler Design
Illustrator
Dale Verzaal

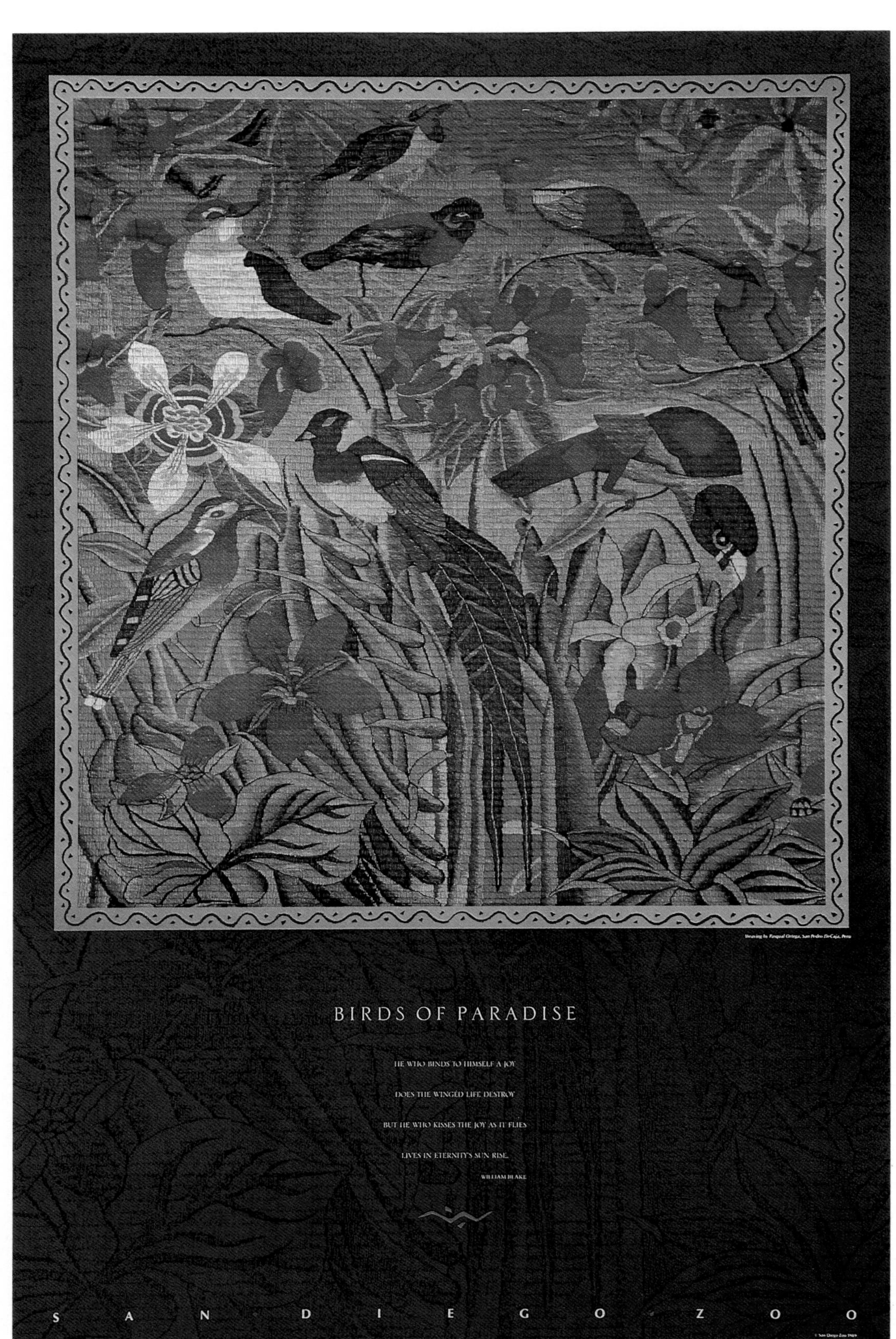

Butterflies of the Endangered Rain Forests
©Vizaal
SAN DIEGO ZOO

San Diego Zoo
California, USA

Art Director
Brenda Bodney
Designers
Brenda Bodney, Maurya Siedler
Design Firm
Bodney + Siedler Design
Illustrator
Dale Verzaal

Flowers of the Endangered Rain Forests
©Verzaal
SAN DIEGO ZOO

Patrice Ceisel/John G. Shedd Aquarium

Sea World of Florida Orlando, Florida

Over the next three years, Sea World in Orlando, Florida will be undergoing a US$2 million thematic graphics implementation program. The project serves to replace the assortment of existing graphics and architectural styles that have evolved since the park's inception in 1973.

With an area of 219 acres and some 2,500 aquatic and aerial creatures that reside here, Sea World is unique in its natural quality of settings and attractions when compared to the other tourist theme parks in the area. The design criteria includes the use of natural forms, patterns and colours of the oceanic environment. Here is a glimpse of what the new Sea World will look like in three years.

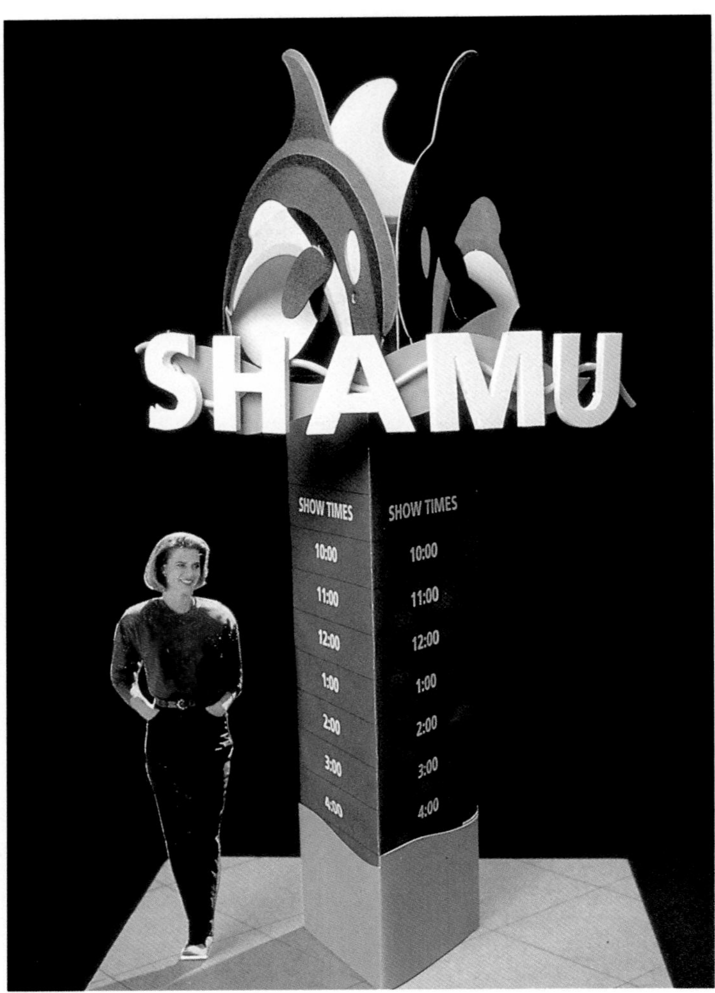

Art Director
Richard A. Foy
Designer
Bryan R. Gough
Design Firm
Communication Arts Incorporated

Representative Plan
Front Elevation
Seaworld Queuing Line Sculpture Study

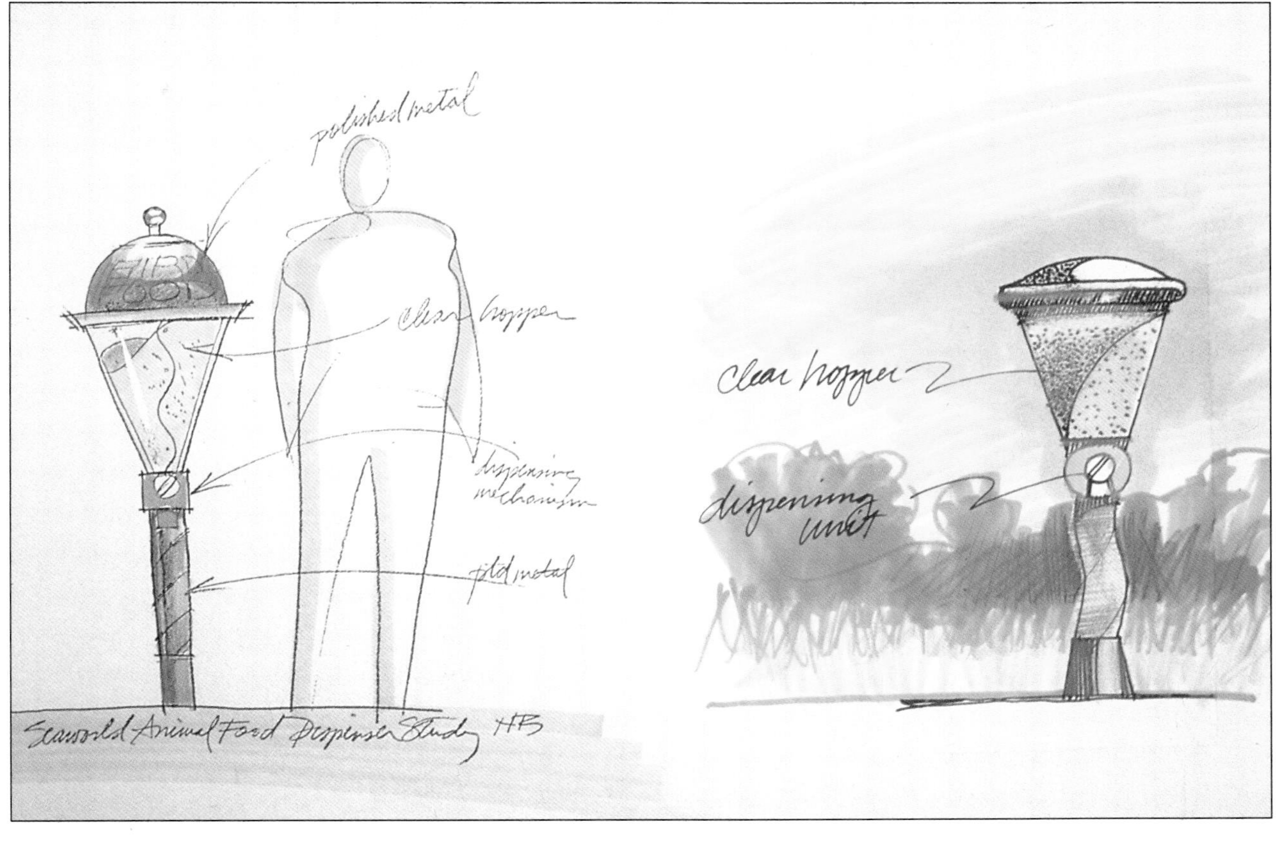
polished metal
clear hopper
dispensing mechanism
Seaworld Animal Food Dispenser Study
Clear hopper
dispensing unit

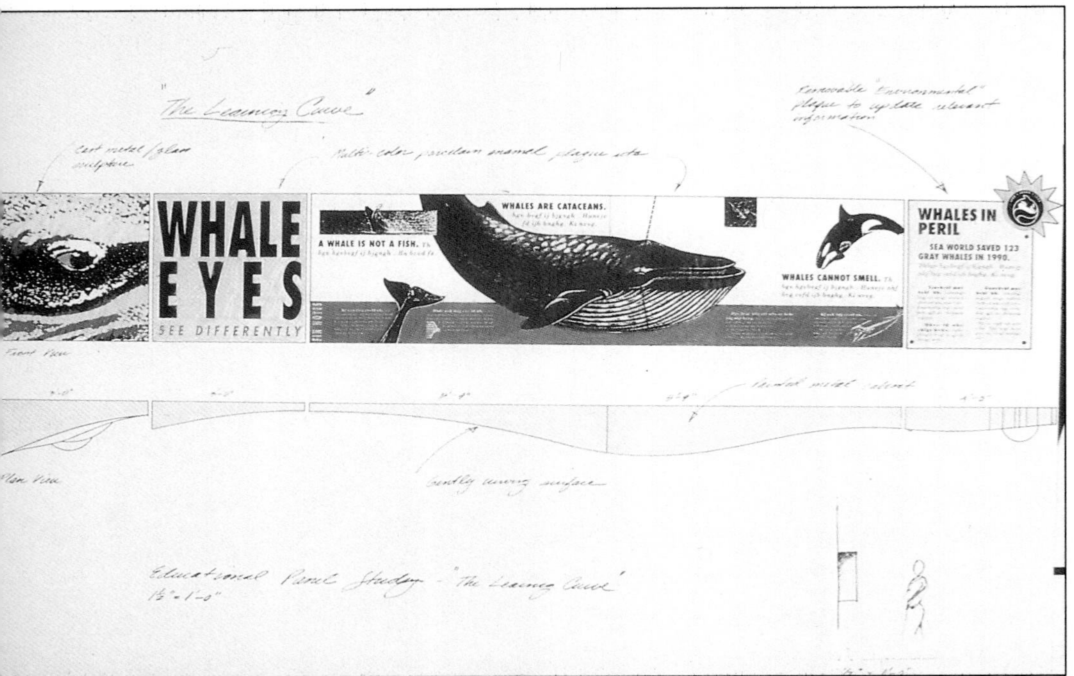

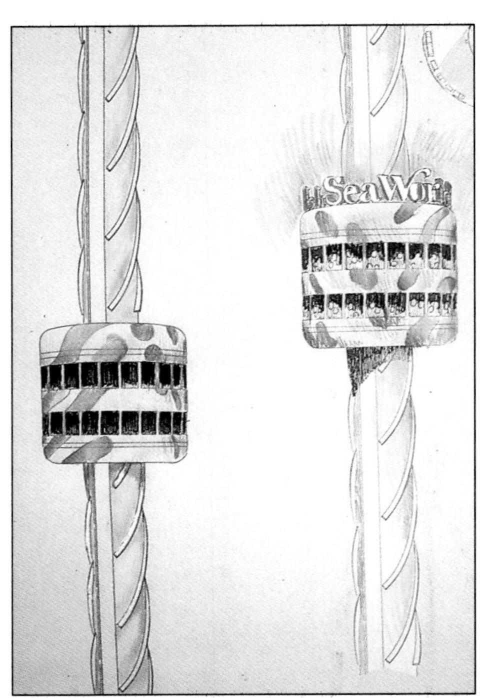

Edward Lines, Jr./John G. Shedd Aquarium

John G. Shedd Aquarium Chicago, USA

In 1931 Chicago became home to the world's largest aquarium, thereby fulfilling the dream of John G. Shedd, who died before his project could be completed. Ocean water had been moved by rail from Key West at great expense. But difficulties such as this in the original construction phase pale in comparison to those encountered during the recent expansion.

In April 1991 the transformation was complete: Chicago now boasts "an ocean by the lake" - the world's largest indoor marine mammal habitat. This US$ 45 million oceanarium was constructed entirely on landfill in Lake Michigan. More than 3 years elapsed before the facility was ready to receive the animals which had been collected

Architects
Lohan Associates

and trained elsewhere. The goal was to create a living lesson in ecology. The 2 million gallon main pool recreates the environment of the Pacific Northwest, complete with trees and rocky cliffs. Educational exhibits tackle questions such as how animals can keep warm under water.

The John G. Shedd aquarium has approximately 5000 animals in the collection. The oceanarium is home to 5 sea otters, 4 dolphins, 2 beluga whales, 3 harbour seals, and about 25 penguins.

Inside the Oceanarium, a 1000-seat amphitheatre with the north temperate rainforest and touch tide pool straight ahead

Keeping Warm Exhibit in underwater viewing gallery – an exhibit about the insulating properties of fur, feathers and blubber.

Photographers
Jon Miller, Hedrich-Blessing

Penguin shore interpretive sign, explaining distribution of various penguin species world-wide. Sign is adjacent to penguin habitat in underwater viewing gallery.

Photographer
Edward Lines, Jr.

Moving Through Water and Feeding Interpretive Exhibits in underwater viewing gallery – "streamlining game" island in the centre foreground, with hands-on experiment illustrating that streamlined shapes offer less resistance than non-streamlined shapes when moving through a dense medium like water.

Photographers
Jon Miller, Hedrich-Blessing

Interpretive exhibits in underwater viewing gallery, showing Introductory area at left and Breathing and Diving exhibit at right.

Photographers
Jon Miller, Hedrich-Blessing

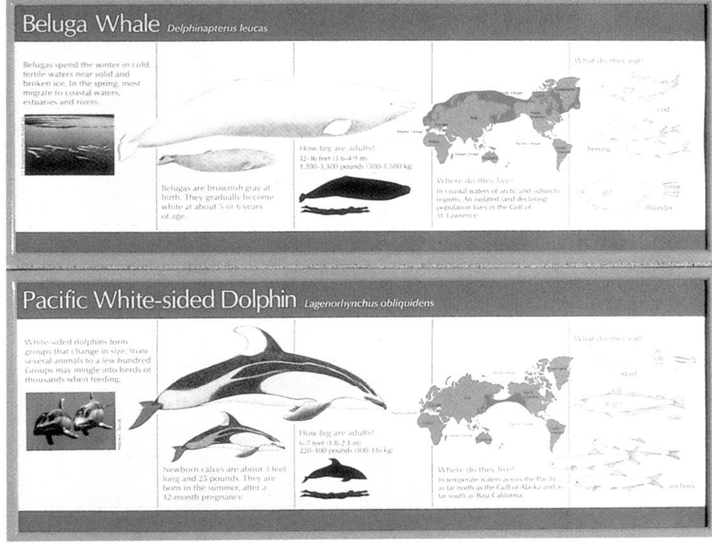

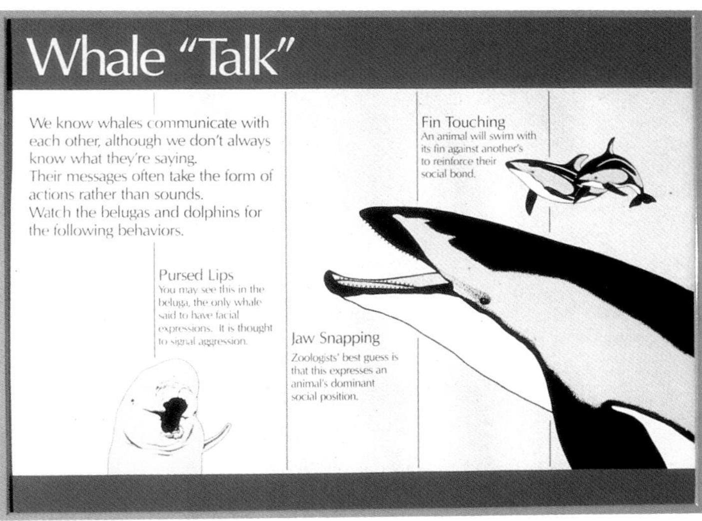

Beluga whale identification panel

"Window note" on cetacean communications at underwater viewing windows

Pacific white-sided dolphin identification panel

Photographer
Edward Lines, Jr.

Nature trail through temperate rain forest at the north end of Oceanarium habitat, showing Jarrah wood walkway, Sitka spruce and western hemlock trees.

Photographer
Edward Lines, Jr.

Looking south on coastal walkway into secluded bay (at left) and seal bight (barely visible at right) with fallen tree at top of photo and temperate rain forest ahead.

Photographers
Jon Miller, Hedrich-Blessing

Signs along the nature trails in the oceanarium.

Photographer
Edward Lines, Jr.

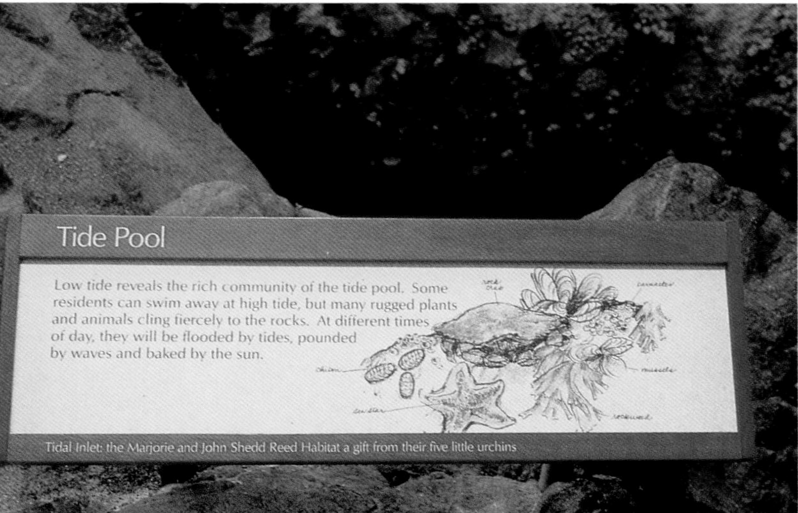

Tide Pool
Low tide reveals the rich community of the tide pool. Some residents can swim away at high tide, but many rugged plants and animals cling fiercely to the rocks. At different times of day, they will be flooded by tides, pounded by waves and baked by the sun.
Tidal Inlet: the Marjorie and John Shedd Reed Habitat a gift from their five little urchins

Temperate Rain Forest
Lush forests of Sitka spruce, western hemlock and other evergreen trees grow along the Pacific coast from Northern California to Alaska where the climate is mild and rainfall is plentiful. These coastal rain forests are home to some of the largest and oldest trees on our continent.

Promotional material – mug, button, brochure, T-shirt

Opening Celebration invitation

Poster

Art Directors
Paul Bluestone, J. Bacal, M. Delfini
Designers
M. Delfini, Matt Kirchman, Susan Sunvidge
Illustrators
Byron Gin, William Peterson, Evelyn Wulthers
Copywriters
Karen Furnmeyer, Carol Garfinkel, Peg Kern

OCEANARIUM

SHEDD AQUARIUM CHICAGO

Press kit and poster

Art Directors
Bryan Sanzotti, Eileen Noren
Designer
Eileen Noren
Design Firm
Design Horizons International
Illustrator
Jim Ruskowski
Copywriter
Jean Baker

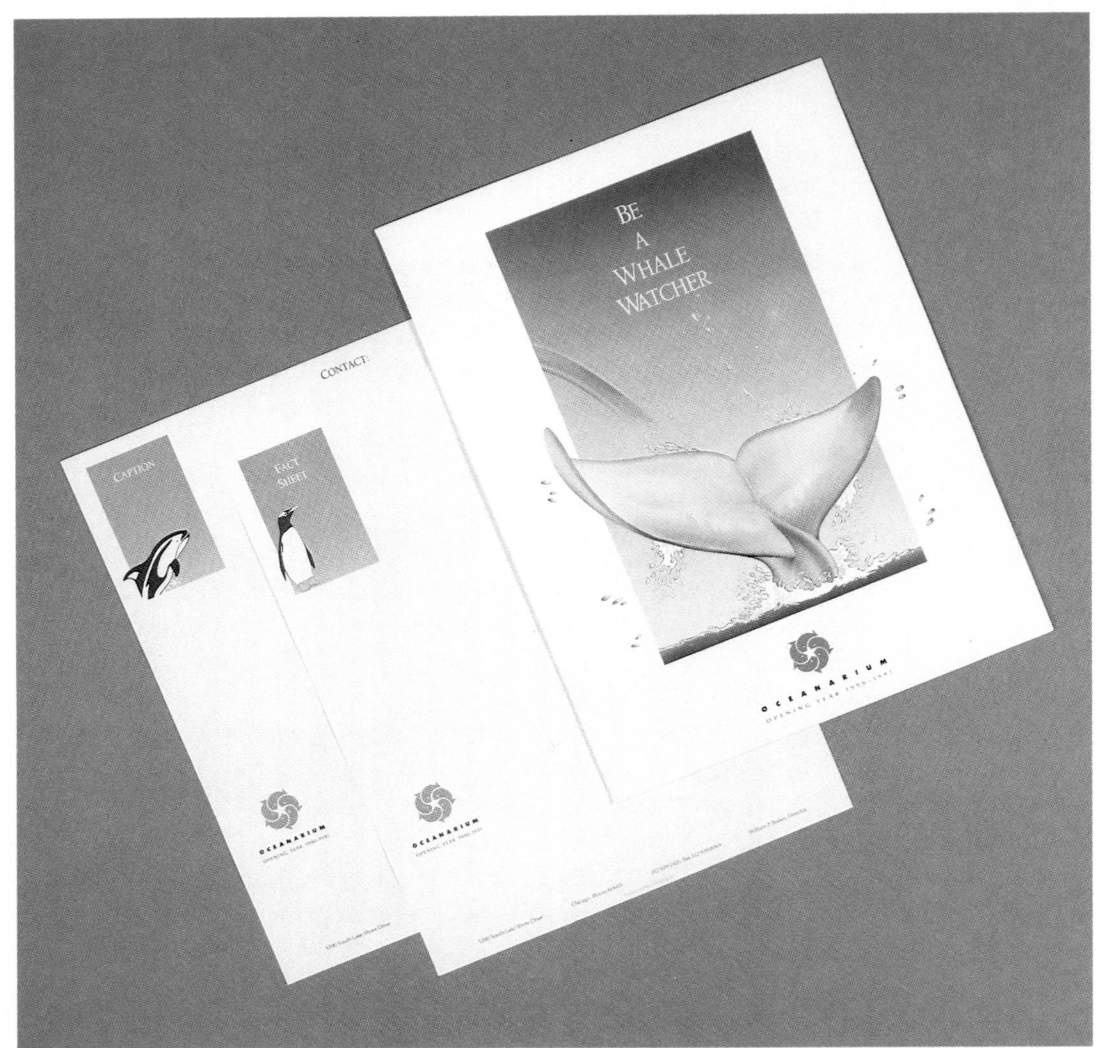

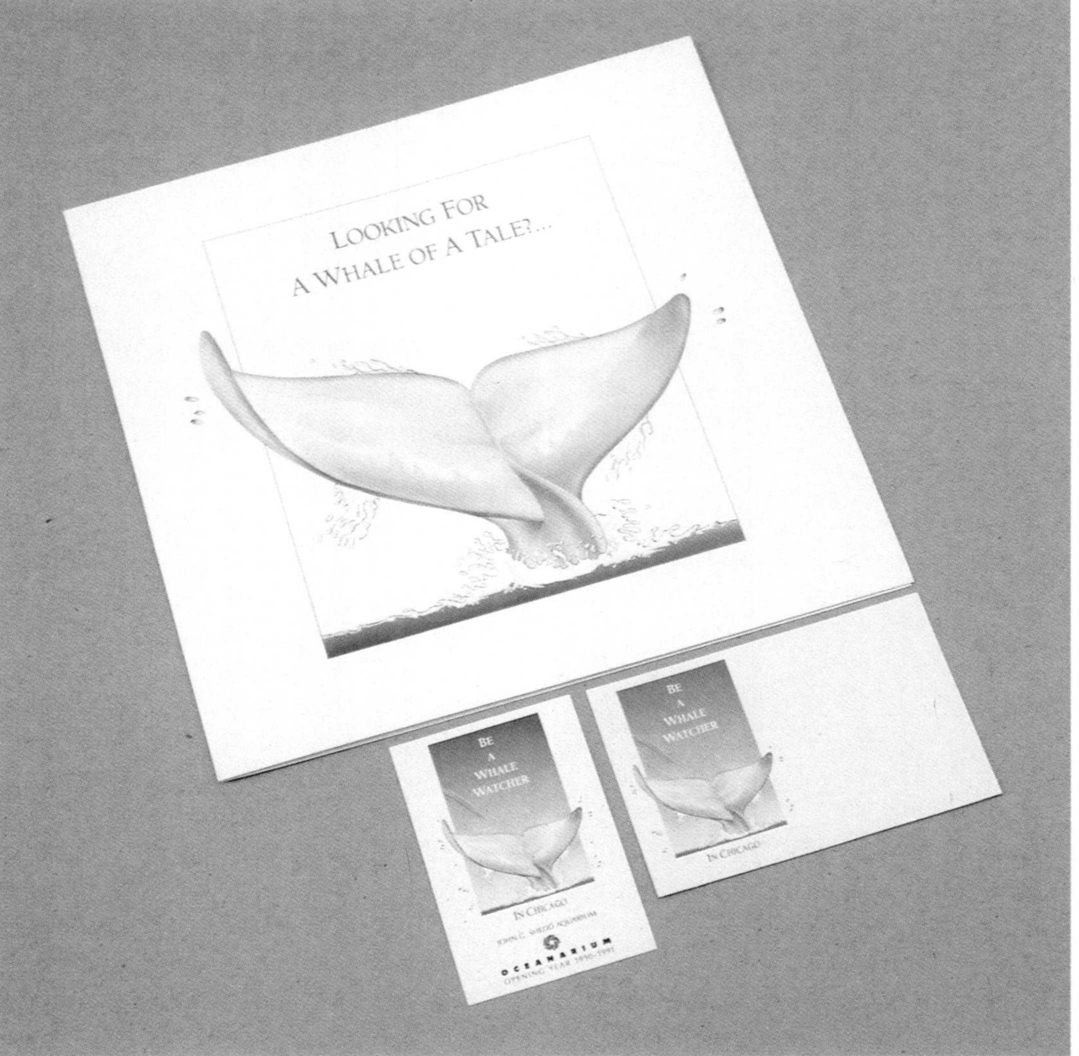

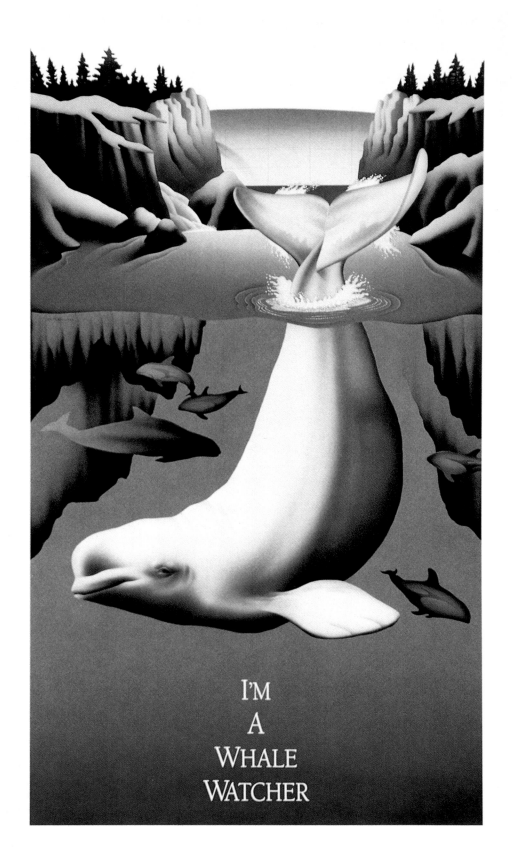

I'M
A
WHALE
WATCHER

JOHN G. SHEDD AQUARIUM

OCEANARIUM

OPENING YEAR 1990-1991

JOHN G. SHEDD AQUARIUM South Lake Shore Drive, Chicago, Illinois

Christmas card

1990 Annual report

Opening Gala invitation

Art Director
Paul Bluestone
Designers
Matt Kirchman, Susan Johnson, M. Delfini
Illustrator
Lohan Associates
Copywriter
Peg Kern

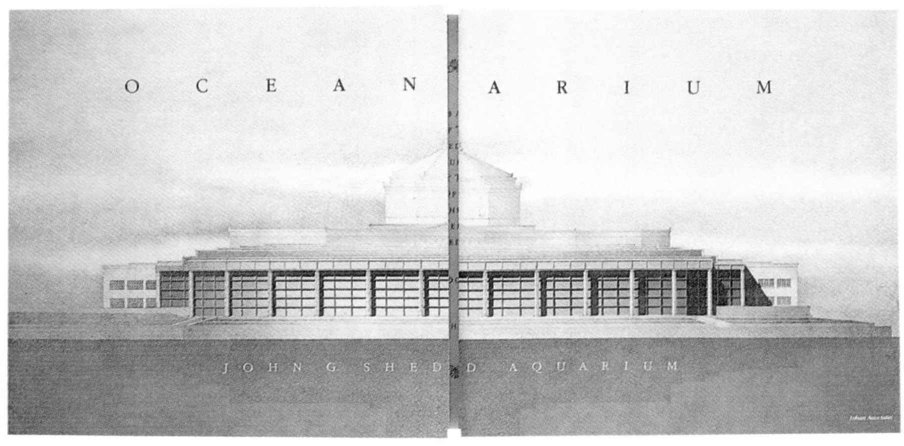

Various print material

Art Director
Paul Bluestone
Designers
Sally Smith, Matt Kirchman, M. Delfini
Illustrators
Lohan Associates, Linda Wilson
Photographers
Hedrich Blessing, Patrice Ceisel, Marcie C. Tarvid
Copywriters
Barbara Ceiga, William P. Braker, Paula Resk, Antonella Gianni

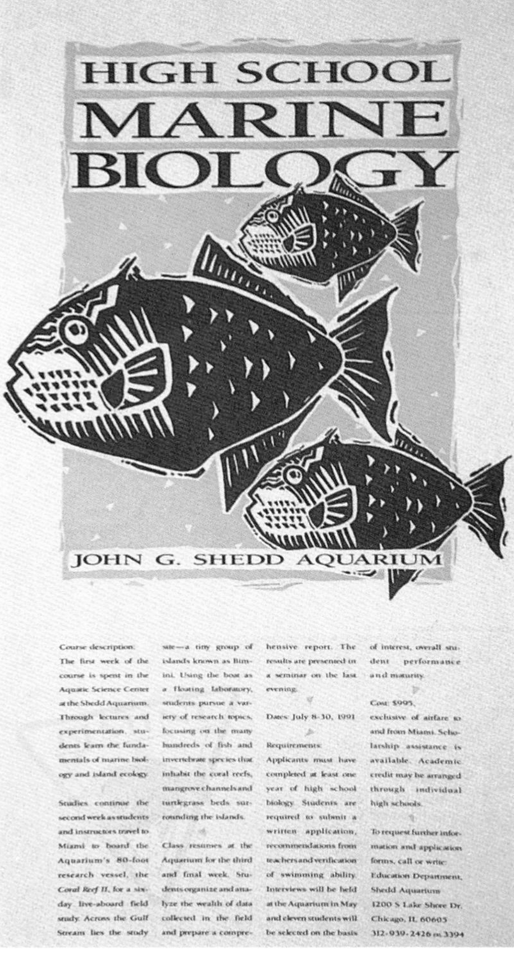

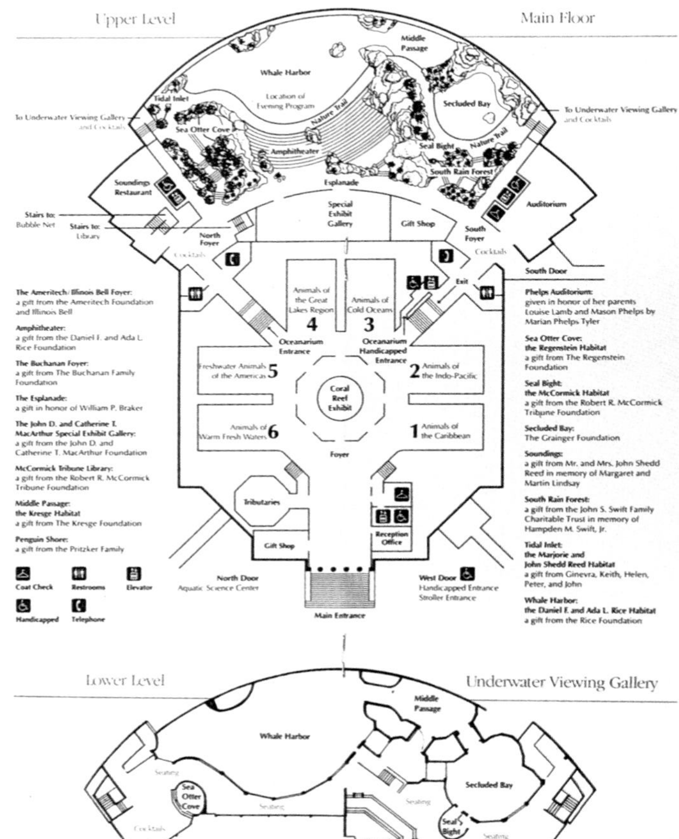

Various print material

Art Director
Paul Bluestone
Designers
Sally Smith, Matt Kirchman
Illustrators
Lohan Associates, Sally Smith, Matt Kirchman
Photographer
Marcie C. Tarvid
Copywriters
William P. Braker, Peg Kern
Editor
Charles R. Feldstein

Carl Roessler – FPG/Masterfile

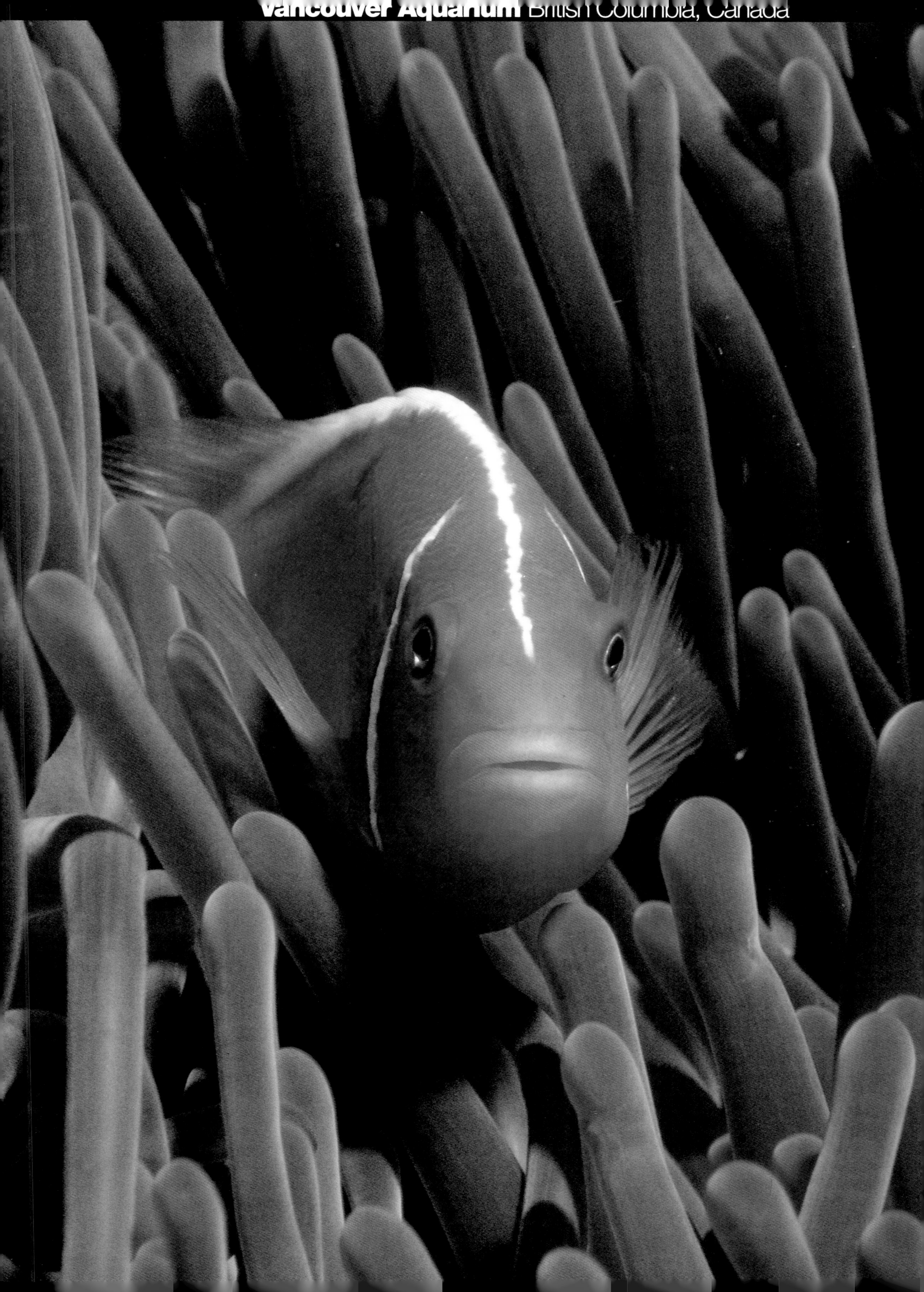

Vancouver Aquarium British Columbia, Canada

The Vancouver Aquarium is a non-profit, self-supporting institution dedicated to the preservation of aquatic life through education, recreation and research. It enjoys a strong membership of more than 50,000 individuals and is visited by nearly one million people each year.

The Aquarium in many ways reflects the waters of the world. The 9600 animals that make their home at the Aquarium serve as living ambassadors for regions as diverse as the Amazon rainforest and the Arctic Ocean. Unlike many facilities where animals are featured in generalized exhibits, the Vancouver Aquarium focuses upon real places - internationally recognized areas of ecological significance. The ecosystems portrayed in

IMAQ, The Arctic Sea exhibit

Designer
Greg Davies
Copywriter
Debbie Cavenaugh

the interpretive galleries and live animal exhibits become focal points of Aquarium research and educational programs. The Aquarium features specially trained biological interpreters who move throughout the ecosystem exhibits, exploring with the public observable events such as fish breeding and territorial displays. Discussion moves from the animals in the Aquarium habitats to the behaviour of animals in the wild ecosystems they represent.

A graphics budget is established a year in advance. It is a fluctuating amount based on the needs of all aquarium departments, projects planned and availability of funds. Large projects have historically had 7% of the overall budget assigned to the graphic component. It is hoped that this percentage will increase.

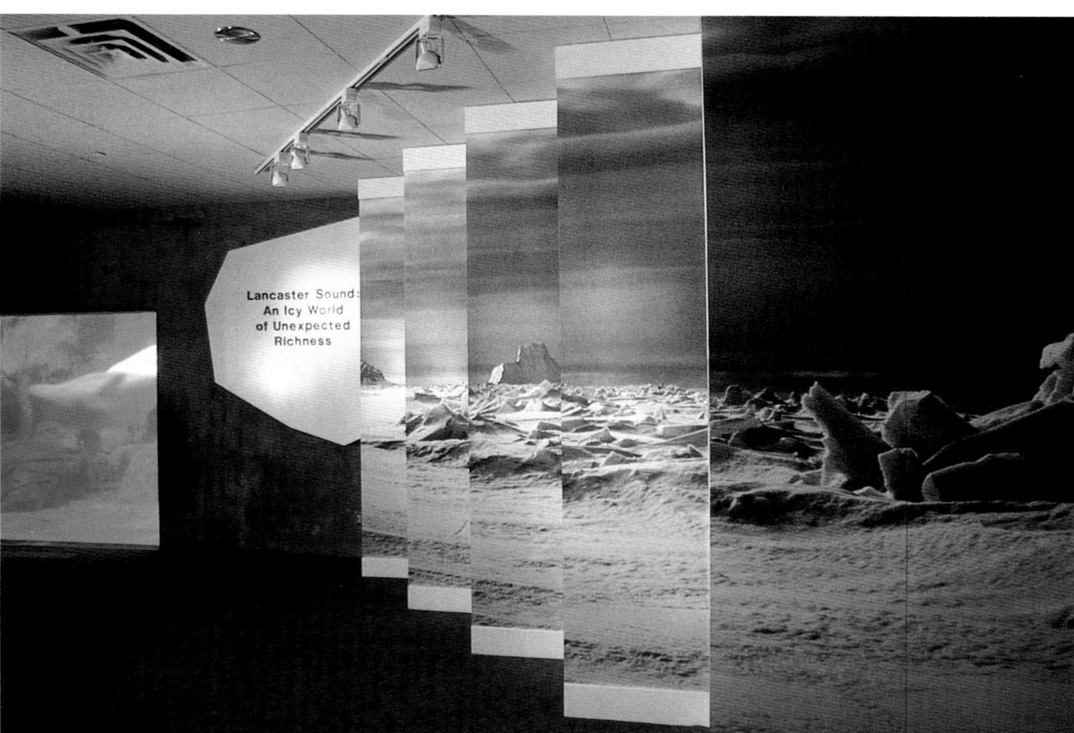

Killer whale exhibit

IMAQ, The Arctic Sea exhibit

Exterior enamel graphics – sea otters

Arctic Canada display associated with live beluga exhibit

Designer
Greg Davies
Photography
Finn Larsen
Copywriters
Sharon Proctor, Debbie Cavenaugh, Elin Kelsey, Nancy Baron

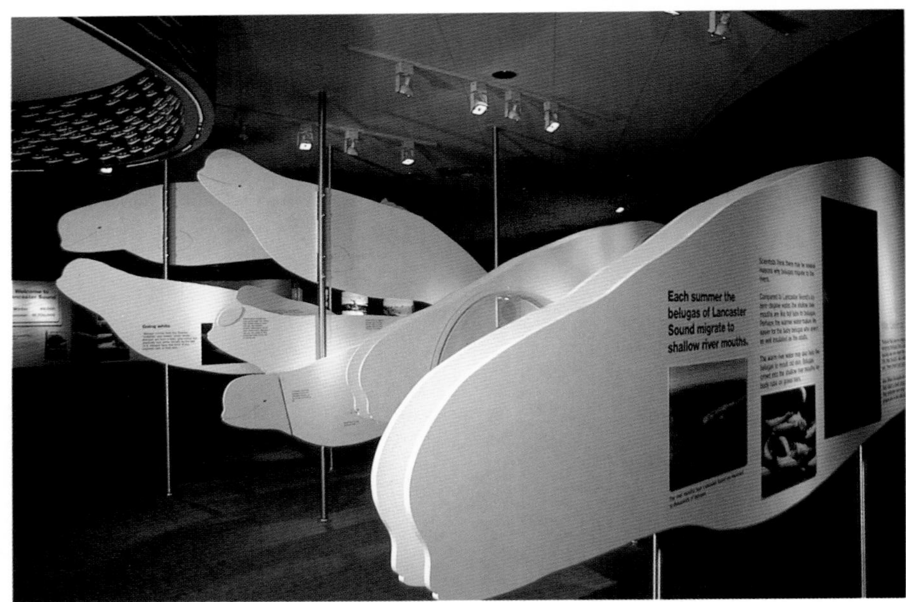

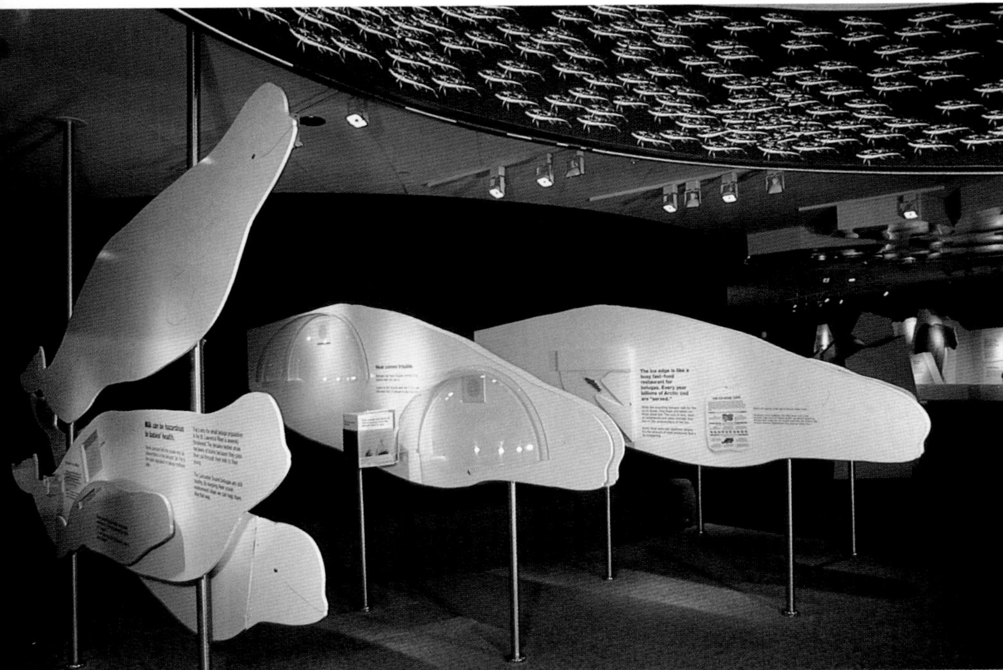

Arctic Canada display associated with live beluga exhibit

Designer
Greg Davies
Copywriters
Nancy Baron, Elin Kelsey, Sharon Proctor

Spawning salmon exhibit

Designer
Greg Davies

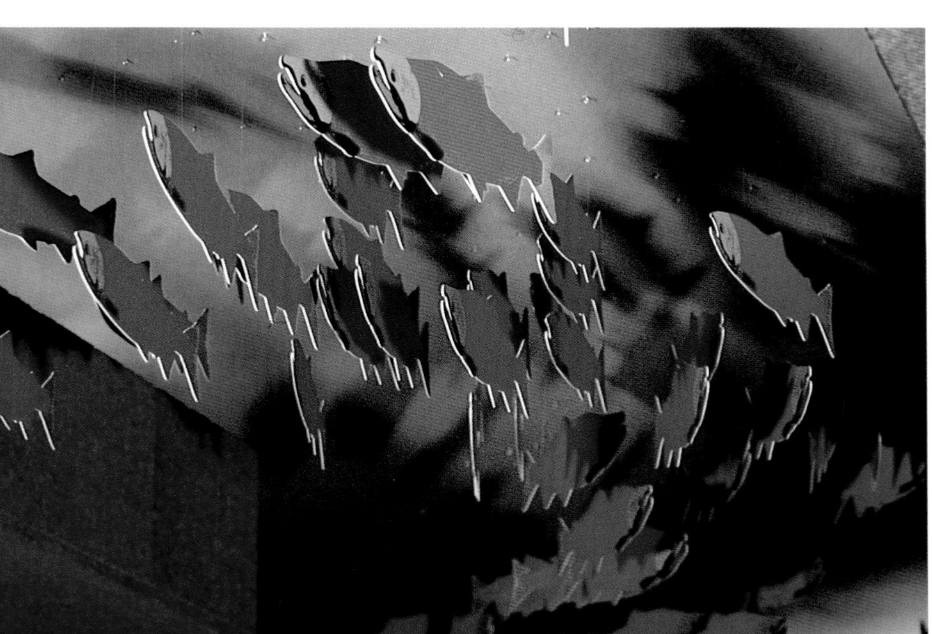

Arctic Canada display associated with live beluga exhibit

Designer
Greg Davies
Copywriters
Nancy Baron, Elin Kelsey, Sharon Proctor

Exterior banners and bus promotion

Designer
Greg Davies
Illustrator
Ron Reward

George Calef/Masterfile

Metro Toronto Zoo
Ontario, Canada

Creative & Art Director
Geoffrey B. Roche
Design Agency
Chiat/Day/Mojo inc.Advertising
Illustrator
Doug Martin
Copywriter
Joe Alexander

Metro Toronto Zoo
Ontario, Canada

Creative Director
Geoffrey B. Roche
Art Directors
Geoffrey B. Roche,
Duncan Milner
Design Agency
Chiat/Day/Mojo inc.Advertising
Illustrator
Doug Martin
Copywriter
Joe Alexander

Marineland Los Angeles, California, USA

Creative Director
Paul Waddell
Designers
Susan Westre, Dorothy Allard
Design Agency
Evans
Copywriter
Bill Schohl

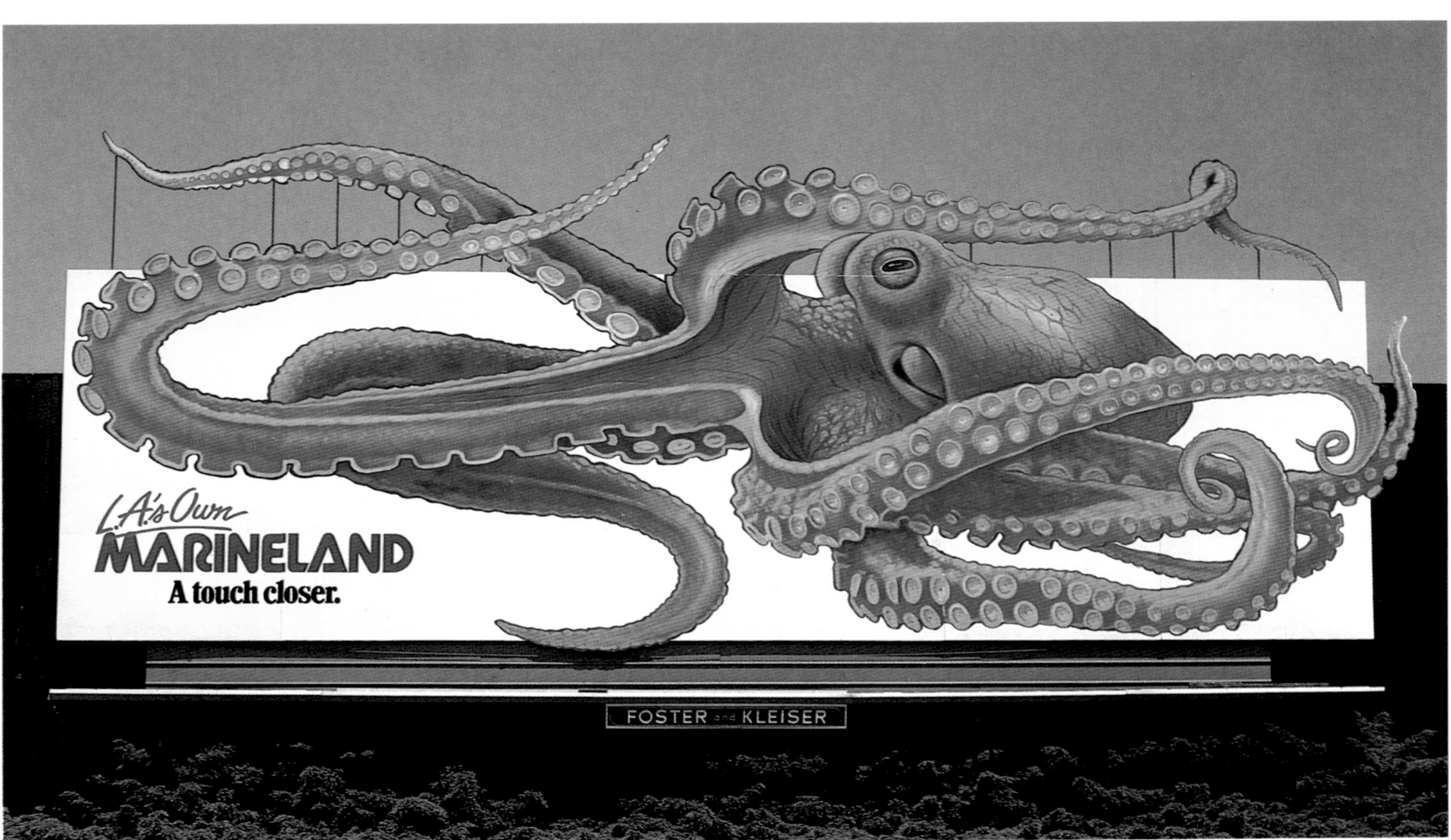

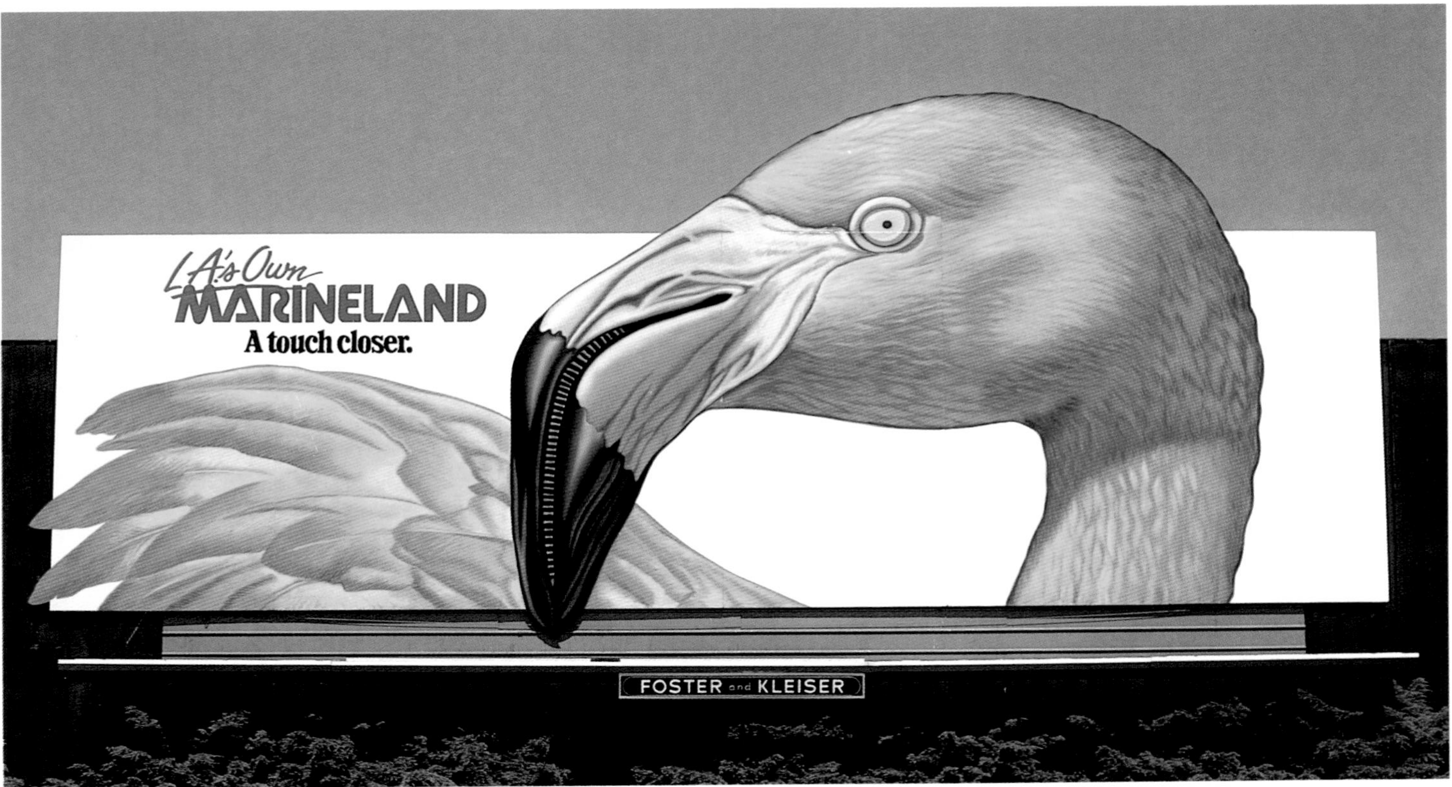

Tracy Aviary
Salt Lake City, Utah, USA

Art Director
Ron Stone, Evans Advertising
Designers/Copywriters
Jeff Olsen, Dick Brown,
Bryan DeYoung
Design Firm
The Weller Institute for the Cure
of Design, Inc.
Illustrator
Don Weller

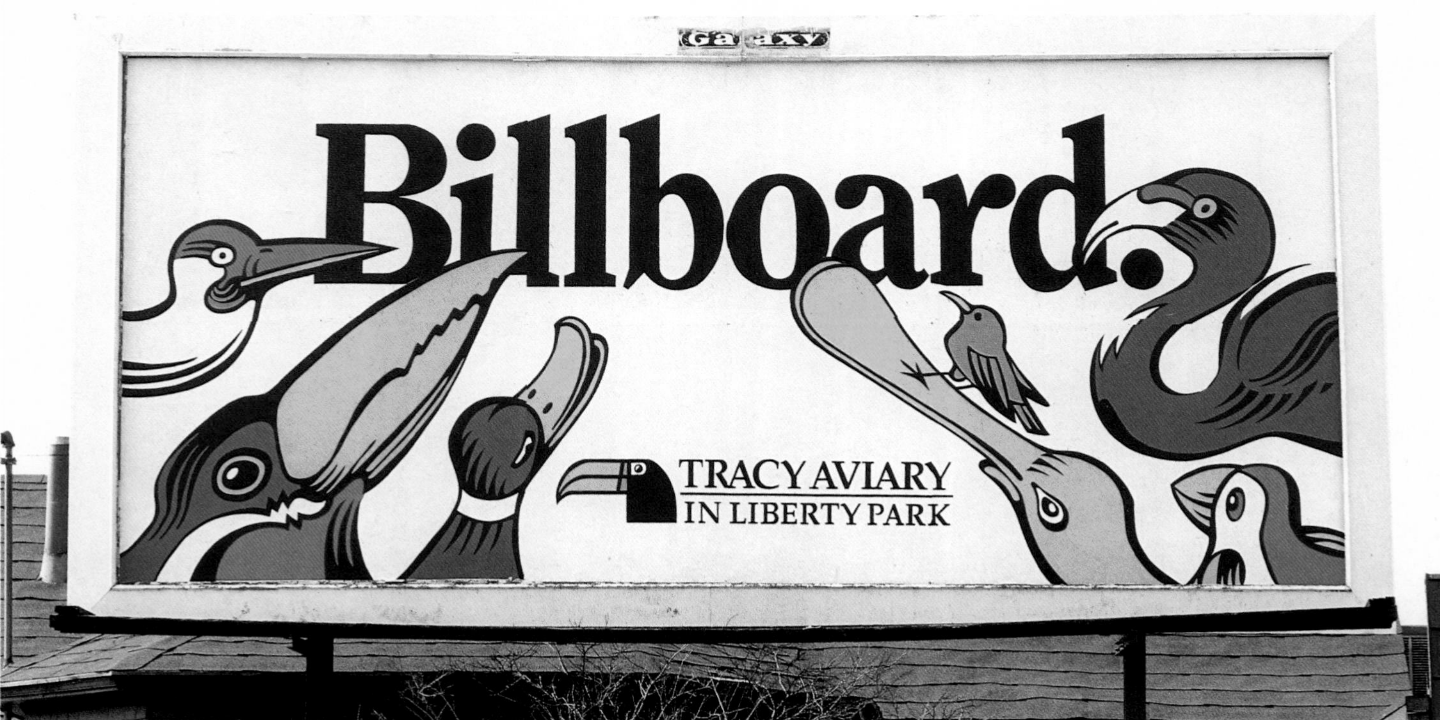

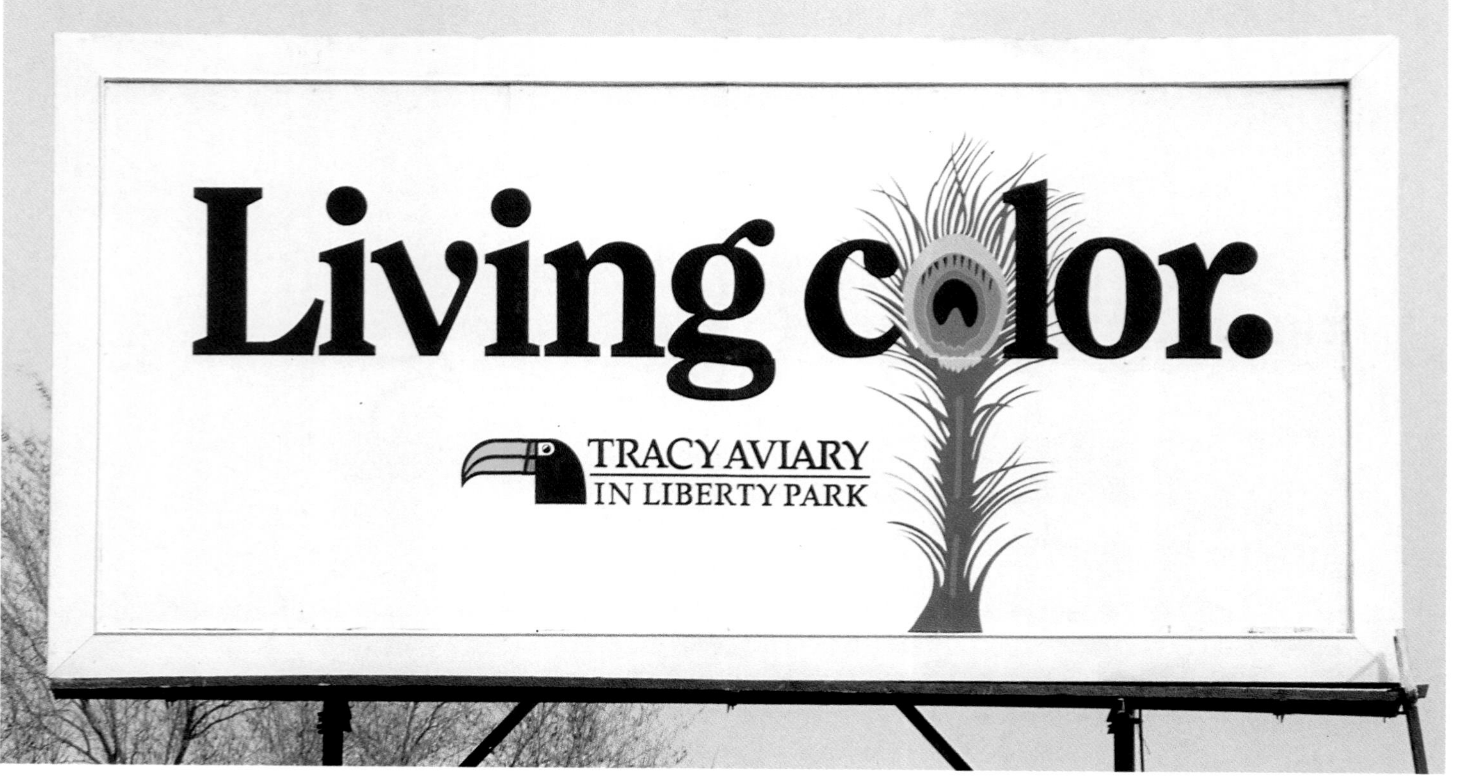

Tracy Aviary
Salt Lake City, Utah, USA

Art Director
Ron Stone, Evans Advertising
Designers/Copywriters
Jeff Olsen, Dick Brown,
Bryan DeYoung
Design Firm
The Weller Institute for the Cure
of Design, Inc.
Illustrator
Don Weller

Los Angeles Zoo
California, USA

Art Director/Designer
Mikio Osaki
Design Agency
Poindexter/Osaki/Nissman
Illustrator
Brain Zick
Copywriter
Mikio Osaki

San Antonio Zoological Gardens & Aquarium
Texas, USA

Designers
Mark Mayfield, Gloria Merlo
Design Firm
FingerPrints, Inc.
Illustrator
Gloria Merlo
Photography
Mark Mayfield

Get tickled pink

The San Antonio ZOO

"This place is a zoo"!

Gorillas in our midst

The San Antonio ZOO

"This place is a zoo"!

St. Louis Zoo
Missouri, USA

Design Firm
Bartels, Carstens & Associates
Illustrator
Braldt Bralds

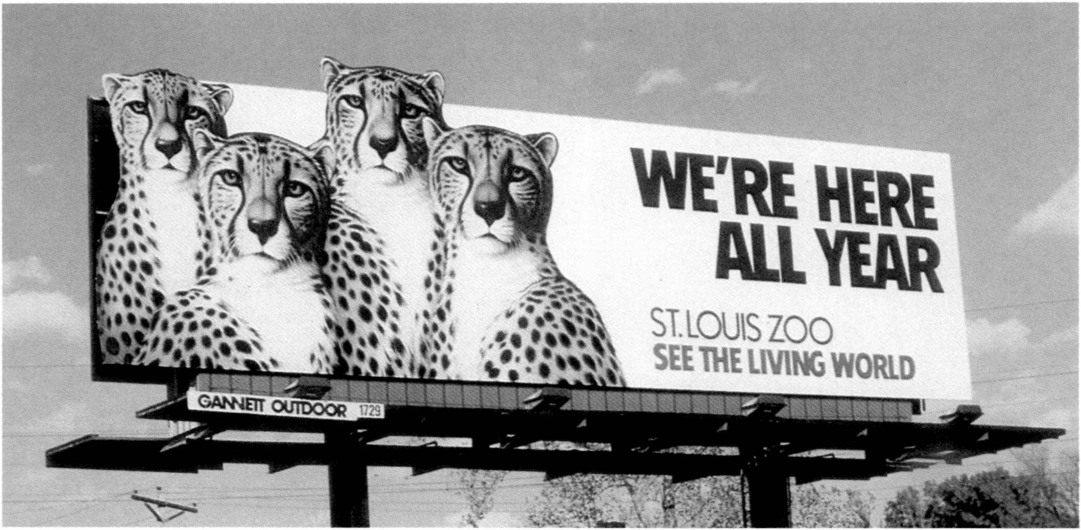

Cincinnati Zoo
Ohio, USA

Art Director/Designer
Teresa Newberry, Dave Bukvic
Design Agency
Mann Bukvic Associates
Illustrators
Doug Henry, David Groff
Copywriters
Debbie Effler, Dave Bukvic

Sea World of California
California, USA

Creative Director
John Armistead
Art Director
Jeff Weekley
Design Agency
DMB&B
Illustrator
Gary Norman
Copywriter
Gary Alpern

Seattle Aquarium
Washington, USA

Art Director
Ron Hansen
Designer
Ron Hansen
Design Agency
Ron Hansen & Partners
Illustrator
Bart Bemus
Copywriters
Ron Hansen, Ed Leinbacher

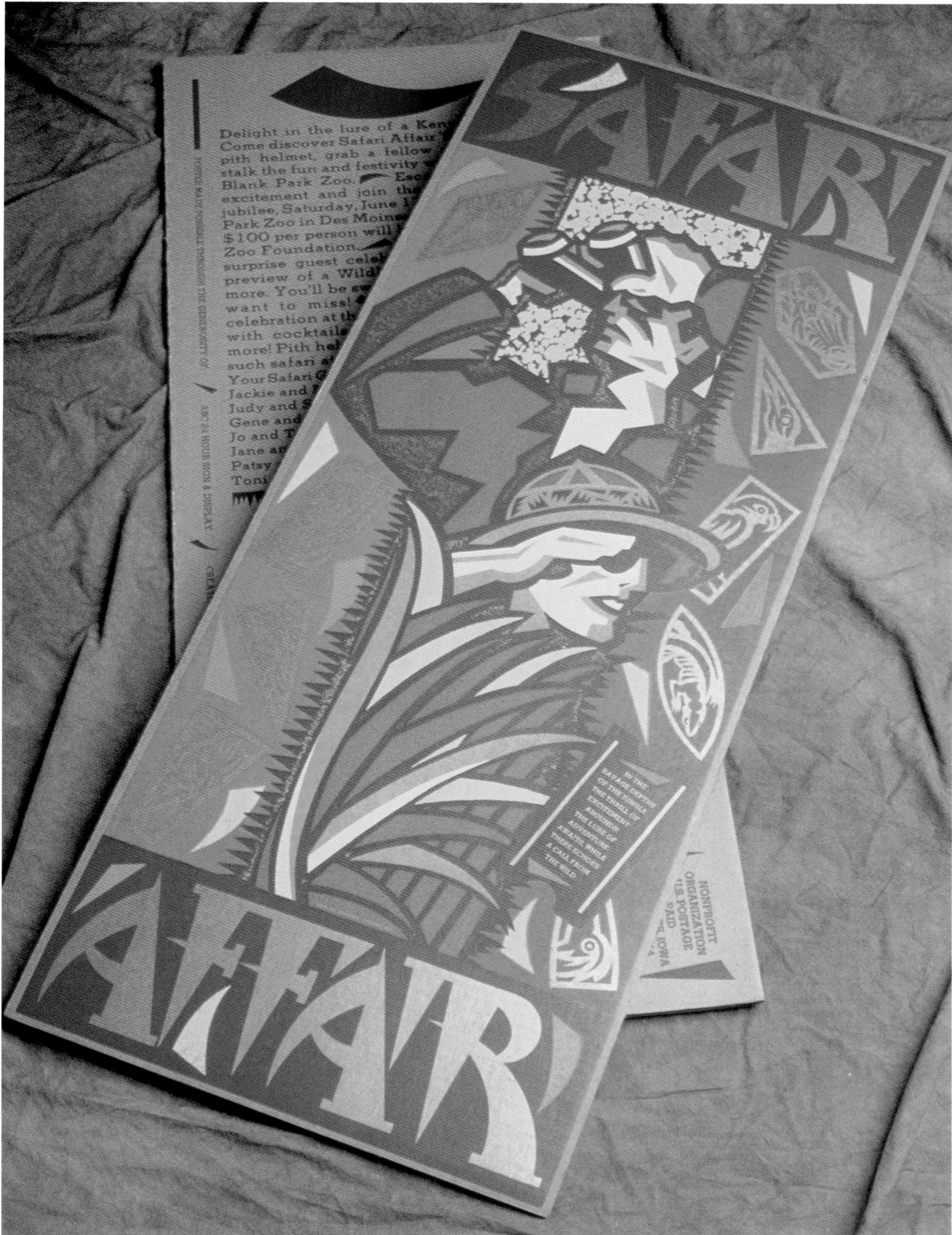

Blank Park Zoo
Des Moines, Iowa, USA

Designer/Illustrator
John Sayles
Design Agency
Sayles Graphic Design, Inc.
Copywriter
LeAnn Koerner

Brookfield Zoo
Illinois, USA

Designer
Hannah Jennings
Illustrator/Copywriter
Hannah Jennings

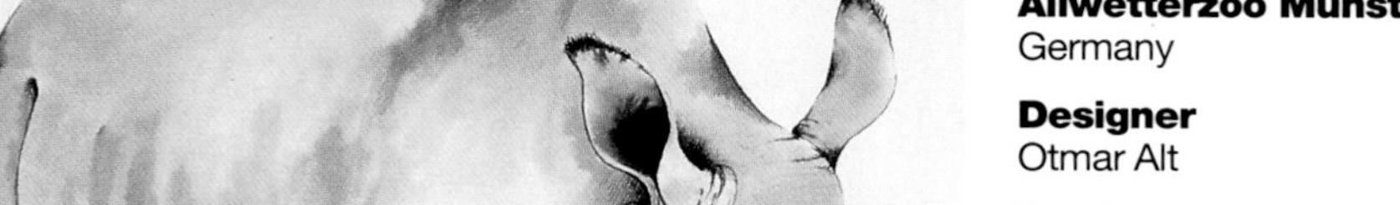

Allwetterzoo Münster
Germany

Designer
Otmar Alt

Designer
Thea Ross

Copenhagen Zoo
Frederiksberg, Denmark

Designer/Illustrator
Marianne Ostergaard

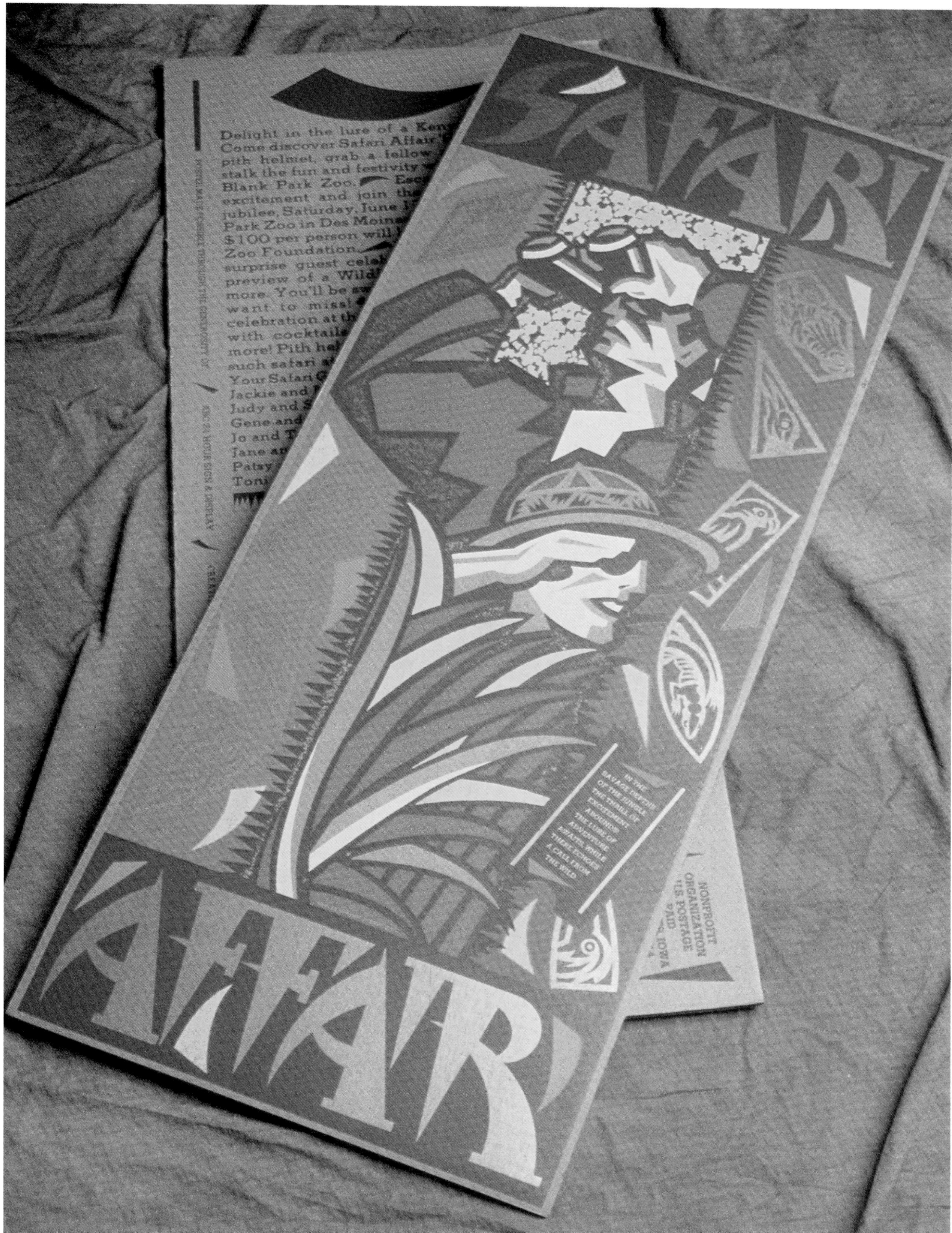

Blank Park Zoo
Des Moines, Iowa, USA

Designer/Illustrator
John Sayles
Design Agency
Sayles Graphic Design, Inc.
Copywriter
LeAnn Koerner

Brookfield Zoo
Illinois, USA

Designer
Hannah Jennings
Illustrator/Copywriter
Hannah Jennings

Allwetterzoo Münster
Germany

Designer
Otmar Alt

Designer
Thea Ross

Copenhagen Zoo
Frederiksberg, Denmark

Designer/Illustrator
Marianne Ostergaard

ZOO
...vilde oplevelser!

Cincinnati Zoo
Ohio, USA

Art Director/Designer
Dan Bittman
Design Firm
Design Team One, Inc.
Illustrator
Lou Specker

Sedgwick County Zoo
Wichita, Kansas, USA

Art Director/Illustrator
Cam Woody
Design Agency
Lida Advertising
Illustrator
Jennifer Hewitson

San Francisco Zoological Gardens
California, USA

Art Director
Marty Neumeier
Design Firm
Neumeier Design Team
Designer/Illustrator
Sandra Higashi

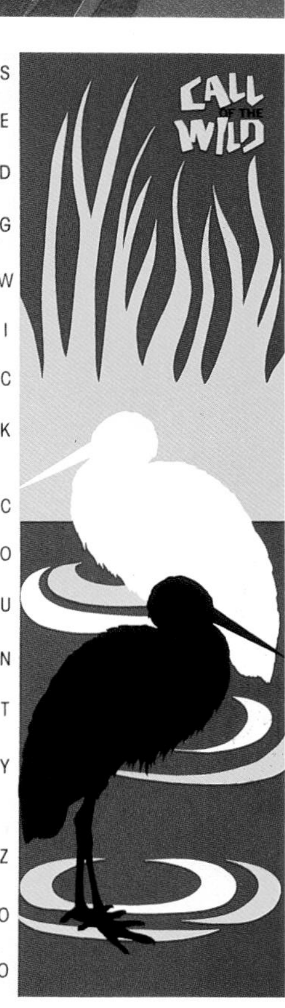

Kings Island Wild Animal Habitat
Cincinnati, Ohio, USA

Art Director/Designer
Dan Bittman
Design Firm
Design Team One, Inc.
Copywriter
Bob Reese, Sara Boone

Seattle Aquarium
Washington, USA

Art Director/Designer
Sharon Dean
Design Firm
Stimpson - Clarke
Photographer
Chris Huss
Copywriter
Jim Cowles

Seattle Aquarium
Washington, USA

Art Director
Rayne Beaudoin
Designer
Tycer Fultz Bellack
Design Firm
Yutaka K. Sasaki/Innov
Illustrator
Yutaka Sasaki

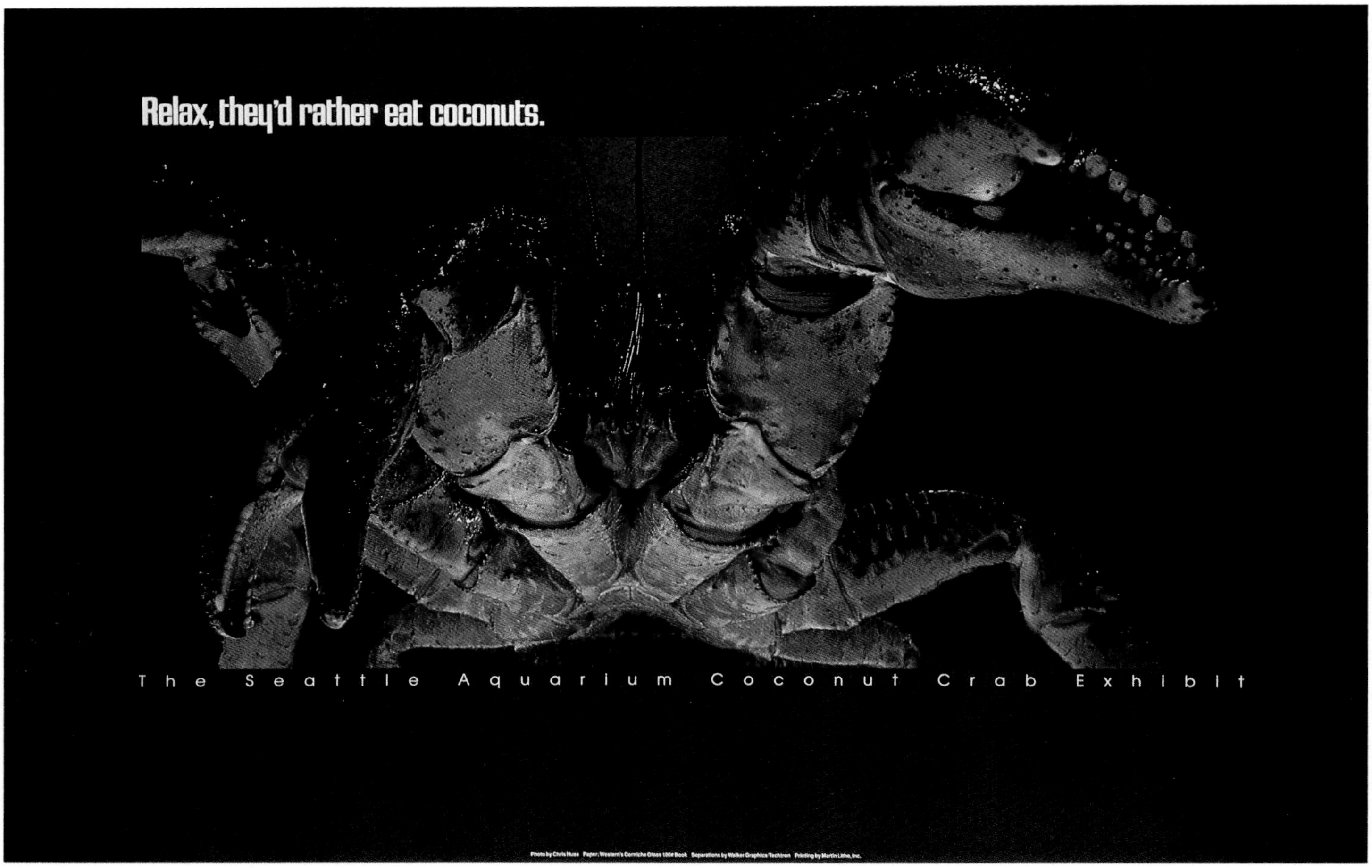

Relax, they'd rather eat coconuts.

The Seattle Aquarium Coconut Crab Exhibit

Photo by Chris Huss Paper: Western's Corniche Gloss 100# Book Separations by Walker Graphics Techtron Printing by Martin Litho, Inc.

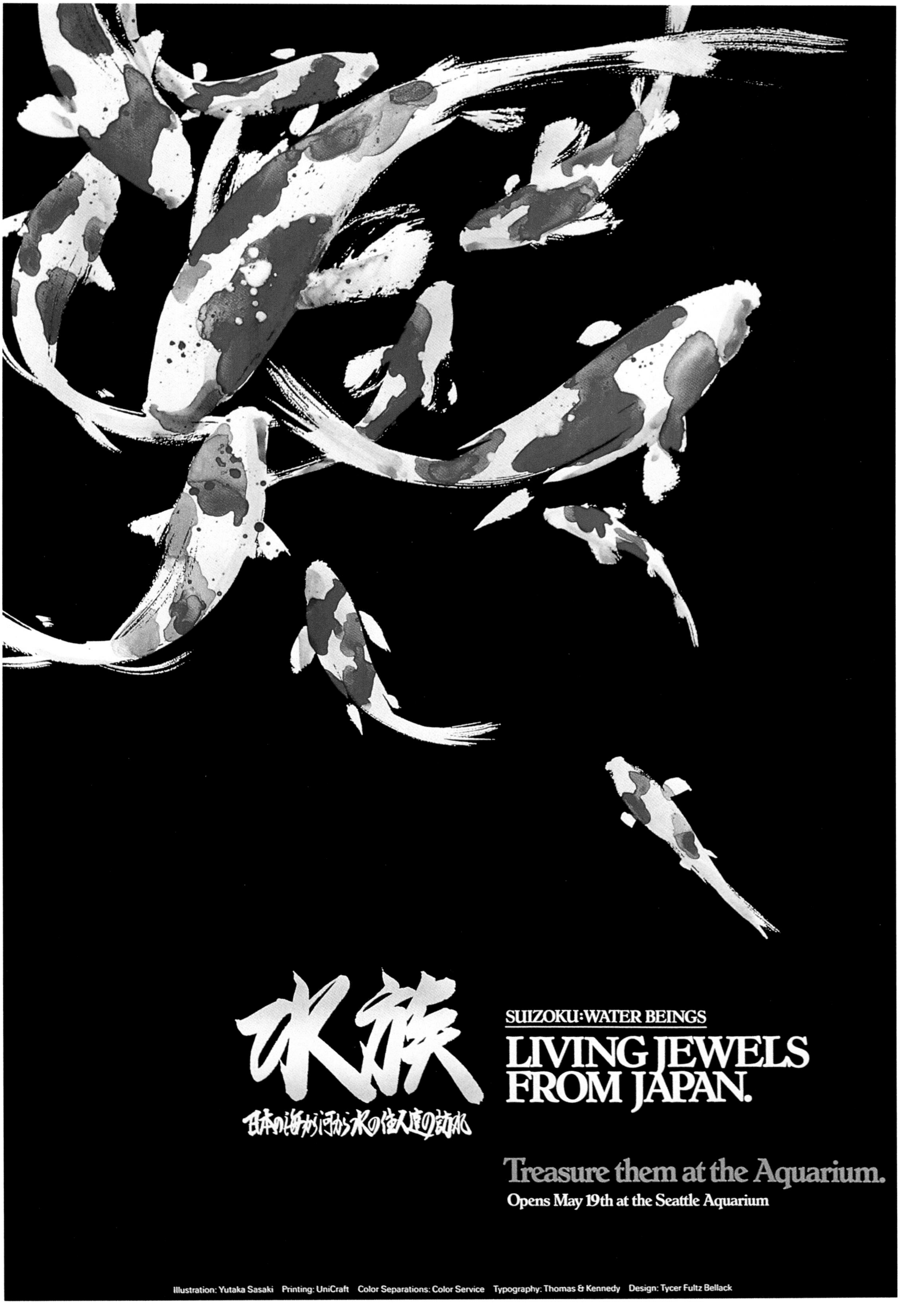

SUIZOKU: WATER BEINGS

LIVING JEWELS FROM JAPAN.

Treasure them at the Aquarium.

Opens May 19th at the Seattle Aquarium

Illustration: Yutaka Sasaki   Printing: UniCraft   Color Separations: Color Service   Typography: Thomas & Kennedy   Design: Tycer Fultz Bellack

Tracy Aviary
Salt Lake City, Utah, USA

Art Director
Ron Stone, Evans Advertising
Designers
Jeff Olsen, Dick Brown, Bryan DeYoung
Design Firm
The Weller Institute for the Cure of Design, Inc.
Illustrator
Don Weller
Copywriters
Jeff Olsen, Dick Brown, Bryan DeYoung

Good-looking chicks.

TRACY AVIARY
SALT LAKE CITY

George Calef/Masterfile

Roger Williams Park Zoo
Providence, Rhode Island, USA

Design Firm
Malcolm Grear Designers

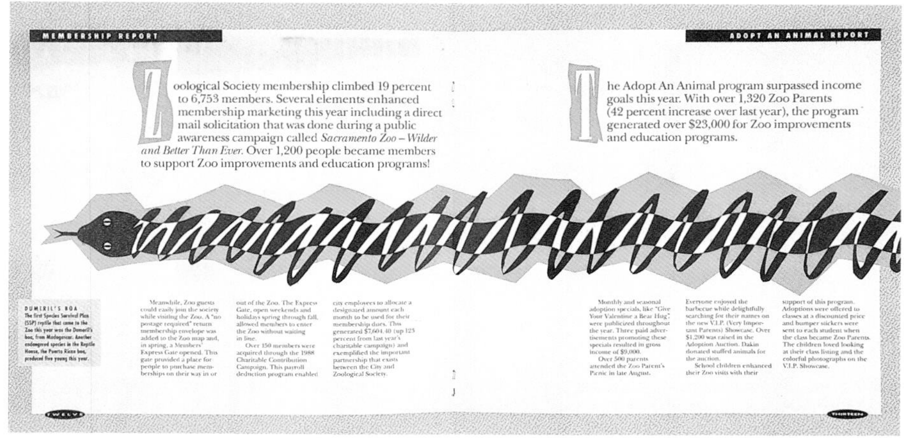

Sacramento Zoo
California, USA

Art Director
Pat Rooney
Designer
Pat Rooney
Design Firm
Tackett – Barbaria Design
Illustrator
Joyce Mansfield Syfstestad

Sacramento Zoo
California, USA

Art Director
Steve Barbaria
Designer
Steve Barbaria
Design Firm
Tackett – Barbaria Design
Illustrator
Steve Barbaria

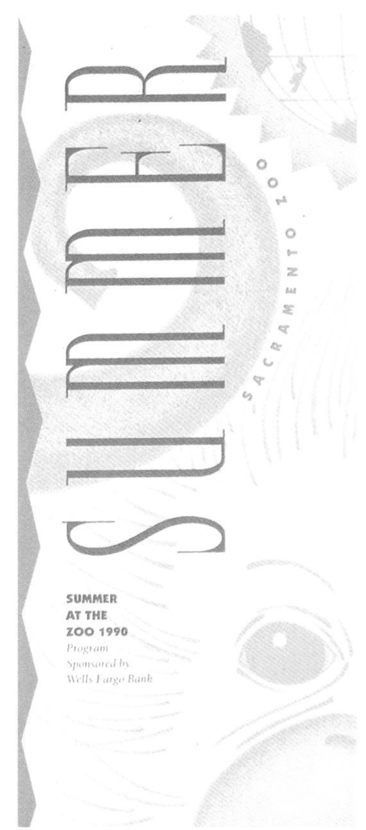

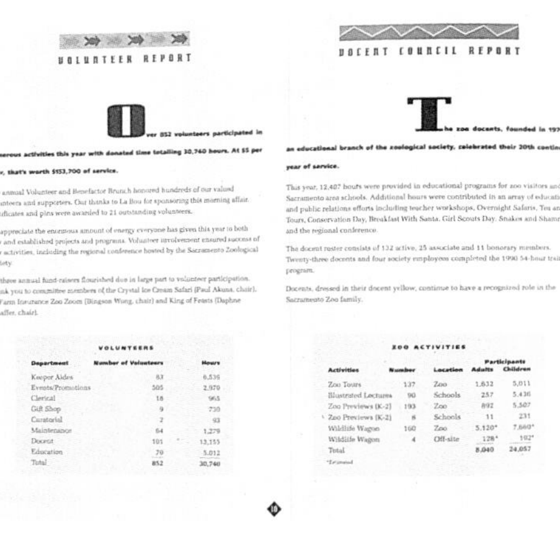

VOLUNTEER REPORT

Over 852 volunteers participated in numerous activities this year with donated time totalling 30,740 hours. At $5 per hour, that's worth $153,700 of service.

The annual Volunteer and Benefactor Brunch honored hundreds of our valued volunteers and supporters. Our thanks to La Bou for sponsoring this morning affair. Certificates and pins were awarded to 21 outstanding volunteers.

We appreciate the enormous amount of energy everyone has given this year to both new and established projects and programs. Volunteer involvement ensured success of new activities, including the regional conference hosted by the Sacramento Zoological Society.

All three annual fund-raisers flourished due in large part to volunteer participation. Thank you to committee members of the Crystal Ice Cream Safari (Paul Akuna, chair), CalFarm Insurance Zoo Zoom (Bingson Wong, chair) and King of Feasts (Daphne Schaffer, chair).

VOLUNTEERS

Department	Number of Volunteers	Hours
Keeper Aides	83	6,536
Events/Promotions	505	2,970
Clerical	18	965
Gift Shop	9	730
Curatorial	2	93
Maintenance	64	1,279
Docent	101	13,155
Education	70	5,012
Total	852	30,740

DOCENT COUNCIL REPORT

The zoo docents, founded in 1970 as an educational branch of the zoological society, celebrated their 20th continuous year of service.

This year, 12,407 hours were provided in educational programs for zoo visitors and in Sacramento area schools. Additional hours were contributed in an array of education and public relations efforts including teacher workshops, Overnight Safaris, Tea and Tours, Conservation Day, Breakfast With Santa, Girl Scouts Day, Snakes and Shamrocks and the regional conference.

The docent roster consists of 132 active, 25 associate and 11 honorary members. Twenty-three docents and four society employees completed the 1990 54-hour training program.

Docents, dressed in their docent yellow, continue to have a recognized role in the Sacramento Zoo family.

ZOO ACTIVITIES

Activities	Number	Location	Participants Adults	Participants Children
Zoo Tours	137	Zoo	1,632	5,011
Illustrated Lectures	90	Schools	257	5,436
Zoo Previews (K-2)	193	Zoo	892	5,507
Zoo Previews (K-2)	8	Schools	11	231
Wildlife Wagon	160	Zoo	5,120*	7,660*
Wildlife Wagon	4	Off-site	128*	192*
Total			8,040	24,057

*Estimated

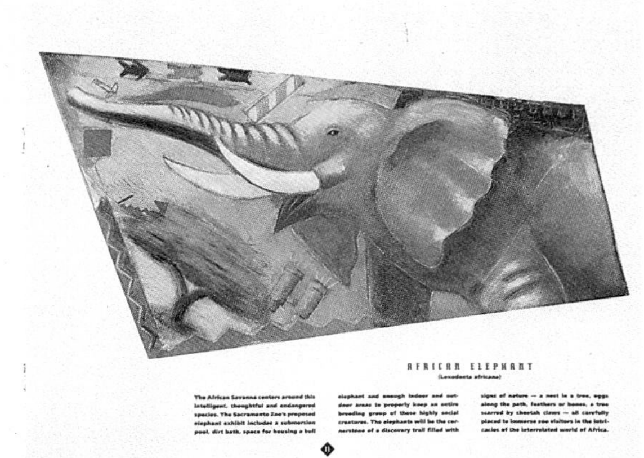

Sacramento Zoo
California, USA

Art Director
Steve Barbaria
Designer
Steve Barbaria
Design Firm
Tackett – Barbaria Design
Illustrator
Joyce Mansfield Syfstestad

New Indianapolis Zoo
Indiana, USA

Art Director
Joseph Smith
Designer
William Hendrickson
Design Firm
Garrison Jasper Rose & Co.
Illustrator
Andrea Eberbach
Copywriter
Kevin Sutton

Brookfield Zoo
Illinois, USA

Designer
Edie Emmenegger

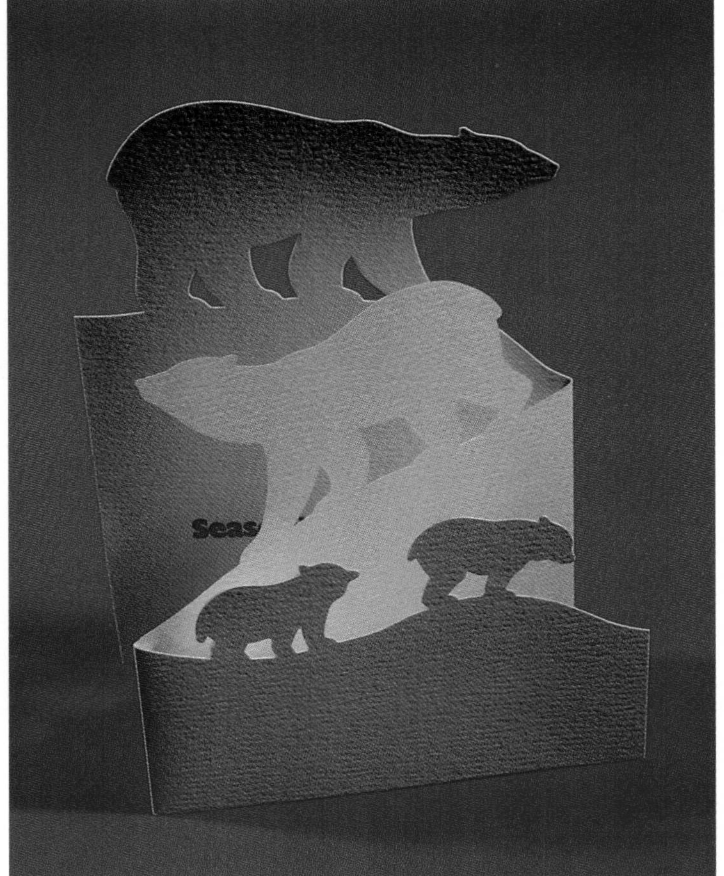

Buffalo Zoological Gardens
New York, USA

Designer
Terrence S. Ortolani
Design Firm
Ortolani & Co.
Copywriter
Lauricella Public Relations

Antwerp Zoo
Belgium

Design Firm
Euro Color Creative
Photographer
Luc Peeters

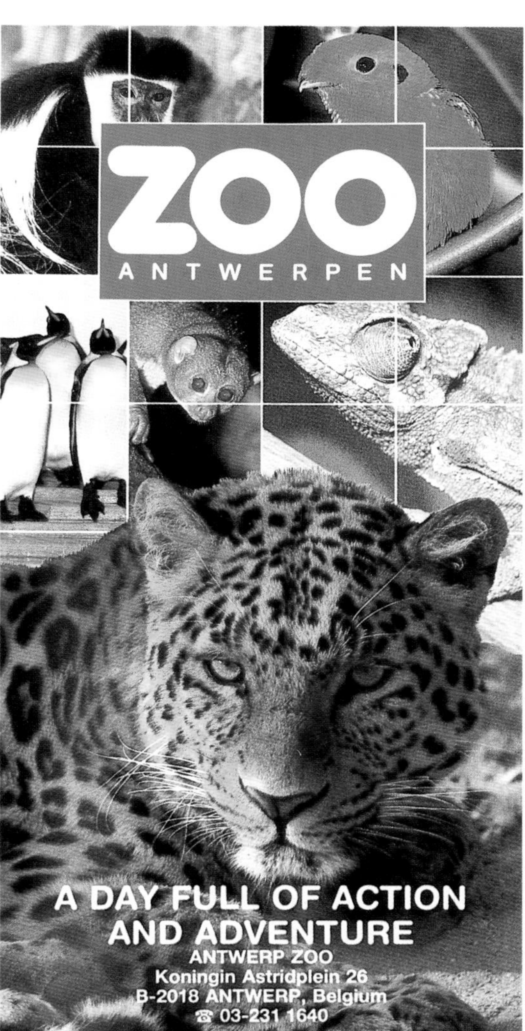

Okinawa Expo Aquarium
Japan

Art Director
Takaaki Matsumoto,
Michael McGinn
Designer
Takaaki Matsumoto
Design Firm
M Plus M Incorporated

Art Director/Designer
Robbii
Design Firm
Metagraphics
Photographer
Gerry Ellis

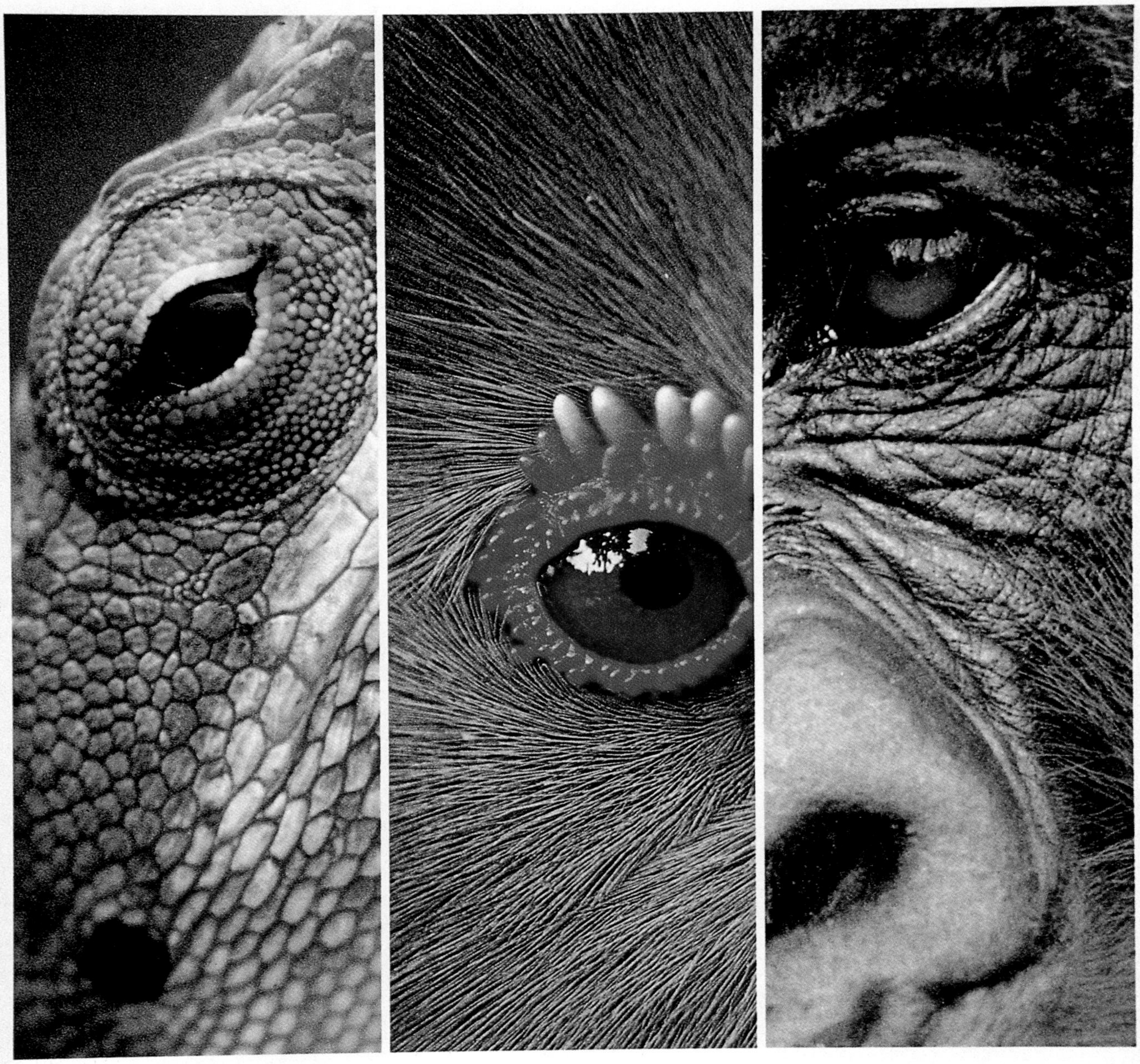

ELLIS WILDLIFE COLLECTION

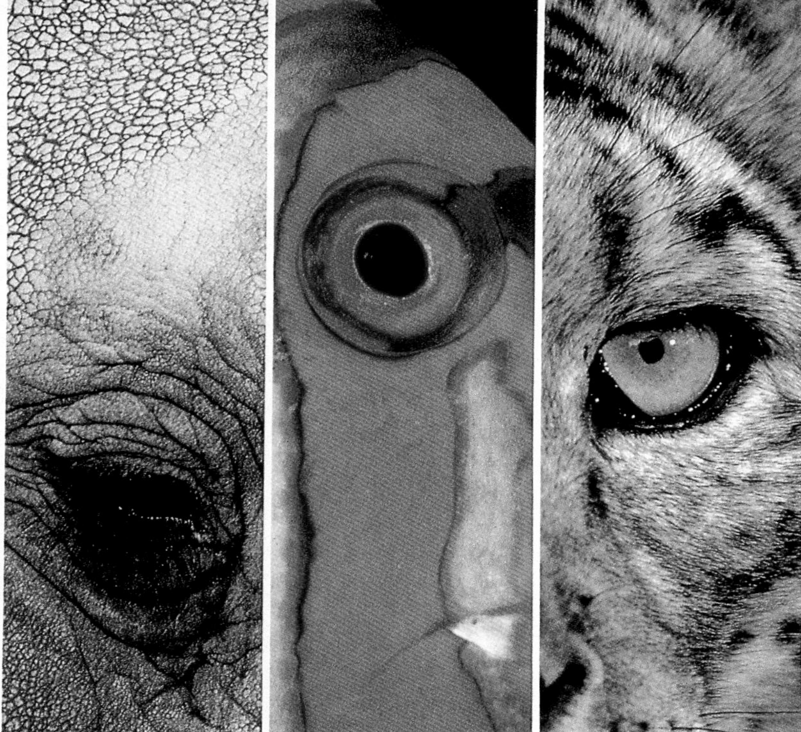

69 Cranberry Street, Brooklyn NY 11201 • 718-935-9600 • 1-800-622-WILD • FAX 718-935-9031

Printed in Japan

ELLIS WILDLIFE COLLECTION

69 Cranberry Street
Brooklyn Heights, New York 11201
718-935-9600 • 1-800-622-WILD

Lincoln Park Zoological Gardens
Chicago, Illinois, USA

Art Directors
Susan Reich, Anne Boyle
Designer
Anne Boyle
Design Firm
Green Planet Creative Group
Photographer/Copywriter
Susan Reich
Illustrator
Joe Taylor

Kings Island Wild Animal Habitat
Cincinnati, Ohio, USA

Art Director
Dan Bittman
Designer
Dan Bittman
Design Firm
Design Team One, Inc.
Copywriters
Bob Reese, Sara Boone

Miami Metrozoo
Florida, USA

Designer
Laura Sartucci
Design Firm
Metrozoo Design Department

Seattle Aquarium
Washington, USA

Art Director
Rayne Beaudoin
Designer
Tycer Fultz Bellack
Design Firm
Yutaka K. Sasaki/Innov
Illustrator
Yutaka K. Sasaki

City of New York Parks & Recreation Natural Resources Group
New York, USA

Art Director/Designer
April Cass
Design Firm
April Cass Design
Illustrators
Robert Villani, Frank Ippolito
Copywriters
Todd Miller, Lisa Mack, Michael Feller

Jamaica Bay, Queens

Only twenty miles from Manhattan, the Jamaica Bay Wildlife Refuge is a world apart, where more than 325 species of birds find food and shelter. The refuge was acquired by New York City in 1938. In 1974, the Jamaica Bay Wildlife Refuge was incorporated into the newly formed Gateway National Recreation Area. Now managed by the National Park Service, the refuge encompasses 9,155 acres of islands, open water, dunes, and salt marsh.

In summer, wading birds, including great blue, little blue, and tricolored herons, and great and snowy egrets, feed in the shallows and mudflats. The osprey has been making a strong comeback at the refuge – a pair has nested, but not bred, for the past two summers – after decades of decline tied to the use of the now-banned pesticide DDT. In winter, thousands of ducks, geese, and other waterfowl congregate in Jamaica Bay's relatively protected waters. Each fall and spring, waves of migrating shore-birds descend on the bay's mudflats to feed.

Most of the refuge is composed of saltmarsh islands that are off limits to the general public. Visitors are welcome at the refuge headquarters, where several trails allow for a panoramic view of the marshes, and a variety of other habitats created and maintained to attract diverse bird species. A free permit, required to visit the grounds, may be obtained at the refuge headquarters. Ask for maps and check the log for recent bird sightings.

Transportation

Subway: A or C train to Broad Channel; then walk west to Cross Bay Boulevard and north about a mile to the refuge entrance.

Bus: The Q53 runs north-south along Cross Bay Boulevard between Horace Harding Boulevard and the Rockaways. Take bus to refuge entrance.

Car: Belt Parkway to Cross Bay Boulevard south. Head south, cross bridge, and look for parking lot entrance 1 1/4 miles ahead on the right.

Perhaps the most widespread of breeding herons in our area's salt marshes, the green-backed heron nests in trees and shrubs near water.

10

Inwood Hill Park, Manhattan

Inwood Hill Park, a 196-acre oasis at the northern tip of Manhattan, features the last remnant of the tidal marshes that once surrounded Manhattan Island. The marsh receives a mixture of fresh water flowing from the upper Hudson River and salt water from the ocean's tides. The mix of salt and fresh waters, called brackish water, has created an environment unique in the city. While the low marshes of Jamaica Bay and Long Island Sound are pure stands of *Spartina alterniflora*, Inwood Hill Park's low marsh also contains big saltwater cordgrass *(Spartina cynosuroides)* and two species of bullrush.

Between the low marsh and the park path are a number of marsh plants rare elsewhere in the city, including water hemp, salt marsh bullrush, and seabeach dock. Marsh elder, swamp rose mallow, and groundsel bush also grow here.

A broad, expansive mudflat runs from the marsh to the channel of the Harlem River Ship Canal. Great blue herons frequent the flat in winter. Great and snowy egrets are common visitors from spring through fall. You can often hear the chattering of a belted kingfisher as it flies overhead, hovers, and then drops into the water, emerging with a wriggling fish in its oversized bill.

Hudson River
Henry Hudson Bridge
0 1/4 mile
N

Transportation

Subway: IND A train to 207th Street or Dyckman Street; IRT #1 train to 207th Street or 215th Street.

Bus: M-100 to Dyckman Street or 207th Street.

Car: Henry Hudson Parkway to Dyckman Street exit; east on Dyckman to Broadway; north on Broadway to 207th Street; west to Seaman Avenue.

11

Sedgwick County Zoo
Wichita, Kansas, USA

Art Director
Sonia Greteman
Designers
Sonia Greteman, Mitzie Walden, Denise Brueggeman
Design Firm
Gardner Greteman Milkulecky
Illustrators
Sonia Greteman, Mitzie Walden

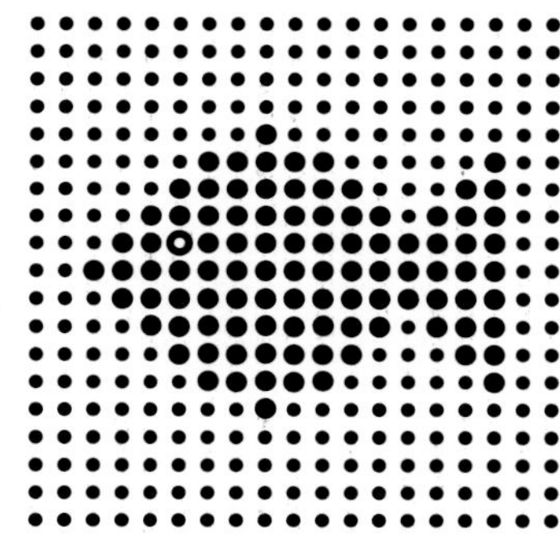

New York Aquarium

Designer
Elie Aliman

Woodland Park Zoological Gardens

Designer
Keith Yoshida

Sacramento Zoo

Designer
Steve Barbaria

Tennessee Aquarium

Designer
Tom Geismar

Edmonton Valley Zoo

Designer
Wei Yew

Aquarium of Metropolitan Toronto

Designer
Tom Geismar

Como Zoo

Designer
Susan Hanson

Okinawa Expo Aquarium

Designer
Takaaki Matsumoto

San Diego Zoo
California, USA

Art Director
Brenda Bodney
Designers
Brenda Bodney, Maurya Siedler
Design Firm
Bodney + Siedler Design
Photographer
Chris Wimpey

Fantastic Felines
It's the cat's meow. Six fantastical kitties adorn this easy-care Laurel Burch sweatshirt. Made in USA. 50/50, cotton/acrylic. M, L, XL **#P11385 $38** (members $34.20)

Call Toll-Free
1-800-628-3179
Within area code (619) 586-1657

A Horse of a Different Color
Oh, the detail and beauty. Nothing compares to hand carving and painting. And it shows in this running horse, inspired by the art traditions of Southeast Asia. It even has two hidden compartments. **#D33477 $72** (members $64.80)

Rainforest Crunch
Eat it up, it's Rainforest Crunch. The all-natural, all-delicious Cashew and Brazil nut buttercrunch that puts your money where your mouth is: a portion of the profits go to preserve the world's rainforests. Made in USA. **#S02155 $18** (members $16.20)

African Grassland Sweatshirt & T-shirt
It's a San Diego Zoo exclusive. And a salute to the wonderful, wild animals of the grasslands. Made in USA. Sweatshirt 50/50, cotton/polyester. T-shirt 100% cotton. Adult sweatshirt S, M, L, XL **#C04122 $18.95** (members $17.06) Child XS, S, M, L **#C04126 $14.95** (members $13.46) Adult T-shirt S, M, L, XL **#C03966 $10.95** (members $9.86) Child S, M, L **#C03971 $7.95** (members $7.16)

Wood Safari Necklace & Earrings
All the color and beauty of a safari, captured in wood and beads. The necklace was designed and created especially for your San Diego Zoo. With wood animals from Africa. And beads from the Philippines. Necklace & earrings set **#J10848 $55** (members $49.50) Necklace only **#J10835 $49** (members $44.10) Earrings only **#J10849 $6** (members $5.40)

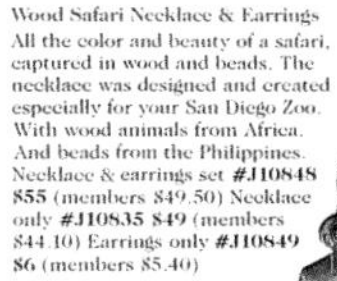

Take Home a Classique
This one's strictly for the birds. The Plush Toucan Classique, another huggable, lovable, collectible friend from Dakin. **#T11577 $58** (members $52.20)

SATISFACTION GUARANTEED
Ordering by phone or mail is so easy. And it's all guaranteed. If for any reason you're unhappy with anything you order, we'll exchange it or refund your money. It's that simple.

San Francisco Zoological Society
California, USA

Art Directors
James Cross, Ken Cook
Designer
Ken Cook
Design Firm
Cross Associates
Illustrator/Photographer
Steve Underwood and various

SAN FRANCISCO ZOOLOGICAL SOCIETY
FOR MEMBERS OF THE SAN FRANCISCO ZOOLOGICAL SOCIETY, AN ORGANIZATION DEDICATED TO INSTILLING A LIFELONG COMMITMENT TO WILDLIFE CONSERVATION.
ZOO Views
SAN FRANCISCO
VOLUME 1 ISSUE 1 SEPT / OCT 1988

Sunshine's Little Sunshine

San Francisco's new baby gorilla, Binti Jua, was too tiny to fly as cargo, so she rode up front in the cockpit. The pilots were a little leery at first, but the cuddly seven-pound infant, wrapped up in her baby blanket, won them with her charm.

Dusty Lombardi, children's zoo and nursery supervisor at Columbus Zoo in Ohio, was entrusted with bringing the precious bundle to San Francisco. "She was the perfect traveler," Lombardi says. "She had two in-flight feedings and barely made a sound. By the time we reached the Rocky Mountains, the pilots were showing her the sights."

(continued on page 2)

The Zoo's siamangs have something special to hoot about. Their newest baby, born October 21, set two world records for the Zoo: the most siamang births at any zoo—17—and the most births for any pair—12. Since 1967, the siamang parents have had babies every two years.

The San Francisco Zoo has two family groups of siamangs—one near the Plaza Cafe and the other near Koala Crossing—and has had enormous success with breeding these lesser apes. In 1984, San Francisco had the first recorded birth of siamang twins.

"It's very important to maintain the family group," said Senior Keeper Carol Martinez. "The siamangs learn normal siamang behavior and the role of the parents in raising offspring."

Siamangs live in the canopy of the tropical rain forests of Sumatra and the Malay Peninsula. They travel by brachiating (swinging hand over hand). As an adaptation to life in the trees, siamangs' arms are longer than their legs, spanning up to five feet in a large adult.

Siamangs can swing so rapidly, they almost appear to fly. Efficient and graceful in the trees, they are awkward on the ground, sometimes walking with their hands held high overhead for balance.

Until the newest siamang gets a bit older and the mother less protective, the infant is difficult to see. At about six months, the baby will begin venturing away from the mother. Until then, look for the siamang that keeps her legs pulled up when she swings through the exhibit. Then, watch carefully and you'll see the baby clinging to her fur and peeking out over the mother's knees.

By Kathleen Harper

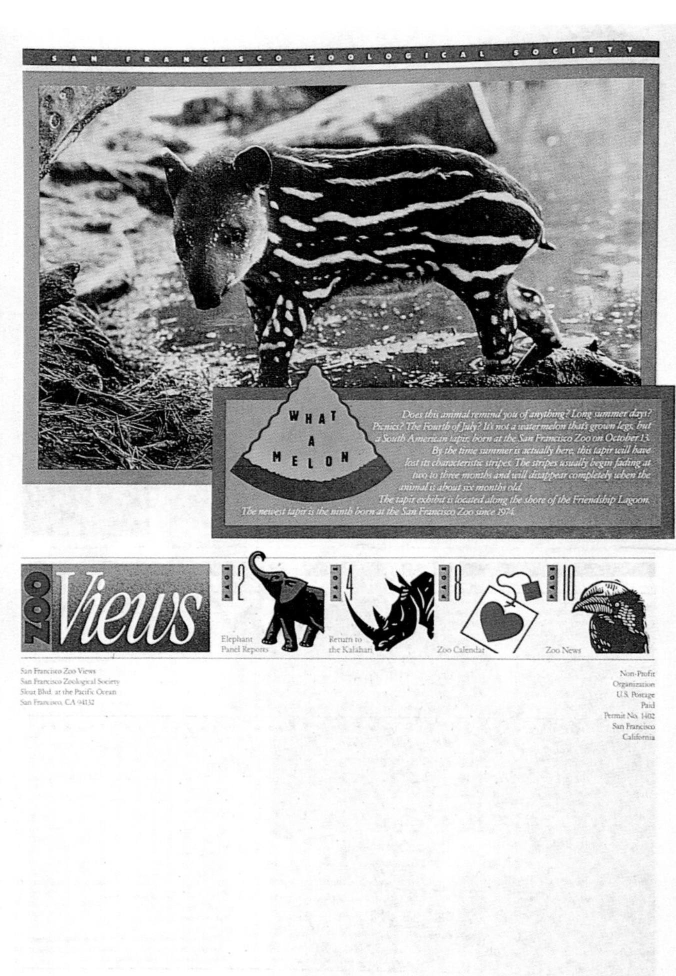

WHAT A MELON

Does this animal remind you of anything? Long summer days? Picnics? The Fourth of July? It's not a watermelon that's grown legs, but a South American tapir, born at the San Francisco Zoo on October 13.

By the time summer is actually here, this tapir will have lost its characteristic stripes. The stripes usually begin fading at two to three months and will disappear completely when the animal is about six months old.

The tapir exhibit is located along the shore of the Friendship Lagoon. The newest tapir is the ninth born at the San Francisco Zoo since 1974.

San Francisco Zoo Views
San Francisco Zoological Society
Sloat Blvd. at the Pacific Ocean
San Francisco, CA 94132

Non-Profit
Organization
U.S. Postage
Paid
Permit No. 1402
San Francisco
California

SAN FRANCISCO ZOOLOGICAL SOCIETY

ZOO
Views
SAN FRANCISCO
FOR MEMBERS OF THE SAN FRANCISCO ZOOLOGICAL SOCIETY, AN ORGANIZATION DEDICATED TO INSTILLING A LIFELONG COMMITMENT TO WILDLIFE CONSERVATION.

VOLUME 1 ISSUE 2 NOV/DEC 1988

Bald Eagle Breeding Program Welcomes New Chicks

The ponderosa pine reaches 140 feet into the Northern California sky, surrounded by a panorama of lakes, rivers and forests, home territory for a pair of bald eagles.

The uppermost boughs cradle their nest—a six-foot structure, strong enough to support a grown man. This nest is one of two in the state chosen to provide chicks for the Zoo's bald eagle breeding project.

California's bald eagle captive breeding program was initiated at the San Francisco Zoo in 1986. Each May, federal, state and San Francisco Zoo biologists survey all bald eagle nests in the state. Depending on the number of chicks hatched, California Department of Fish and Game and United States Fish and Wildlife Service biologists determine if it is appropriate to move chicks from wild nests into the breeding program. In 1988 two chicks, from Siskiyou County and Butte County, joined the Zoo's project.

In early June, a ten-person team, including Zoological Society field biologist George Carpenter, raptor veterinarian Russell Tucker, and eagle specialists Robert Lehman and Philip Detrich, traveled to Northern California for the delicate task of bringing a bald eagle chick to the Zoo.

The team started its quest early in the morning, hiking with all its gear to the remote eagle territory. Carpenter set up a base from which he could observe the operation, while Lehman and Detrich, skilled in mountaineering techniques and veterans of more than one hundred eagle climbs, set up for the climb. Lehman began the two-hour ascent of the imposing ponderosa

BALD EAGLES GROW QUICKLY. THIS TEN-WEEK-OLD CHICK IS ALREADY ADULT-SIZED, BUT IT WILL BE AT LEAST FOUR YEARS BEFORE IT GETS ITS DISTINCTIVE WHITE HEAD.

(continued on page 2)

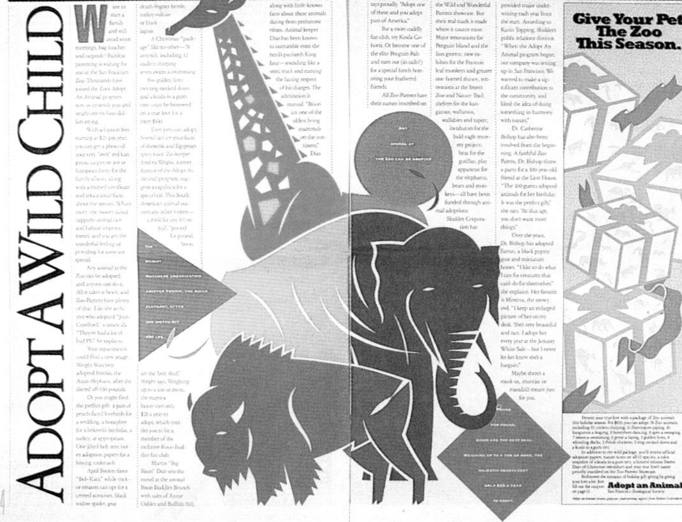

The Elephant Review

Margaret Burks

Elephant Panel Report

Bringing Up Binti

Return to the Kalahari

By Nancy Jacobs

Mark & Delia Owens

Mark and Delia Owens take the next step toward protecting Africa's—and the world's—heritage. With a passion born of dedication and visionary optimism, the Owenses have lived and worked together in one of the world's harshest environments for most of their 15 years of marriage. Authors of the international bestseller *Cry of the Kalahari*, Mark and Delia have made African wildlife the focus of their life's work. More than just researchers, they are crusaders—working to preserve and restore the wild places threatened by poachers and foreign development.

Mark and Delia Owens first went to Africa in 1974, determined to set up a wildlife research project in a "pristine wilderness" while such a thing still existed. Concerned by reports of Africa's disappearing wildlife, the Owenses hoped to gather facts that would help in the development of conservation programs where none currently existed. For seven years they studied the desert lions and brown hyenas of the Central Kalahari Desert of Botswana. Known as the "Great Thirst," their study area was a tract of land larger than Ireland but peopled only by themselves.

Based in a valley called "Deception," the Owenses learned new and exciting details about the inhabitants of a drought ecology, in some cases overturning conventional theory. They were able to prove, for example, that brown hyenas are far from solitary animals. In fact, these elusive scavengers live in social clans and raise their young communally—70 percent of the cubs reaching maturity in one group were "adopted" orphans. Their lion studies exploded other myths. Male lions—previously thought to depend on their female "harem" for food—actually hunt for themselves 80 percent of the time. And the animal with the largest range in the Kalahari proved to be the leopard.

In 1985, when Mark and Delia Owens spoke in San Francisco about their Kalahari experiences they necessarily minimized the extent of the disasters befalling African wildlife; at that time they were still trying to return to Botswana after being expelled by government officials for publicly urging changes in wildlife policies. Last October the San Francisco Zoological Society again sponsored the Owenses for a Wildlife Conservation Series lecture about their ongoing scientific and conservation efforts in Africa. This time, the picture they painted was less rosy.

"Sugar-coating the story of African wildlife is dishonest ...all is *not* well in Eden. The question we *should* be asking is 'What has gone wrong?'" says Mark. The Owenses believe that much of what has gone wrong in Africa is due to well-meaning but misguided efforts by Western governments to promote economic growth in developing nations. By introducing foreign technologies and animal species—cattle-ranching, for example—into barely-understood ecologies, the natural balance has been disastrously upset. In Botswana, the Owenses discovered that cattle-fencing was preventing migrating wildebeest from reaching water during times of drought, causing entire herds—60,000 animals in 1983 alone—to die of thirst.

But the Owenses persevered, and their efforts led to considerable international pressure. The result is some good news for wildlife in Botswana. The Central Kalahari Game Reserve—at one time threatened with cattle development—has been saved. The fences are slowly coming down, and waterholes are being drilled to help the besieged wildebeest survive future droughts. Cattle development throughout Botswana is being curbed, and Mark and Delia Owens have been allowed to return to their beloved Kalahari to check up on the animals they had come to love so well.

After completing their doctoral degrees at the University of California at Davis in 1984, Mark and Delia set out to return to Africa for further study of large predators. This time their dream was larger. Scanning the map of Africa, they looked for a place where they could work *with* local officials to develop wildlife as an economic resource for the native peoples displaced by reserves and barred from their traditional hunting grounds.

At first glance, Zambia seemed the best choice, boasting 19 large national parks. In reality, however, only four of these parks proved to have any wildlife remaining. "The animals in the other parks had been poached out of existence," explains Mark. Indeed,

> SUGAR-COATING THE STORY OF AFRICAN WILDLIFE IS DISHONEST. ALL IS *NOT* WELL IN EDEN.

North Luangwa National Park had literally been written off by Zambian officials as too remote to defend from poachers—more than 75,000 elephants had already been killed for ivory. But to Mark and Delia, the Luangwa Valley proved to be ideal.

Compared to the Kalahari, the Luangwa Valley is positively lush, with a large river system providing a permanent oasis for all manner of wildlife. The Owenses will be studying seasonal movement patterns of predators and their prey along the river floodplains. "In Botswana we studied how animals survived drought and extremely scarce food supplies," explains Delia. "In Luangwa we have the opposite situation; we'll be looking at how animals manage to co-exist in an extremely competitive environment, where the lions, leopards, and other large predators are living practically on top of one another."

With permission from the Zambian government, Mark and Delia are working to set up a research center while beginning to rehabilitate the North Luangwa Park. One of their primary goals is to develop the park for tourism, with all revenues going directly to the local villagers. Already several village headmen are vying for the chance to build airstrips, and overall enthusiasm for the Owens Foundation and their projects is running high.

"One of the most exciting aspects of this project is the opportunity to provide the locals with sources of income other than poaching," Mark elaborates. "The elephants are already gone from the Luangwa Valley, but there's still a viable population of black rhinoceros." Intensively poached for their horns, black rhinos are severely endangered throughout Africa. "The only hope for these animals is to make them valuable to the people who live around them."

Funded primarily by the Frankfurt Zoological Society, Mark and Delia believe strongly that similar organizations—as well as individuals—can help tip the balance in favor of wildlife in Africa. "We'd like to start an 'Adopt A Game Warden Camp' program," says Delia. "There's only one camp for the entire North Luangwa Park, and they're pitifully under-equipped. They have no vehicles, and the entire ammunition supply for the year is a single bullet per warden. Yet they still go out after poachers."

Despite their love for the wildlife, Mark and Delia aren't starry-eyed romantics; they understand that, at least for the present, a reasonable approach to conservation plans include controlled hunting, for subsistence and to bring tourist dollars. "But we keep stressing the value of *live* animals," says Delia. "You can only shoot or eat an animal once... but you can show it to tourists over and over again."

Meanwhile, they are building their own camp and airstrip and beginning their predator research. Their scientific goals include understanding the needs of Zambian wildlife throughout different seasons and conditions so game reserve boundaries can be redrawn along less arbitrary lines. But the Owenses also know that pure scientific knowledge isn't enough. "Some researchers just move on when their study animals are killed by poachers," says Mark. "We can't do that; we want these animals to be here in the future. They are part of the world's heritage."

Poached to the brink of extinction, black rhinos are critically endangered. The population has been so decimated that black rhinos in some parts of Africa must be watched over by armed guards. Rhinoceros horn—twice as valuable, ounce for ounce, as gold—is sought after for folk medicines and dagger handles.

Winter White Sale

White Tiger $500 Regularly $1,000
Snow Goose $20 Regularly $25
Snowy Owl $100 Regularly $250
Polar Bear $500 Regularly $1,000
Mute Swan $25 Regularly $30
Snow Leopard $500 Regularly $1,000
American White Pelican $30 Regularly $50

Take advantage of Adopt An Animal's blizzard of bargains! Adopt one or more of the Zoo's white furred or feathered animals and save 50%. If you ever wanted to parent a polar bear, shelter a snow leopard or house a snowy owl, now's the time to do it.

Zoo parents receive an adoption folio with official adoption papers, nature notes and a wallet-sized color snapshot.

As with all white sales, the money goes toward home decor: Adopt An Animal program proceeds are used for habitat improvements at the Zoo.

For more information, call 415/661-2023.
Hurry! Sale ends February 28.

Adopt An Animal
San Francisco Zoological Society

The Adopt An Animal Program receives generous underwriting support from Shaklee Corporation.

Zoo Parent Market

Run Wild in Zoo Shoes

Make tracks in Zoo Shoes. Animal faces cover the velcro fastenings, and matching animal tracks cross the bottom. Zoo Shoes come in koala olive, tiger orange and frog green. Also available are blue raccoons, black and white penguins and gray monkeys. Children's sizes only, 1 to 12. $25.

Night Lights

Light a dark hall or soothe a small child to sleep with Lizard Lights. Ten red, gray and black four-inch lizards crawl along an 18-inch string and shine a blinking or solid light. $19.75.

Rainy Day Fun

What to do when the kids can't go outdoors and "I'm bored" is the chronic complaint? Fill their time with fun from the Zoo Shop.

Winter Fun **is a book filled with stories to read, comics to giggle over, puzzles to enjoy, jokes to tell, games to play, and science projects to astound friends. From the editors of Owl Magazine. $7.95.**

Piece together Prince Charles, the Zoo's rare white tiger, and his sister Whiskers, in this 1,000-piece jigsaw puzzle, measuring 23 inches by 29 inches. $8.50. The Zoo Shop has puzzles of penguins, primates, pandas, parrots and much more. $7.50 to $23.

Now that the children are happily occupied, bundle up in front of the fire to read *Cry of the Kalahari*, the national bestseller by Mark and Delia Owens. The book describes Mark and Delia's adventures and challenges during their seven years in the Kalahari Desert of Africa. $7.95.

SAN FRANCISCO ZOOLOGICAL SOCIETY

CARING FOR ELEPHANTS

For those of you who may not be aware, on October 1, a veterinary technician was injured while treating Tinkerbelle, the Zoo's 22-year-old Asian elephant. The technician's pelvis was fractured. The elephant reacted instinctively and suddenly when the technician reached into the elephant's mouth and evidently touched a sensitive area. The elephant did not "rampage."

Charges of animal abuse were made by one keeper, who stated the elephants were "routinely beaten." This is not true. I regret the negative publicity generated by one keeper, which does all of us, and the Zoo itself, a grave injustice.

The present policy of the San Francisco Zoo, and essentially all others, is to work Asian elephants in a daily routine in order to best (and most safely) handle, move and medically treat them. It is considered sound practice and we have had no injuries in the past five years. The present elephant team is caring, sensitive and highly trained.

I know that many of you have met the elephant keepers, and I would encourage those of you who have not to come observe the elephant handlers working with their animals. Your first-hand experience will speak for itself.

In fact, the primary elephant keepers attend the annual Elephant Management Workshop with their colleagues from all over the world to exchange information, techniques and philosophy on all aspects of elephant exhibition, handling, breeding and conservation. No other species has as much professional attention devoted to it, and elephant handlers are notoriously devoted to their animals. This is true in San Francisco as well.

Given the emotional climate and the nature of the accusations, I have asked three elephant specialists to review our protocol and report to the Recreation and Park Commission within 30 days. This review does not indicate lack of confidence in the Zoo's staff, but was done to ensure objective assessment.

Members of the panel are Dale Tuttle, director of the Jacksonville Zoo and chairman of the American Association of Zoological Parks and Aquariums' (AAZPA) Species Survival Plan for Asian elephants; Dr. William Boever, head veterinarian at the St. Louis Zoo and chairman of AAZPA's Ethics Committee; and Michael Keele, assistant curator at the Washington Park Zoo in Portland, which is internationally recognized for its elephant program.

The AAZPA is currently re-examining elephant protocols nationally to review policy appropriate for conservation and exhibit needs. We believe our current practices to be sound, with high regard for safety and the dignity and welfare of the animals.

You should also know that a new elephant exhibit is planned in Phase I of Zoo 2000, which will get the elephants off concrete and into a naturalistic exhibit worthy of them and of their keepers. It will be you, the members of the Zoological Society, who can make this happen.

SAUL L. KITCHENER
ZOO DIRECTOR

(Continued from page 1)

while Detrich coordinated the climb from below.

Once up, fully supported by the huge pine nest, Lehman placed one of the two five-week-old, six-pound nestlings into a heavy, padded canvas bag. At that age, the eaglets are mature enough to be moved, yet young enough not to be frightened by the activity.

As quickly and carefully as possible, the chick was lowered to the biologists waiting below. Slightly confused, but generally calm, the bird was placed in the shade where it rested comfortably while it was observed by Tackett.

After Lehman descended, the bird was loaded into a padded front pack (like the ones used to carry babies) for the hike down the hill. "We are very careful that the chick is not jostled or overheated," said Carpenter. Excess heat is more of a problem than cold, since bald eagles are adapted to cold climates.

Meanwhile, the adult eagles circled the tree, perched and watched. Carpenter, at an observation point about a mile from the nest, watched to see that the parents returned to care for the remaining youngster. "Eaglets can't smell and apparently can't count," he noted. "By the end of the day they always come back. They take care of the nestling in the tree, and we take care of the other one."

Back at the road, the bird was put into a jumbo animal carrier with pine needles on the floor to make it feel at home. The young bird spent its first night away from the nest in its own air-conditioned hotel room, before being flown to San Francisco the next day.

At the San Francisco Zoo, the young eagles are raised in off-exhibit conservation aviaries. To avoid disturbances and imprinting on humans, they have visual and vocal access to adult bald eagles, but no direct human contact. The eaglets are monitored by closed circuit television and fed through ports in the side of the aviary. They consume more than one pound of filleted quail, rats and chicken a day.

When they mature in about five years, the birds will become breeding stock for California's captive breeding program. "A bald eagle in captivity has a much greater chance of reproducing than one in the wild," explained Carpenter. "We can protect them from starvation, disease and injury." Wild birds have a one-in-ten chance of reproducing; captive birds have a nine-in-ten chance.

Chicks from the Zoo's breeding project are expected in 1991. As part of the statewide recovery program, they will be released into areas of California where the bald eagle formerly nested.

The Zoo's project will consist of six pairs of bald eagles, housed in the Avian Conservation Center, currently planned as part of Zoo 2000. The State of California awarded the Zoological Society a $175,000 grant from the Environmental License Plate Fund to design the facility.

"Bald eagles once nested throughout the state, but now are concentrated in the northernmost counties of California—about one-third of their former range," said Carpenter. The bald eagle population, which declined sharply during the 1950s and 1960s, is now increasing slowly. The number of known breeding pairs has increased from fewer than 30 in the 1960s to approximately 70 in 1988. The goal of the recovery program is to double the number of breeding pairs and increase the number of young that survive.

The two-year-old bald eagle breeding project is managed by the Zoological Society's Avian Conservation Program, active in the field of raptor conservation for ten years. More than 100 birds of prey—including Harris' hawks, red-shouldered and red-tailed hawks, barn owls and great horned owls—have been raised at the Zoo and released into their natural habitats.

Financial support for the project comes from the Fireman's Fund Insurance Company Foundation, Zoological Society members and the Adopt An Animal fund. —*Ellen Newman*

BALD EAGLE
California Range Depletion

From The Bay Bridge To Santa Catalina

New Home for San Francisco's First Peregrine Falcon Chick

THE SAN FRANCISCO BAY BRIDGE IS AN UNLIKELY WILDLIFE HABITAT. YET THIS SPRING A PAIR OF PEREGRINE FALCONS FOUND THE STEEL GIRDERS A GOOD SUBSTITUTE FOR THEIR USUAL ROCKY AERIES. • THEIR NEST WAS FIRST SIGHTED EARLY IN THE BREEDING SEASON. ZOO VOLUNTEER DAVID GREGOIRE KEPT THE NEST SITE UNDER OBSERVATION, LOOKING FOR SIGNS OF YOUNG. AFTER A COUPLE OF MONTHS, ACTIVITY AROUND THE NEST SLOWED DOWN, AND THE OBSERVERS ASSUMED THAT THE ADULTS HAD ABANDONED THE NEST. • IMAGINE, THEN, JOHN AIKIN'S SURPRISE WHEN HE GOT A CALL FROM A FIREMAN AT THE SAN FRANCISCO FIREBOAT DOCK, REPORTING THAT A PEREGRINE FALCON CHICK HAD FALLEN OFF THE BAY BRIDGE. AIKIN, DIRECTOR OF THE AVIAN CONSERVATION PROGRAM, CHUCKLED AND SAID, "IT MUST BE A KESTREL," BUT WENT TO THE DOCK TO INVESTIGATE. • "THE FIREMAN BROUGHT ME INTO A LITTLE ROOM WHERE THEY HAD CORNERED THE BIRD, AND MY JAW DROPPED." AIKIN WAS LOOKING AT THE FIRST PEREGRINE FALCON EVER HATCHED IN URBAN SAN FRANCISCO. APPARENTLY THE ADULTS HAD ABANDONED THEIR FIRST NEST AND HAD MADE A SECOND ATTEMPT AT A NEW SITE. • AFTER BRINGING THE BIRD BACK TO THE ZOO AND MAKING IT AS COMFORTABLE AS POSSIBLE, AIKIN CALLED THE PEREGRINE FUND AT UC SANTA CRUZ, AND APPROPRIATE FEDERAL AND STATE AGENCIES TO FIND THE BEST PLACE FOR THE CHICK. • "WE COULDN'T PUT THE BIRD BACK IN THE NEST BECAUSE IT WOULD AGAIN BE IN JEOPARDY OF FALLING INTO THE BAY," SAID AIKIN. • IT WAS DETERMINED THAT THE BEST SPOT FOR THE YOUNG RAPTOR WAS ON SANTA CATALINA ISLAND, A HISTORIC PEREGRINE HABITAT. A GROUP OF YOUNG BIRDS, ABOUT THE SAME AGE AS THE CHICK, WERE SCHEDULED TO BE RELEASED IN THE AREA IN THE NEXT FEW DAYS. • THREE DAYS AND AN AIRPLANE AND BOAT RIDE LATER, THE CHICK WAS RELEASED ALONG WITH THE OTHER YOUNG FALCONS ON A STEEP CLIFF ABOVE THE ROARING PACIFIC. RAPTOR BIOLOGISTS PROVIDED FOOD FOR THE BIRDS WHILE THEY LEARNED TO HUNT. THE SAN FRANCISCO FALCON PREFERRED TO ROOST ALONE, BUT WAS OBSERVED FEEDING AND FLYING WITH THE OTHERS. • PEREGRINE FALCONS ONCE NESTED THROUGHOUT THE WORLD, EXCEPT ANTARCTICA, BUT BY 1973 DDT POISONING AND PERSECUTION LEFT THE SPECIES SEVERELY ENDANGERED. THERE WERE ONLY TWO PEREGRINE NESTS IN CALIFORNIA IN THE 1970S. ACTIVE CONSERVATION AND CAPTIVE BREEDING PROGRAMS HAVE IMPROVED THE SITUATION. "WITH FEWER THAN 100 PEREGRINE NESTS IN THE STATE, THIS CHICK'S SURVIVAL AND SUCCESSFUL RELEASE ARE IMPORTANT TO THE RECOVERY OF THE SPECIES," SAID AIKIN. • RELOCATION COSTS FOR THE PEREGRINE CHICK WERE UNDERWRITTEN BY BECHTEL ENVIRONMENTAL, AND PILOT AND ZOO DOCENT JOHN LONDEL FLEW THE BIRD TO SOUTHERN CALIFORNIA.

DOCENTS CELEBRATE Twenty YEARS

ASK ME 20

Twenty years ago the Beatles were together, miniskirts were at their height, ecology became a household word—and the San Francisco Zoological Society's Docent Council was born.

"In 1968, about a half dozen housewives who were deeply concerned about the increasing number of endangered species saw the San Francisco Zoo as an educational forum for wildlife conservation," recalls Education Director Brandy Pound, "and they felt the community had an obligation to supply the manpower for this effort."

Supported by the Zoo, this small volunteer group set about trying to teach themselves to be docents. They asked the Zoo director, animal keepers and local college professors to talk to their small class—and even took turns teaching each other.

Mavis Lang, 1970 docent class graduate, recalls, "In the early years, the docents in the class prepared the fact sheets and even gave lectures. We ran our own office too. It was in a place we called 'the Ivory Tower,' above the kitchen, so we got all the horsemeat smells. We handled all the tour bookings. We used bullhorns when leading tours; sometimes they didn't work."

From these beginnings, the Docent Council evolved into a formal program with nearly 200 active volunteers. Each has completed an intensive 14-week training course and tag-along apprenticeship. "The course is quite inclusive and the final exam isn't easy," Lang says.

Over the years, the Docent Council has steadily expanded its services from giving Zoo tours to school groups and Zoo visitors to include a children's summer school program and Zoomobile, an outreach program that brings animals to schools, senior citizens centers and convalescent homes.

Pound notes that today's docents, ranging in age from 18 to 79, are as committed to wildlife education as the founding members were. The training class, which runs from January to April, is now conducted on Wednesdays or Saturdays. The weekend class is invariably filled to capacity.

"When the program first began, most docents were retired or homemakers," she says. "Today, you name the occupation, we have someone who does it. They volunteer their precious leisure time to the program."

The reasons individuals join the docent program are varied. Lee Bailey, Class of '73, says her interest was piqued while on a teaching sabbatical in Japan. "A young man from my class took me to the insect zoo at Ueno Park, and that got me started. I always liked animals but never had a pet. When I retired, I thought this would be wonderful. I can have another career. I go to the Zoo to learn something."

Jean Curtner, Class of '77, had been volunteering for other causes, but felt she needed a change. "I asked myself where is the happiest place on earth," she recalls. "It is where children and animals meet—at the Zoo. I felt I could make a contribution."

Guy Littman, Class of '81, drives in from his Santa Rosa home. An accountant, Littman says, "Originally, I had weekday time and was looking for things to do in a volunteer way. I've been interested in ecology and conservation, and a part of me has always wanted to be a teacher."

Some people come in pairs. Joe and Connie Aschero, Class of '79, were the first husband and wife team to take the docent class. Connie thought it would help overcome her fear of birds; now she actually looks forward to having a hawk perch on her arm. The Ascheros' favorite assignment is staffing the Zoomobile. "We're probably frustrated teachers at heart," Joe admits. "We take animals like alligators, boa constrictors, hedgehogs, iguanas, hawks and bobcats out to the schools to teach kids." Sometimes the lesson is on him. "In one class I was trying to make the point that snakes use their tongues to catch scents in the air," he recalls. "I asked one kid, 'How do you think snakes smell?' and the kid answered, 'Not very nice.'"

The enjoyment received by conveying wildlife education is its own reward, most docents claim. "Knowing that I can show these wonderful animals to children satisfies something in me. We teach them conservation," says Lang.

It has given greater dimension to the Zoo as well. "The Zoo is flourishing," notes Bailey. "It draws tremendous crowds compared to 15 years ago. I think part of it is a result of our educational services."

This December the docents will celebrate their 20th year at a dinner, to be held appropriately enough—in the Lion House with the king of beasts.—*Delphine Hirasuna*

The San Francisco Zoological Society's 1988 Good Egg Award, given to the year's outstanding volunteer, went to Lillian Bentley—docent, philanthropist, penguin hand-rearing and avian team volunteer.

From her beginning involvement with the docent program eight years ago, Lillian has done everything from wrapping packages for Christmas with the Animals to oiling the Avian Conservation Program's hinges and locks, from cleaning rabbits and rats to feeding the raptors to hand-rearing penguins. "To tell you the truth," she says, "I can't remember how I got into it."

Even when Lillian isn't working as a docent, she always has her docent sash. "It gives you credibility when you ask people to get down from the railing around Gorilla World or Wolf Woods," she says. "They just don't believe you when you say it's dangerous."

What Bentley enjoys most about volunteering at the Zoo is working with the people—and judging by the standing ovation she received when accepting the Good Egg Award, people enjoy working with her too. —*Kathleen Harper*

GOOD EGG AWARD

San Francisco Zoological Society
California, USA

Art Directors
James Cross, Ken Cook
Designer
Ken Cook
Design Firm
Cross Associates
Illustrator/Photographer
Steve Underwood and various

St. Louis Zoological Park
Missouri, USA

Art Director
David Chiow
Designer
David Chiow
Editor
Jerry Sears
Copywriter
Dorothy Brockhoff

ZUDUS

SOMETHING TO CELEBRATE

PROLONGED HOLIDAY

EHRLICH ON ECOLOGY

SUMMER FUN

SIBERIAN CONNECTION

Tiger Tag Polo Benefit

MEET THE ALLIGATOR SNAPPING TURTLE

A Colorful Stroll: The Wildlife Art Walk

A Behind-The-Scenes Peek

ST. LOUIS ZOO FRIENDS ASSOCIATION

THE LIVING WORLD

THE LIVING WORLD IN PERSPECTIVE

NEW CENTER SOUNDS A CLARION CALL FOR CONSERVATION

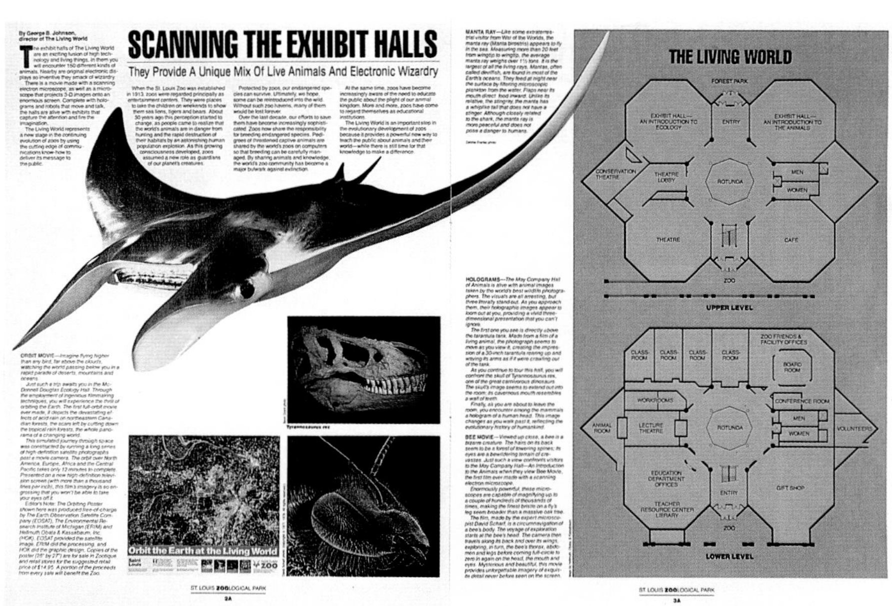

SCANNING THE EXHIBIT HALLS

They Provide A Unique Mix Of Live Animals And Electronic Wizardry

Orbit the Earth at the Living World

THE LIVING WORLD
FOREST PARK
EXHIBIT HALL— AN INTRODUCTION TO ECOLOGY
ENTRY
EXHIBIT HALL— AN INTRODUCTION TO THE ANIMALS
CONSERVATION THEATRE
THEATRE LOBBY
ROTUNDA
MEN
WOMEN
THEATRE
CAFE
ZOO
UPPER LEVEL
CLASS-ROOM
ZOO FRIENDS & FACILITY OFFICES
BOARD ROOM
WORKROOMS
CONFERENCE ROOM
ANIMAL ROOM
LECTURE THEATRE
ROTUNDA
VOLUNTEERS
EDUCATION DEPARTMENT OFFICES
GIFT SHOP
ENTRY
TEACHER RESOURCE CENTER LIBRARY
ZOO
LOWER LEVEL

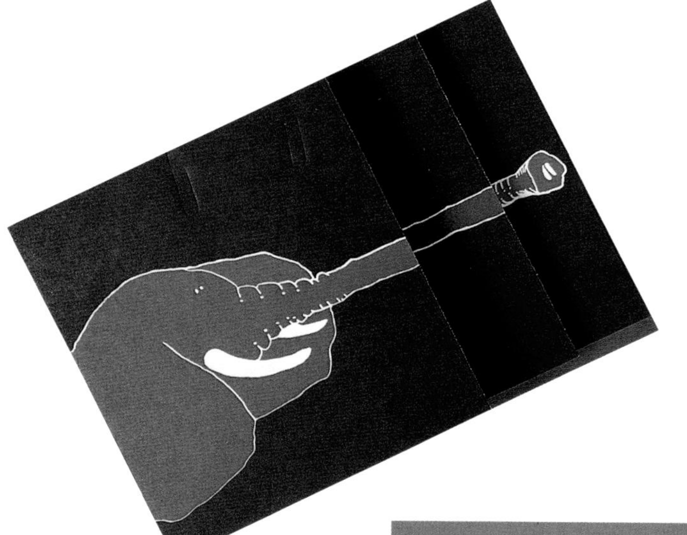

Woodland Park Zoological Gardens
Seattle, Washington, USA

Art Director
Keith Yoshida
Designers
Keith Yoshida, Trisha Hyodo
Illustrators
Keith Yoshida, Paul Macapia, Trisha Hyodo, Rosemary Woods
Copywriters
Keith Yoshida, Sherry Rind, Hank Klein

THE ALASKA JUNGLE PARTY

JUNGLE PARTY

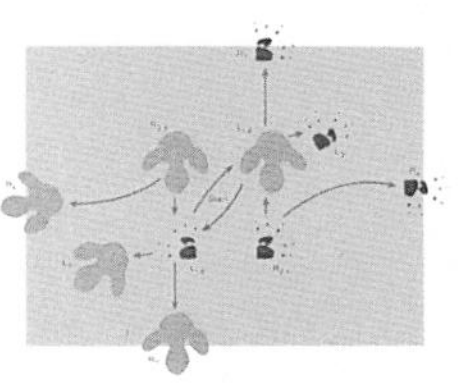

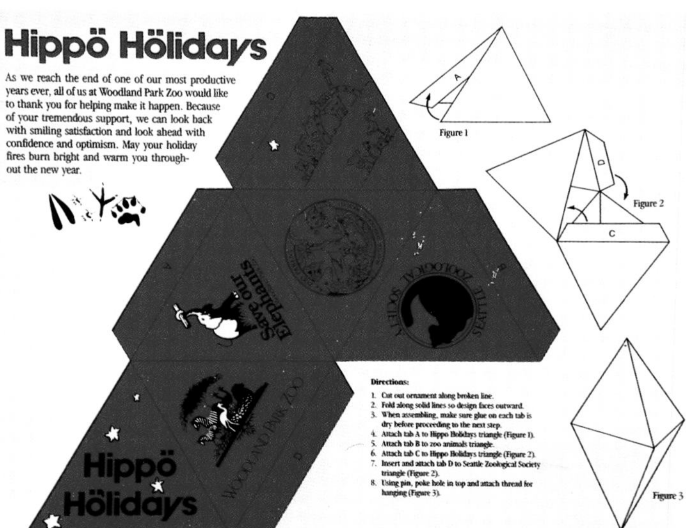
Hippö Hölidays
As we reach the end of one of our most productive years ever, all of us at Woodland Park Zoo would like to thank you for helping make it happen. Because of your tremendous support, we can look back with smiling satisfaction and look ahead with confidence and optimism. May your holiday fires burn bright and warm you through-out the new year.
Figure 1
Figure 2
Figure 3
Directions:
1. Cut out ornament along broken line.
2. Fold along solid lines so design faces outward.
3. When assembling, make sure glue on each tab is dry before proceeding to the next step.
4. Attach tab A to Hippo Holidays triangle (Figure 1).
5. Attach tab B to zoo animals triangle.
6. Attach tab C to Hippo Holidays triangle (Figure 2).
7. Insert and attach tab D to Seattle Zoological Society triangle (Figure 2).
8. Using pin, poke hole in top and attach thread for hanging (Figure 3).
Save our Elephants
WOODLAND PARK ZOO
Hippö Hölidays

ADOPT A WOODLAND PARK ZOO ANIMAL

Becoming the parent of an 3,400 pound bundle of joy is easier than you'd think.

Because now you can adopt any animal in the zoo, from a two-toed sloth to a four-ton elephant, as a member of the Seattle Zoological Society's Zoo Parent program.

ALL YOU HAVE TO DO IS LOOK PROUD.

Just decide which animal you want to adopt from the list below, and then fill in the attached application and send us your tax-deductible yearly fee.

We'll send you a certificate of adoption, a Zoo Parent decal and an invitation to a special Zoo Parent party. And whenever you come to the zoo, you'll see your name listed on our Zoo Parent showcase. If you contribute $250 or more, we'll also send you a framed 8 x 10 color photograph of your animal.

And since all animals continue to stay at the zoo, you won't have to worry about feeding, walking or caring for them. We'll even clean up their rooms.

WE PROMISE THEY'LL ALL BEHAVE LIKE WILD ANIMALS.

All funds raised by our Zoo Parent program go to a good cause. We'll use them to improve the habitats of our zoo's animals. Some of the projects planned include building a tapir pool, improving the orangutan exhibit and constructing a new facility for our birds of prey.

So you'll be helping us give our animals a place to live that's as much like their natural homes as possible. Which is something they'll all be wild about.

YOU CAN VISIT YOUR PRIDE AND JOY 365 DAYS A YEAR.

Most parents like to visit their animals whenever they come to the zoo. The folks at the front entrance will tell you where to find them.

Just remember, zoo animals are living things and their lives are subject to change. If your animal leaves the zoo for any reason, we'll inform you and let you choose a new animal.

STICK YOUR NECK OUT. GIVE SOMEONE A GIRAFFE.

An animal adoption makes a great gift for any occasion. Or any person, school class, business or organization.

And even though some of the animals on the list may have already been selected by other people, they're all happy to have more than one set of parents. So send in your application today.

Here's a partial list of our animals. If you'd like to be a Zoo Parent for one not included here, just let us know.

182 PETS YOU'LL NEVER HAVE TO CLEAN UP AFTER

ZOO PARENT APPLICATION FORM
ANIMAL TO BE ADOPTED: ____
Name to be on certificate and showcase ____
Your Name: ____ Phone ____
Your Address ____
City, State, Zip ____
I wish to make a Zoo Parent gift for:
Name ____ Phone ____
Address ____
City, State, Zip ____

Method of Payment:
☐ Check enclosed payable to Seattle Zoological Society
☐ VISA
☐ AMERICAN EXPRESS
☐ MASTER CARD
Card number ____
Expiration date ____
Signature ____
1 year Zoo Parent Fee: $ ____
☐ Yes, I'd also like to join the Seattle Zoological Society. Membership fee $20.00.
Total enclosed: $ ____
For more information about Zoo Parents please call 789-6060.

Perth Zoo
Australia

Art Director
Rick Lambert
Designer
Arlene Lockwood
Design Firm
Rick Lambert Design Consultants
Illustrator
Kathy Morgan
Copywriter
Sam Leland

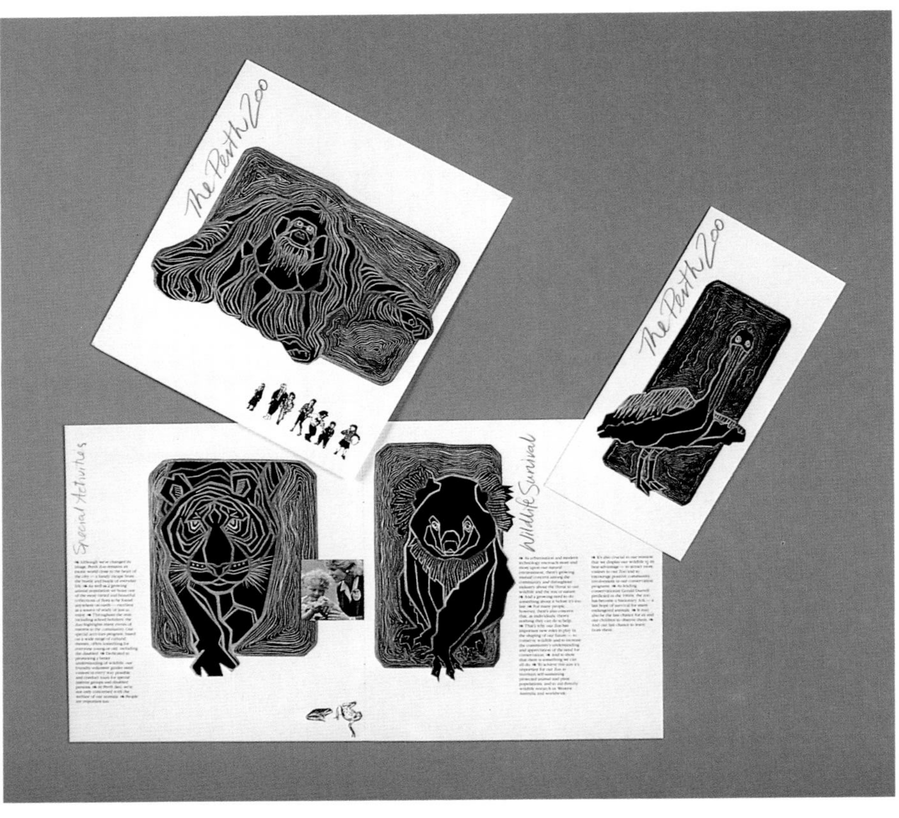

Cleveland Metroparks Zoo
Ohio, USA

Art Director
Cherie Valentine
Designer
Cherie Valentine
Design Agency
WYSE Advertising
Photographer
Andy Russetti
Prop
Mary McMahon
Copywriter
Chuck Withrow

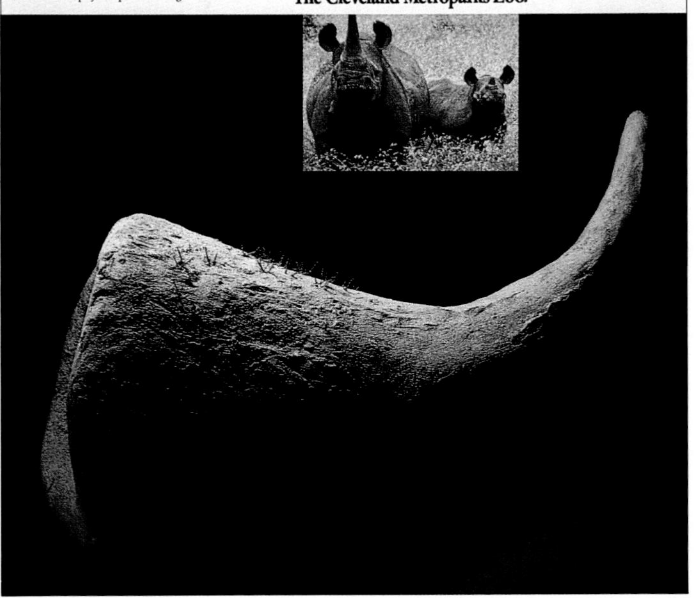

George Calef/Masterfile

Baltimore Aquarium
Maryland, USA

Designer
Tom Geismar
Design Firm
Chermayeff & Geismar
Associates
Illustrator
Tom Geismar

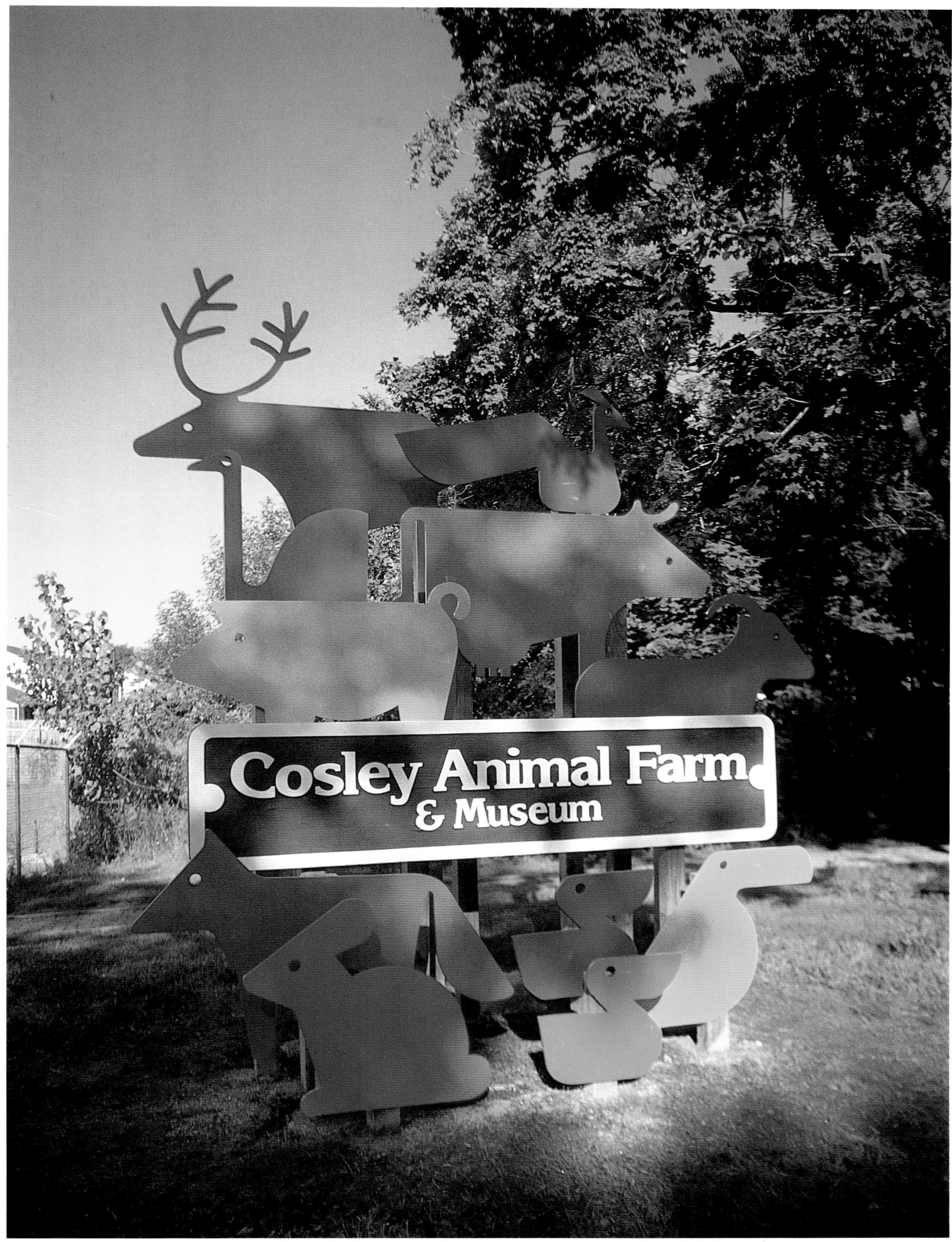

Cosley Animal Farm & Museum
Wheaton, Illinois, USA

Art Director/Designer
Richard Wittosch
Design Firm
Directional Design

Busch Gardens
Zoological Park
Tampa, Florida, USA

Design done by in-house graphics department of the Park

Illustrator
Lynn Ash
Sign fabricator
Jonathan Jones Sign Co.

All these painted signs are executed on 2" x 6" tongue and groove planks

15' X 17' Elephant identification sign

6' x 10' North American eagle identification sign with copy blocks of vinyl lettering

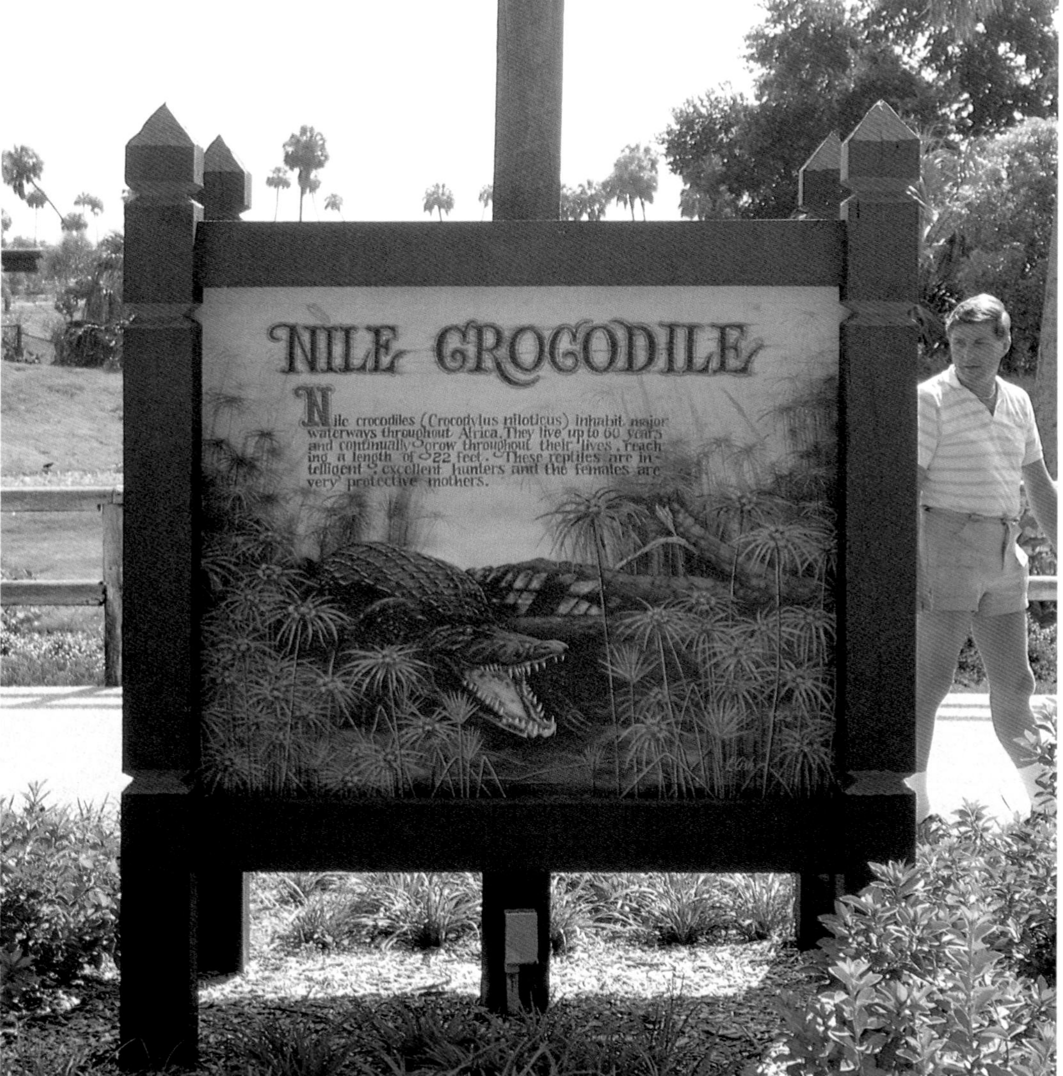

All these painted signs are executed on 2" x 6" tongue and groove planks

8' X 10' Pelican identification sign

5' x 7' Chilean flamingo identification sign

5" x 7" Nile crocodile identification sign

Brookfield Zoo
Illinois, USA

Designers
Tamar Rosenthal, Hannah Jennings
Illustrators/Sculptors
Edie Emmenegger, Emin Asanovski
Copywriter
Judee Hanson

Detroit Zoological Park
Michigan, USA

Porcelain enamel interpretive panels for chimpanzee exhibit

Designer
Joe Clark
Design Firm
Coe Lee Robinson Roesch
Illustrator
Jeffrey Terreson
Copywriters
Jon Coe, Barbara McGrath

Fort Wayne Children's Zoo
Indiana, USA

The use of the globe as an interactive device which provides a unique lesson on wildlife and geography

Designer
Cheryl Piropato
Design Firm
Image Exhibits
Illustrator
Victoria Piebenga
Copywriter
Cheryl Piropato

Quebec Zoological Garden
Canada

Design
Ministère du Loisir, de la Chasse et de la Pêche

Miami Metrozoo
Florida, USA

Designers
William Tuttle, Design staff
Design Firm
Metrozoo Design Department
Illustrator
Renee Campbell

Rio Grande Zoo
Albuquerque, New Mexico, USA

The zoo's sign system is designed to direct, identify and inform without competing with the major focal point – the animals. Hence, the use of the natural warmth of wood as opposed to the austerity of metal or plastic.

Designer
Ray Darnell
Illustrators
Ray Darnell, Deborah Morgan

Sea Life Park Hawaii
Hawaii, USA

Designer
Richard Reese
Design Firm
Richard Reese Designs
Illustrators
Grover Ishii, Todd Mayfield
Copywriter
Charles Seaborn

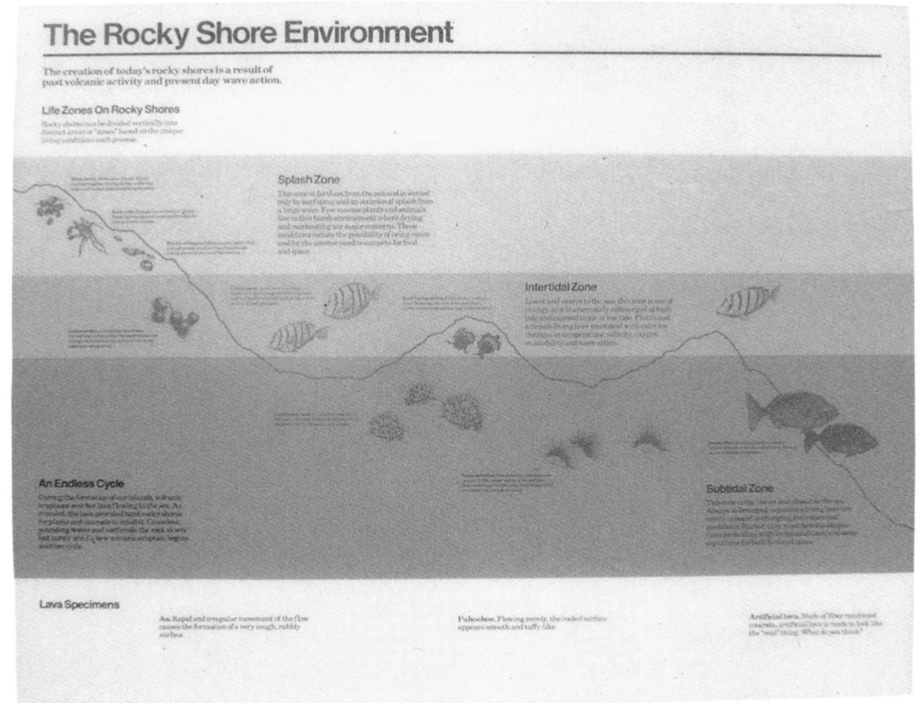

St. Louis Zoo
Missouri, USA

Pole-mounted banner campaign announcing the opening of The Living World

Designer
Ken Wehrman
Design Firm
Wehrman & Co.
Photographer
Chuck Dresner

St. Louis Zoo
Missouri, USA

Zoomobile

Designer
Ken Wehrman
Design Firm
Wehrman & Co.
Photographer
Emily Routman

St. Louis Zoo
Missouri, USA

Parents Program kiosk – displays updated quarterly

Design Firm
Hellmuth, Obata & Kassabaum, Inc.

Wildpark Langenberg
Zürich, Switzerland

Designer
Angelika Bomhard
Design Firm
Angelika Bomhard
Illustrator
Angelika Bomhard
Copywriter
Angelika Bomhard

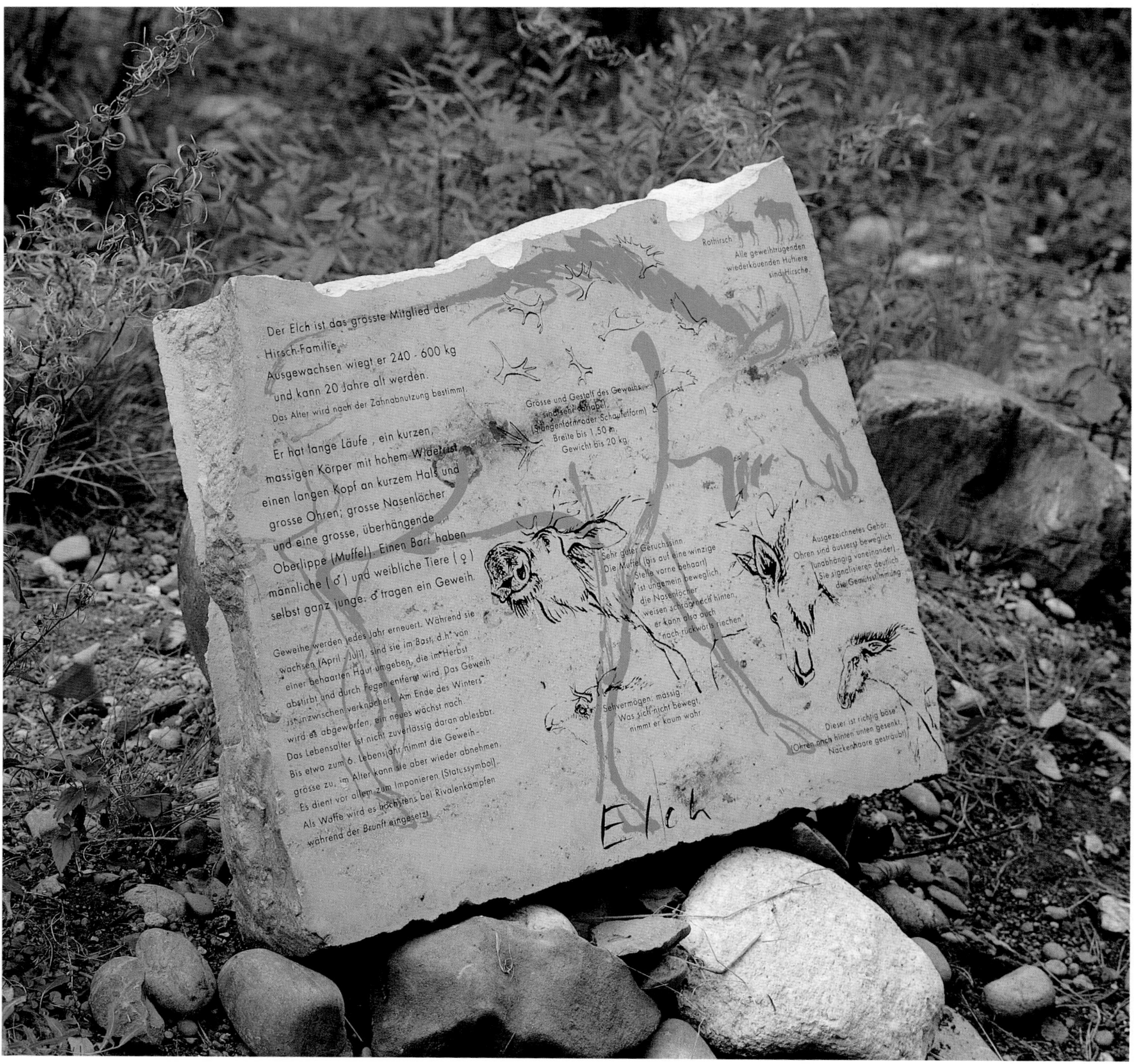

Identification sign in front of elk enclosure – silkscreen on rock ca. 600 x 550 x 100mm

Information signs – Please do not feed the animals & Please do not touch the animals

Information sign at a place where visitors can leave their dogs – Parking for dogs

Poster

Sacremento Zoo
California, USA

Art Director
Kim Tackett
Designer
Steve Ball
Design Firm
Tackett – Barbaria Design

Roger Williams Park Zoo
Providence, Rhode Island, USA

Large hands-on globe at entrance and exit of Tropical America building – entrance globe indicates current areas of rainforest while exit globe indicates how much less rainforest remain at the present rate.

Design
Department of Public Parks

Edinburgh Zoo
Scotland

Art Director
Rodger Stanier
Designer
Guy Gumm
Design Firm
The Leith Agency
Copywriter
Gerry Farrell

Patrice Ceisel/John G. Shedd Aquarium

Index

Art Directors, Designers, Illustrators, Photographers, Copywriters

Addresses of zoos, aquaria, aviaries and wildlife parks

Allwetterzoo Münster
Sentruper Str. 315
D-4400 Münster
Germany

Antwerp Zoo
K. Astridplein 26
Antwerp 2018
Belgium

Audubon Zoological Garden
6500 Magazine Street
New Orleans, LA 70178
U.S.A.

Baltimore National Aquarium
Pier 3, 501 East Pratt Street
Baltimore, MD 21202
U.S.A.

Baltimore Children's Zoo
Druid Hill Park
Baltimore, MD 21217
U.S.A.

Blank Park Zoo of Des Moines
7401 SW 9th Street
Des Moines, Iowa 50315
U.S.A.

Bronx Zoo
New York Zoological Society
185 Street & Southern Blvd.
New York, NY 10460
U.S.A.

Brookfield Zoo
Chicago Zoological Society
Brookfield, IL 60302
U.S.A.

Buffalo Zoological Gardens
Delaware Park
Buffalo, NY 14214
U.S.A.

Busch Gardens Zoological Park
3605 Bougainvillea Blvd.
Tampa, FL 33612
U.S.A.

Carl Hagenbecks Tierpark
Postfach 540 930
Stellingen
D-2000 Hamburg 54
Germany

Central Park Zoo
New York Zoological Society
830 Fifth Avenue
New York, NY 10021
U.S.A.

Cincinnati Zoological Gardens
3400 Vine Street
Cincinnati, OH 45220
U.S.A.

Cleveland Metroparks Zoo
3900 Brookside Park Drive
Cleveland, OH 44109
U.S.A.

St. Paul's Como Zoo
Midway Parkway & Kaufman Dr.
Saint Paul, MN 55103
U.S.A.

Copenhagen Zoo
Sdr. Fasanvej 79
DK-2000 Frederiksberg
Denmark

Cosley Animal Farm & Museum
1356 Gary Avenue
Wheaton, IL 60187
U.S.A.

Dallas Zoo
621 East Clarendon Drive
Dallas, TX 75201
U.S.A.

Detroit Zoological Park
8450 West Ten Mile Road
Royal Oak, MI 48068
U.S.A.

Edinburgh Zoo
Royal Zoological Society of Scotland
Murrayfield
Edinburgh, Lothian EH12 6TS
England

Fort Wayne Children's Zoo
3411 Sherman Boulevard
Fort Wayne, IN 46808
U.S.A.

Healesville Sanctuary
Badger Creek Road
Healesville
Melbourne, Victoria 3777
Australia

The New Indianapolis Zoo
1200 West Washington Street
Indianapolis, IA 46222
U.S.A.

John G. Shedd Aquarium
1200 South Lake Shore Drive
Chicago, Il 60605
U.S.A.

Jurong Birdpark
Jurong Hill
Jalan Ahmad Ibrahim
Singapore 2262
Republic of Singapore

Kings Island Wild Animal Habitat
6300 Kings Island Drive
Kingsland, OH 45034
U.S.A.

Los Angeles Zoo
5333 Zoo Drive
Los Angeles, CA 90027
U.S.A.

Miami Metrozoo
12400 S.W. 152 Street
Miami, FL 33177
U.S.A.

National Zoological Park
Smithsonian Institution
3000 Connecticut Avenue, NW
Washington, DC 20008
U.S.A.

New England Aquarium
Central Wharf
Boston, MA 02110
U.S.A.

Okinawa Expo Memorial Park Aquarium
Motobu-cho
Okinawa-ken 10460
905-03 Japan

Osaka Aquarium/Kaiyukan
Tempozan Harbor Village
1-1-10 Kaigan Dori
Minato-ku, Osaka
Japan

Philadelphia Zoo
The Zoological Society of Philadelphia
34th Street and Girard Avenue
Philadelphia, PA 19104
U.S.A.

The Phoenix Zoo
Post Office Box 52191
Phoenix, AZ 85072
U.S.A.

The Pittsburgh Zoo
P.O. Box 5250
Pittsburgh, PA 15206
U.S.A.

Quebec Zoological Garden
8191 avenue du zoo
Charlesbourg, Quebec
G1G 4G4
Canada

Rio Grande Zoo
903 Tenth Street, S.W.
Albuquerque, NM 87106
U.S.A.

Roger Williams Park Zoo
Elmwood Avenue
Providence, RI 02905
U.S.A.

Royal Melbourne Zoological Gardens
Elliott Avenue
Parkville
Melbourne, Victoria 3052
Australia

Sacramento Zoological Society
3930 West Land Park Drive
Sacramento, CA 95822
U.S.A.

San Antonio Zoo
3903 N. St. Mary's Street
San Antonio, TX 78212
U.S.A.

The Zoological Society of San Diego
Post Office Box 551
San Diego, CA 92112
U.S.A.

San Francisco Zoological Society
Sloat Blvd. at the Pacific Ocean
San Francisco, CA 94132
U.S.A.

Sea Life Park Hawaii
Makapuu Point
Waimanalo, HI 96795
U.S.A.

Sea World of Florida
7007 Sea World Drive
Orlando, FL 32821
U.S.A.

The Seattle Aquarium
Pier 59, Waterfront Park
Seattle, WA 98101
U.S.A.

Sedgwick County Zoo and Botanical Garden
5555 Zoo Boulevard
Wichita, KS 67212
U.S.A.

St. Louis Zoo
Forest Park
Saint Louis, MO 63110
U.S.A.

Tennessee Aquarium
701 Broad Street
Tivoli Center
Chattanooga, TN 37402
U.S.A.

Metro Toronto Zoo
P.O. Box 280
West Hill, Ontario M1E 4R5
Canada

Tracy Aviary
Liberty Park
589 East 1300 S.
Salt Lake City, UT 84105
U.S.A.

Valley Zoo
13315 Buena Vista Road
Edmonton, Alberta T5R 5R1
Canada

Vancouver Aquarium
P.O. Box 3232
Vancouver, B.C. V6B 3X8
Canada

Wildpark Langenberg
8135 Langnau am Albis
Langnau, Zürich 8135
Switzerland

Woodland Park Zoological Gardens
5500 Phinney Avenue North
Seattle, WA 98103
U.S.A.

Zoo Atlanta
800 Cherokee Avenue, S.E.
Atlanta, GA 30315
U.S.A.